DISCA

SIR PHILIP SIDNEY

The Maker's Mind

SIR PHILIP SIDNEY

The Maker's Mind

Dorothy Connell

CLARENDON PRESS · OXFORD
1977

Oxford University Press, Walton Street, Oxford OX2 6DP

OXFORD   LONDON   GLASGOW   NEW YORK
TORONTO   MELBOURNE   WELLINGTON   CAPE TOWN
IBADAN   NAIROBI   DAR ES SALAAM   LUSAKA   ADDIS ABABA
KUALA LUMPUR   SINGAPORE   JAKARTA   HONG KONG   TOKYO
DELHI   BOMBAY   CALCUTTA   MADRAS   KARACHI

British Library Cataloguing in Publication Data

Connell, Dorothy
  Sir Philip Sidney.
  1. Sidney, *Sir* Philip – Criticism and interpretation
  821'.3   PR2343   77–30167

ISBN 0 19 812081 8

*Printed in Great Britain by
William Clowes & Sons Ltd., London, Beccles and Colchester*

Contents

Maps

Introduction: The Renaissance Maker

IN HIS brief thirty-two years, Sir Philip Sidney was courtier, poet, lover, soldier, politician, patron, scholar, and religious devotee. His protean spirit is mirrored in a brilliant and varied group of literary remains: letters, essays, sonnets and other verse (including a versification of the Psalms), and the two *Arcadias* in prose. To introduce a study of Sidney there could be no better epigraph than Pico's joyful phrase about man: 'Who would not admire this our chameleon?'

A reminder of the spirit of Pico della Mirandola is apt because he first formulated in the Renaissance an influential concept of man which Sidney later used and adapted. It is the idea of man as a maker. In the famous *Oration on the Dignity of Man* Pico advances the theory that the key to man's greatness is his God-given power to 'make' himself—the power freely to act, to create and, like the chameleon, to transform his own nature. In the *Oration* God is imagined revealing this power to man at the Creation:

We have made thee neither of heaven nor of earth, neither mortal nor immortal, so that with freedom of choice and with honor, as though the maker and molder of thyself, thou mayst fashion thyself in whatever shape thou shalt prefer.[1]

Sidney extended the concept of the maker to argue in special praise of the poet. In *A Defence of Poetry* the term itself is derived by Sidney from Greek and English sources and is presented with a lively display of humanist and nationalist pride:

The Greeks called him a 'poet', which name hath, as the most excellent, gone through other languages. It cometh of this word ποιεῖν, which is, to make: wherein, I know not whether by luck or wisdom, we Englishmen have met with the Greeks in calling him a maker: which

---

[1] Translated by Elizabeth Livermore Forbes, in *The Renaissance Philosophy of Man*, edited by Ernst Cassirer, Paul Oskar Kristeller, and John Herman Randall, Jr. (Chicago, 1948), p. 225.

name, how high and incomparable a title it is, I had rather were
known by marking the scope of other sciences than by any partial
allegation.[1]

Although the influence of Pico is not acknowledged, a relationship can clearly be inferred between Sidney's well-known description of the power of the poet–maker and the broader creative
power which Renaissance humanists, following Pico, ascribed to
man generally: '. . . he goeth hand in hand with nature, not en-
closed within the narrow warrant of her gifts, but freely ranging
only within the zodiac of his own wit' (*Defence*, p. 78). Later in
the essay Sidney makes the connection explicit between the poet's
power as a maker and that of all mankind. At the same time Sidney,
like Pico, defines the source and the limits of human creativity in
the higher creativity of God.

Neither let it be deemed too saucy a comparison to balance the highest
point of man's wit with the efficacy of nature; but rather give right
honour to the heavenly Maker of that maker, who having made man
to His own likeness, set him beyond and over all the works of that
second nature: which in nothing he showeth so much as in poetry,
when with the force of a divine breath he bringeth things forth sur-
passing her doings. . . .

(*Defence*, p. 79)

These and related passages from *A Defence of Poetry* will figure
later in the discussion of Sidney's conception of poetry. But the
idea of the maker is also a useful starting-point for examining
Sidney's thought and work. Sidney's emphasis on a free, exuber-
ant creativity in poets, his sense that such greatness of spirit is not

---

[1] Sir Philip Sidney, *A Defence of Poetry*, in *Miscellaneous Prose of Sir Philip Sidney*,
edited by Katherine Duncan-Jones and Jan van Dorsten (Oxford, 1973), p. 77. Other
page notations in the text from *A Defence of Poetry* will refer to that edition, called
here *Sidney's Miscellaneous Prose*. I have used the title *A Defence of Poetry* which was
chosen by these editors instead of one or the other of the traditional titles for Sidney's
essay—*The Defence of Poesie* or *An Apologie for Poetrie*. I give the editors' reasons:

Sidney may never have contemplated giving his discourse a proper title, but in his
opening paragraph he used the phrase 'a. . .defence of. . .poetry', while the most
authoritative source, Pe, calls itself 'Defence of Poetry'. Unlike the terms 'Apologie'
and 'Poesie' which one finds on the title-pages of O and P, the words 'Defence' and
'Poetry' require no explanation. It is hoped, therefore, that the title *A Defence of
Poetry*, which was also used for the new O.U.P. school edition, will in time replace
its optional alternatives.

(*Sidney's Miscellaneous Prose*, pp. 69–70)

exclusive to poets, deriving rather from the creative power of all men, his recognition that this human power depends on and is limited by God's power, and finally the relationship between his idea and those of other Renaissance thinkers should all be noted. For these exemplify important general qualities of Sidney's thought which are reflected in several different ways in his works.

The chameleon creativity of Sidney and the seemingly contradictory mix of aspirations for man and religious humility in his themes have tended to obscure the perception of the fundamental unity of his ideas. The recent critical attention Sidney has received characterizes him in two separate ways. On the one hand he is perceived as a modern, dramatizing human conflicts in order to cultivate a moral and emotional ambivalence that is unresolved. On the other hand he is seen as a moralist who firmly advances Christian ideals in his poetry.[1] By excluding its opposite, each point of view falls short of dealing with the full range of Sidney's literary imagination. Those critics who focus on the secular and ambivalent in Sidney's poetry tend to dismiss or ignore the religious aspect of his work. Those critics who emphasize the idealism and morality of the poetry tend to ignore Sidney's humorous and sympathetic insistence on the earthly, the fallible, the foolish in life.[2]

[1] For the characterization of Sidney as a modern see David Kalstone, *Sidney's Poetry: Contexts and Interpretations* (Cambridge, Mass., 1965), Neil L. Rudenstine, *Sidney's Poetic Development* (Cambridge, Mass., 1967), and most recently J. G. Nichols, *The Poetry of Sir Philip Sidney: An Interpretation in the Context of His Life and Times* (Liverpool, 1974). These authors concentrate on *Astrophil and Stella* as the thematic and stylistic culmination of Sidney's poetry. For the moral view see John F. Danby, *Elizabethan and Jacobean Poets: Studies in Sidney, Shakespeare, Beaumont and Fletcher* (London, 1965) and Walter R. Davis, 'A Map of Arcadia: Sidney's Romance in Its Tradition', in *Sidney's Arcadia* (New Haven, Conn., 1965). These critics, in contrast to the others, focus on the *Arcadia* of 1593 as being Sidney's most significant work.

[2] Nichols, who focuses on the secular element in Sidney's poetry, admits to perplexity about the religious element of his work: 'The very existence of Sidney's versions [of the Psalms] . . . remains a mystery to me' (p. 50). On the other side Nancy R. Lindheim, in 'Vision, Revision, and the 1593 Text of the *Arcadia*', *English Literary Renaissance*, II. i (Winter 1972), 136–47, argues the dangers of using the composite 1593 edition of the *Arcadia* (Books I–III of the *New Arcadia* coupled with Books III–V of the *Old*, with a few significant revisions) to form a unified interpretation of the story, as Davis and Danby try to do:

Criticism of the *Arcadia* has not consistently recognized that the revisions of the 1590 text are not inherent in the main plot, or even completely harmonious with it, but that they significantly alter the character of the work. Perhaps the most curious result of this is the interpretation of the later books—notably of the debate on suicide between Philoclea and Pyrocles and the princes' acceptance of death as they

A crucial assumption which Sidney made about poetry has also been obscured or forgotten. Several major studies of his work limit their discussions of Sidney's poetic development to the verse from *The Lady of May* and the *Old Arcadia*, and to *Certain Sonnets*, *Astrophil and Stella*, and the Psalms.[1] Sidney states in the *Defence*, however, that for him the poem-form is not at all the defining characteristic of poetry: 'It is not rhyming and versing that maketh poesy. One may be a poet without versing, and a versifier without poetry' (*Defence*, p. 100). Not form, but rather the creative power of the maker is the focal point of his definition:

> . . . indeed that name of making is fit for him, considering that where all other arts retain themselves within their subject, and receive, as it were, their being from it, the poet only bringeth his own stuff, and doth not learn a conceit out of a matter, but maketh matter for a conceit.
>
> (*Defence*, p. 99)

Following Sidney and assuming that the growth of his own power as a maker took place in verse and prose as well, one perceives that the two *Arcadias*—not Sidney's poems—hold the key places in the historical sequence of his poetry. The *Old Arcadia* was written at the opening of Sidney's poetic career, and the revised version was being completed at his death. Thus by accident a comparison between the two versions of *Arcadia* has more than its own intrinsic interest. It has the potential to measure the full extent of change in the poet's mind over time. The sense of Sidney's poetic development is informed, of course, by the study of his other poetry as well, and in all these works it is important to search out the unifying elements that are discoverable in them.

The key element in this search is not the modernity, the morality, or even the originality of Sidney's thought. Indeed it is a quality which has been noted and described—under various titles—as being characteristic of Renaissance thought.[2] In very

---

await trial—as though they really were culminations of the 'earlier' material in the Captivity sequence. . . . The text of Books III–V as it stands will not bear the particular freight of religion and neo-Platonism that is being thrust upon it by analogy with the expanded scope of the Captivity. (p. 140)

[1] For example Kalstone, Rudenstine, Nichols, and Robert L. Montgomery, Jr., *Symmetry and Sense: The Poetry of Sir Philip Sidney* (Austin, Texas, 1961).

[2] My thinking on this point has been influenced primarily by Ernst Cassirer, 'Giovanni Pico della Mirandola', in *Renaissance Essays from the Journal of the History of Ideas*, edited by Paul Oskar Kristeller and Philip P. Wiener (New York, 1968), 11–60; Rosalie L. Colie, *Paradoxia Epidemica: The Renaissance Tradition of Paradox* (Princeton, N.J., 1966); Johan Huizinga, *Homo Ludens: A Study of the Play Element*

general terms I would describe it as an ability to encompass and balance contradictions. Understanding that property of Renaissance thought seems to me essential to understanding Sidney, for it allows ambivalence to coexist with assured values, and morality to embrace a sense of what it is to live as a man.

The creative power of the maker, the idea that man may make himself, for example, is contradictory—a logical impossibility. But in the Renaissance formulation the idea is a paradox, a seeming impossibility made possible by God's gift. Sidney's habit of mind more than Pico's seems to have been to focus on the paradoxical element. On one hand in the *Defence* Sidney extols the seemingly unlimited power of the maker. On the other hand he perceives the limits of that human power. It gives 'no small arguments to the credulous of that first accursed fall of Adam, since our erected wit maketh us know what perfection is, and yet our infected will keepeth us from reaching unto it' (*Defence*, p. 79).

Sidney is clear about the limitations of fallen mankind, yet faith and a genial humour combine to make his vision of the world a positive one. This general attitude and the fact that it is characteristic of the period may be summed up and illustrated by comparing *A Defence of Poetry* with two quintessential works of the Renaissance, Erasmus's *Praise of Folly* and Castiglione's *Book of the Courtier*.[1]

Erasmus, as a man of reason, exposes and censures human folly. But in the involuted and paradoxical plan of his work, he also gives Folly herself the power to reason, and she finds a higher wisdom in foolishness that touches the defects of mankind with a divinely unreasoned grace. Men cannot help being fools, she argues, even learned men like 'my friende Erasmus'. More-

in Culture (Boston, 1960); Walter Kaiser, *Praisers of Folly: Erasmus, Rabelais, Shakespeare* (Cambridge, Mass., 1963); Erwin Panofsky, *Renaissance and Renascences in Western Art* (New York, 1960) and other writings; and John Stevens, *Music and Poetry in the Early Tudor Court* (London, 1961).

[1] To preserve the Renaissance context of my argument I have used wherever possible English translations that would have been available to Sidney and his contemporaries, although Sidney would not have needed them for Latin, French, Italian, or probably Spanish. *The Praise of Folie* was translated by Sir Thomas Chaloner in 1549 and the *Book of the Courtier* was translated by Sir Thomas Hoby in 1561. Sidney's access to at least this last translation is assured by the fact that Hoby's widow Lady Russell was a close friend. In a Latin elegy written by Daniel Rogers to Sidney in 1579, she is mentioned among a group of ladies at court who were 'second mothers' to Sidney. See J. A. van Dorsten, *Poets, Patrons and Professors: Sir Philip Sidney, Daniel Rogers and the Leiden Humanists* (London, 1962), p. 62.

over, Folly shows that Christ, in choosing to take on human form,
was the greatest fool ever. Indeed, the crowning argument of the
work is that 'God hath disposed to save the worlde by foolish-
nesse.'[1] Within the encircling sense of God's redeeming love,
Erasmus finds room for satire and sympathy toward men, for
approval of scholarly pursuits and acceptance of natural bodily
urges, for serious purpose and self-directed humour.

The *Book of the Courtier* is built on the paradox that man can
make himself. Indeed, it is an extended manual of making and
self-making with the stated purpose 'to shape in words a good
Courtier'.[2] In keeping with this larger framework, Castiglione,
as his argument proceeds, points to the places where wisdom
and absurdity meet. For example, in the Fourth Book, Lord
Octavian gives a beautifully reasoned disquisition on the highest
purpose of the courtier, culminating in the proof that even
Aristotle and Plato belong in the ranks of courtly men. Castiglione
calls attention with a smile to the high flight of his speaker:

Here when the Lord Octavian had made a stay, the Lord Gaspar saide:
I had not thought our Courtier had been so worthie a personage. But
since Aristotle and Plato be his mates, I judge no man ought to dis-
daine this name any more.

Yet wote I not whether I may believe that Aristotle and Plato ever
daunced or were Musitions in all their life time or practised other feates
of chivalrie.[3]

The closeness of Lord Octavian's argument to foolishness is
given a playful emphasis here, but for all that neither his reasoning nor the wisdom which it finds is meant to be discounted.

In this connection we should also consider *A Defence of
Poetry*. Sidney's essay is universally admired for its sophisticated

---

[1] *The Praise of Folie*, Chaloner translation, edited by Clarence H. Miller for the
Early English Text Society (London, 1965), pp. 110, 117. All page references to the
Praise of Folly will refer to this translation and edition.

[2] *The Book of the Courtier*, Hoby translation, edited by Burton A. Milligan in *Three
Renaissance Classics* (New York, 1953), p. 266. All page references following in the
notes will be to this translation and edition. Rosalie L. Colie, in *Paradoxia Epidemica*
(pp. 360–1), states that, despite the contradiction in the idea of the maker, 'some
Renaissance men had a kind of belief that man could make himself, and believed
furthermore that to make himself was a lifetime job to which he owed most of his
attention. Castiglione's *Courtier* is in this sense a fundamental paradox, since it is a
handbook of self-making—and as befits such a book, it has many paradoxes within
it.'

[3] *The Book of the Courtier*, p. 589.

and witty style and tone.[1] But these aspects of technique should be further identified as part of the thematic strategy of the work. Following Erasmus and Castiglione, Sidney in turn persuades his reader—with a rhetorical enthusiasm which calls attention to its own excesses—that Christ and Plato were not fools or courtiers but something very like both: they were poets. On the one hand the *Defence* accomplishes its stated purpose with conviction, even with zeal. On the other it points up the limitations of poets and their work. It is certain that Sidney had read the *Praise of Folly* prior to writing *A Defence of Poetry,* for he mentions Erasmus's 'merry' work in the body of the essay itself, and his statement shows he knew that Folly had a deeper meaning 'than the superficial part would promise' (*Defence,* p. 100). Sidney must have seen the description of poets in Erasmus's famous catalogue of fools:

... they shew theim selues to be of my secte, a free kynde of men, that lyke peincters maie feigne what they list, whose studie tendeth naught els, than to fede fooles eares with mere trifles and foolisshe fables. And yet it is a wonderous thyng to see, how through fame therof, they wene to be made immortall, and Gods peres, promisyng others also like immortalitee therby. To this order more than to any other, bothe Self-loue and Adulacion are annexed familiarly, and of no kynde of men am I obserued more plainly, nor more constantly.[2]

At the end of the *Defence,* Sidney echoes both the tone of Folly and, specifically, her mention of the promise of immortality, as he conjures his readers to believe in poets:

... believe themselves, when they tell you they will make you immortal by their verses. Thus doing, your name shall flourish in the printers' shops; thus doing, you shall be of kin to many a poetical preface; thus doing, you shall be most fair, most rich, most wise, most all, you shall dwell upon superlatives ...

(*Defence,* p. 121)

---

[1] For example, Kenneth Muir, *Sir Philip Sidney* (London, 1960), p. 10: 'The value of Sidney's essay ... does not depend on his criticism of his contemporaries. It depends rather on its tone and style, graceful, civilised and urbane....'Also Kenneth Myrick remarks, in *Sir Philip Sidney as a Literary Craftsman,* 2nd edn. (Lincoln, Neb., 1965), p. 82: 'In the *Defence,* however closely Sidney has followed the rules, the humor and the lightness of touch are more pervasive. The art is mature—perfectly deliberate, yet so fully mastered as to give the illusion of unstudied effort.' Another example is O. B. Hardison, Jr., 'The Two Voices of Sidney's *Apology for Poetry*', *English Literary Renaissance,* II.iii (Autumn 1972), 84: 'Everywhere in the *Apology* Ciceronian elevation is softened by Sidney's wit and his colloquial language.'

[2] *Praise of Folly,* p. 73.

The irony here, like Erasmus's, has sweetness as well as sting. The deflation of poets' pretensions is certainly meant to be felt, but it is complicated and balanced by Sidney's sympathy, self-inclusion, and humility. We are all human, and thus we are all, as Sidney says of poets on the same page, 'next inheritors to fools' (*Defence*, p. 121). In a related passage this more tender feeling is brought out clearly as Sidney explains that the purpose of his censure 'is not to take upon me to teach poets how they should do, but only, finding myself sick among the rest, to show some one or two spots of the common infection . . .' (*Defence*, p. 119). The essay, then, expresses charity and disparaging humour towards poets at the same time that it defends them. This happens not simply because Sidney affected an outward pose of *sprezzatura* but, as we have already noted, because he reverenced inwardly and above all else the 'heavenly Maker' (*Defence*, p. 79) of poets, more than those makers themselves.

Held up to the eye of Heaven, the strivings of men may appear to be puny or heroic, deserving of affectionate irony or enthusiastic praise. But in all three works it is an essentially positive view which triumphs. Making poetry, practising courtliness, and living as the Christian fool—all are seen as ways which Heaven has opened for men to gain and teach that virtue which alone makes them acceptable to God.

The poet is one sort of fool, the lover is another, and love is the subject of Sidney's poetry. *The Lady of May*, the *Old Arcadia*, *Certain Sonnets*, *Astrophil and Stella*, and the *New Arcadia* have their differences, yet central to each work is that one great human experience. The first task of this study then must be to look in detail at Sidney's conceptions of love and poetry and to investigate some reasons why he linked them together. We shall see that in writing about love in the poetry, as in writing about poetry in the *Defence*, Sidney recognized the ambiguities inherent in all human endeavour. But with a habit of mind that was characteristic of his age, he looked with wit and hope through those ambiguities toward eternal values which reason could discover and, beyond reason, which faith could affirm.

CHAPTER I

Sidney's Conception of Love

As a necessary first step towards understanding Sidney's conception of love, we must recognize that Sidney perceived and made important allowances in his thinking for earthly experience, and for man's inevitable blunders in the face of it. On this account a well-known passage from the *Defence of Poetry* deserves a closer look:

But when by the balance of experience it was found that the astronomer, looking to the stars, might fall in a ditch, that the inquiring philosopher might be blind in himself, and the mathematician might draw forth a straight line with a crooked heart, then lo, did proof, the overruler of opinions, make manifest that all these are but serving sciences, which, as they have each a private end in themselves, so yet are they all directed to the highest end of the mistress-knowledge, by the Greeks called ἀρχιτεκτονική, which stands (as I think) in the knowledge of a man's self, in the ethic and politic consideration, with the end of well-doing and not of well-knowing only . . .

(Defence, pp. 82–3)

Three centuries of romanticizing about Sidney's chivalric heroism have tended to blur the sense of the words, 'knowledge of a man's self . . . with the end of well-doing', into a rather facile idealism; but the context puts their meaning in close touch with earthly reality. Self-knowledge here clearly implies a consciousness of human defects which can only be learned in 'the balance of experience'. Using Plato's story from the *Theaetetus* about the foolish astronomer, Sidney suggests that well-doing is in fact tested as much by falling in a ditch as by looking at the stars. When Sidney later wrote of Astrophil's love, he chose to describe the experience of his hero in terms of the same story. For love makes Astrophil

> . . . fare like him that both
> Lookes to the skies, and in a ditch doth fall.[1]

[1] *Astrophil and Stella*, No. 19, in the critical edition by William A. Ringler of *The Poems of Sir Philip Sidney* (Oxford, 1962). References in the text by *number* to poems by Sidney will refer to this edition.

The recently-discovered personal letter from Sidney to Edward Denny (dated at the same period as the *Defence*) also couples a detailed discussion of self-knowledge with the acknowledgement of inevitable human failings. The mood—and even the disarming reference to horsemanship—is close to that of Sidney's essay:

To my Nedd Denny therfore, and even soe to my [selfe] (for I doe in this with you, as we doe one to an other in horsemanship; teach before wee have well learned) this I think may be the course, to knowe, what it is we desire to know. And $\frac{t}{y}$ I thinke to be double, the one as concerninge our selves, the other an outward application of our selves. The knowledge of our selves no doubte ought to be most pretious unto us; and therein the holy scriptures, if not the only, are certainly the incomperable Lanterne in this fleshly darkness of ours. . . . To them if you will adde as to the helpe of the second table (I meane $\frac{t}{y}$ which contaynes the love of thy neighbour, & dealing betwixt man & man) some parts of morall Philosophy, I thinke you shall doe very wisely. For in trothe oftentymes wee erre, thinkinge we doe well, as longe as we meane well; where indeed want of knowledge, may make us doe as much wickedness (though not soe wickedly) as they which, even pretensedly cōmit all naughtiness. Thereout therfore may we seeke what it is to be truly juste, truly vallyant, rightly temperate, & rightly friendly, with their annexed quallityes, and contraryes.

(Sidney to Edward Denny, 22 May 1580)[1]

Critics who discount the significance of earthly experience and the allowance for human fallibility in Sidney's general outlook often end up discounting all serious value in his poetry. For example, Malcolm Wallace, author of the important 1915 *Life of Sir Philip Sidney*, concludes that Sidney's 'greatness is not in his works but in his life'.[2] As recently as 1971, Robert Kimbrough has written that 'Sidney's deepest thoughts are not to be found . . . in his art, but in his part of the translation of Du Plessis-Mornay's treatise *The Truth of the Christian Religion*'.[3] Yet the facts

---

[1] John Buxton, 'An Elizabethan Reading-List: An Unpublished Letter from Sir Philip Sidney', *Times Literary Supplement*, 24 March 1972, p. 344.

[2] Malcolm Wallace, *Life of Sir Philip Sidney* (Cambridge, 1915), p. 402.

[3] Robert Kimbrough, *Sir Philip Sidney*, Twayne's English Authors Series, No. CXIV (New York, 1971), p. 33. A more recent consideration of the evidence has concluded that the translation of Duplessis-Mornay, which has long been attributed to Sidney, is a 'doubtful work': 'Either Golding's claim that he took over where Sidney left off is false, or he revised whatever fragment was given him so heavily that it can no longer be regarded as a work by Sidney' (*Sidney's Miscellaneous Prose*, Appendix I. p. 157).

are that Sidney wrote great and deep poetry, and he wrote poetry almost exclusively about love.

Another aspect of Sidney's general view of life is also related to his idea of love. That is his attitude toward earthly beauty. Sidney made a revealing statement about it when he was on his deathbed. The circumstances were not propitious for an affirmation of life: he knew his end was near, his flesh was literally rotting with gangrene, and he was surrounded by religious men who were zealously preparing his soul for another sphere of existence. Yet we find Sidney saying this—'The Lord himself is an infinite spirit, and his providence reacheth unto all things. He is a most good spirit; for otherwise how should the world continue in the beauty it hath?' What is striking is that even to the dying man God's goodness is proved by the beauty of the world as much as by the promise of Heaven. The voice is movingly authentic, and we can more readily believe that it is indeed the voice of Sidney because it departs so far from the bias of the puritan preacher who recorded his words.[1] The idea here is also reminiscent of the argument against atheism given by Pamela in the *New Arcadia*. There, too, a loving appreciation of 'this fayre estate' of the physical world

---

[1] George Gifford, *The Manner of Sir Philip Sidney's Death*, in Sidney's *Miscellaneous Prose*, Appendix III, p. 168. Gifford was a minister who was present at Sidney's death and later published his account as a hagiography of Sidney, with the purpose of showing 'the most special things whereby he declared his unfeigned faith, and special work of grace, which gave proof that his end was undoubtedly happy' (p. 166). But there are discernible gaps in *Sidney's Death* between Gifford's stereotype of the dying Protestant Worthy and several remarks like the one I have quoted which break the stereotype and have the ring of Sidney's real feelings. Note how Gifford turns the tone back towards his own sombre point of view in the lines that follow Sidney's statement:

'He is a most good spirit; for otherwise how should the world continue in the beauty it hath?' This he spoke with vehement gesture and great joy, even ravished with the consideration of God's omnipotency, providence and goodness, *whose fatherly love in remembering him, to chastise him for his soul's health, he did now feel* . . . (p. 168—emphasis mine)

This last is characteristic of the preachers surrounding Sidney in Gifford's account. From the moment of his wound they pursue him with the idea that 'such sharp correction doth come from God for sin, and that a man so chastised is to humble himself, and to seek to assuage God's displeasure' (p. 166). The heavy insistence on religious mortification in the face of Sidney's physical mortification strikes the modern secular reader as somewhat barbarous. But at least Gifford's religious enthusiasm throws into relief the few indications we gain from his work of Sidney's rather different feelings: grinding frustration, a deeper fear of madness than of death, and lingering faith in the beauty of the world even as he was forced to leave it.

provides the foundation for Sidney's proof of the existence of God and of the benevolence and infinitude of His power.

For this goodly worke of which we are, and in which we live, hath not his being by Chaunce. . . .
Chaunce is variable, or els it is not to be called Chaunce: but we see this worke is steady and permanent. If nothing but Chaunce had glewed those pieces of this All, the heavie partes would have gone infinitely downewarde, the light infinitely upwarde, and so never have mett to have made up this goodly bodie.

*   *   *

And if his power be above all thinges, then consequently it must needes be infinite, since there is nothing above it to limit it. . . . If knowledge and power be infinite, then must needs his goodnesse and justice march in the same rancke: for infinitenes of power, & knowledge, without like measure of goodnesse, must necessarily bring foorth destruction and ruine, and not ornament and preservation.[1]

These statements corroborate the evidence of Sidney's dying words that devotion to the 'too much loved earth' (*Defence*, p. 78) had a central place in the beliefs which Sidney held in his maturity. He was not a pantheist, but obviously he had a strong religious feeling about the 'ornament and preservation' of the world. On that point we must distinguish carefully between what Sidney actually said and what others have said about him. Fulke Greville, for example, states that Sidney thought at the end of his life 'that even beauty itself, in all earthly complexions, was more apt to allure men to evill, than to fashion any goodness in them'.[2] This is powerful testimony coming from Sidney's best friend, but it simply does not fit with the *New Arcadia*, Sidney's last original poetic effort, or indeed with his last words. In Greville's own mind, however, the distrust of earthly beauty seems to have been present from the beginning. It recurs as a prominent theme both in his love poems and in his religious verse, both in works 'written in his Youth, and familiar Exercise with Sir Philip Sidney', and in works written after Sidney's death, when Greville was con-

---

[1] *The Countesse of Pembrokes Arcadia*, 1590 edition re-issued and edited by Albert Feuillerat in *The Prose Works of Sir Philip Sidney*, Vol. I (Cambridge, 1965), pp. 407–8, 410. Text references will be to this edition, called here the *New Arcadia*.

[2] Fulke Greville, Baron Brooke, *The Life of the Renowned Sir Philip Sidney* (London, 1652), p. 19. Text references hereafter will be to the *Life of Sidney* in this edition.

templating his *Life of Sidney*.[1] As for Sidney himself, other-world-
liness appears so rarely in his works outside a pair of early sonnets,
'Thou blind man's marke' (*Certain Sonnets*, No. 31) and 'Leave me
ô Love, which reachest but to dust' (*Certain Sonnets*, No. 32), that
the two poems have become conspicuous.[2] As he grew older,
Greville grew ever more insistent that virtuous souls should be
'maids in earth's adulterous bed'.[3] But Astrophil, the Arcadian
princes, Philisides, Amphialus, Strephon, and Klaius—all basically
virtuous men—do not find it possible to follow dicta like those of
Greville in the realm of experience; and experience, in Sidney's
philosophy, was never to be ignored. Life, principally through
the experience of love, thrusts upon all of the heroes of Sidney's
poetry the knowledge that, as he wrote fairly late in his career,

> . . . man's virtue is but part of man,
> And part must follow where whole man doth goe.[4]

Unlike his friend Greville, then, Sidney chose to give a positive
emphasis to earthly things. He did not consider the earth to be
merely a seat of temptations, but an attestation, by its beauty, to
the benevolent power of God. Pamela states the general idea with
an inimitable Sidneian flourish:

> I will not here call all your senses to witnes, which can heare, nor see
> nothing, which yeeldes not most evident evidence of the unspeakable-
> nesse of that Wisedome: each thing being directed to an ende, and an
> ende of preservation: so proper effects of judgement, as speaking, and
> laughing are of mankind.
>
> (*New Arcadia*, Bk. III, p. 409)

'Preservation' is the key word in this passage, and it also appears
significantly in the phrase, 'ornament and preservation', which

---

[1] Quotation from the title-page of Greville's *Certaine Learned and Elegant Workes*,
1633. All references to Greville's poetry in the text and notes will be to the edition
of Geoffrey Bullough, *Poems and Dramas of Fulke Greville, First Lord Brooke*, 2 vols.
(New York, 1945).

[2] Ringler devotes a long paragraph to the travels of these two sonnets during
the nineteenth century, when they were inaccurately separated from the *Certain
Sonnets* series and placed at the end of *Astrophil and Stella* (p. 423). Kalstone has
recently revived the idea that the pair are 'the only possible dramatic resolution for
Astrophil and Stella . . .' (p. 178).

[3] Line 70 from the 'Prologus' to Greville's play *Alaham*, in the Bullough edition,
Vol. II, p. 140.

[4] *Other Poems*, No. 4, in Ringler's edition, lines 421–2. His research shows that
the poem was written around the time of *Astrophil and Stella* (1581–3) and also that
the subject matter is close to the *New Arcadia* (Ringler, p. 494).

forms the climax of the entire argument against atheism (p. 410).
The word in these two contexts implies not only proportion and
wholeness in earthly things, whereby they retain their 'proper
effects', but also continuity, whereby earthly things are spared
from utter destruction, yet remain essentially earthly. God must
be good, Sidney mused on his deathbed, 'for otherwise how should
the world continue in the beauty it hath?'

By understanding the larger reverence on Sidney's part for
worldly beauty and for its preservation on earth, we move still
closer to understanding Sidney's conception of love. In order to
proceed from this point with greater authority, however, I must
briefly leave Sidney himself and explore the wider area of attitudes
to love current generally in the Renaissance. The summary which
follows will be of necessity sketchy and even arbitrary. But at
least I will be dealing throughout with works which Sidney could
conceivably have known; and, wherever possible, I will refer to
works he would definitely have known. Once we have an opening
on the complex subject of Renaissance conceptions of love, it will
be easier to return to Sidney's poetry and to define with greater
clarity and historical accuracy the conception of love which we
find there.

A man of Sidney's education in the Renaissance would have
had available to him an assortment of reading-matter—ancient,
medieval, and modern—about love. These works present several
contrasting views of the subject. For our first example Chaucer's
Troilus and Criseyde is an appropriate choice. It contains, even as
it transcends, traditional medieval attitudes to love; and it was
also influential in conveying those attitudes specifically to Renaissance Englishmen. Recent research has shown that it was a high
duty for lovers and poets of the early Tudor court, as it had been
for Gower's Lover in the *Confessio Amantis*, 'to rede and here of
Troilus'.[1] Sidney himself singles out the *Troilus* for praise as an
old favourite in *A Defence of Poetry*, a fact which suggests that the
importance of the work may have continued in late Tudor
literary and courtly circles. In his poems Sidney shows an acquaintance with another popular medieval work, the *Roman de la Rose*.
There the delicate idealism of love portrayed by Guillaume de

---

[1] This point is argued in detail by Raymond Southall in *The Courtly Makers:
An Essay on the Poetry of Wyatt and His Contemporaries* (Oxford, 1964), especially
Chapter Three.

Lorris rubs against the satirical energy and the exhortations to earthly procreation of Jean de Meun. These are the two strains which Chaucer united in his great 'canon' of love.[1] In the *Troilus* he praises them both as part of the fullness of Eternity:

> God loveth, and to love wol nought werne;
> And in this world no lyves creature
> Withouten love is worth, or may endure.
> *(Troilus and Criseyde*, III. 12–14)[2]

Yet earthly love, in Chaucer's formulation, whether idealized by Troilus or regarded naturalistically by Pandarus, cannot last. Like earth itself, and man, it is destined to vanish:

> O yonge, fresshe folkes, he or she,
> In which that love up groweth with youre age,
> Repeyreth hom fro worldly vanyte,
> . . . and thynketh al nys but a faire
> This world, that passeth soone as floures faire.
> *(Troilus and Criseyde*, V. 1835–41)

The presentation of earthly love in *Troilus and Criseyde* contrasts with the attitude shown in many works of the ancient classical past which were also available to Renaissance readers. Rather than portray love as a fragile and momentary state, these works by and large present love more as a constant (though indeed sometimes troubling) natural force in the world. Even the idealist Plato gives an important place in his *Symposium* to the earthly lore he attributes to the wise old woman Diotima. She instructs Socrates thus:

'For love, Socrates, is not, as you imagine, the love of the beautiful only'.
'What then?'
'The love of generation and of birth in beauty'.
'Yes', I said.
'Yes, indeed', she replied.
'But why of generation?'
'Because to the mortal creature, generation is a sort of eternity and immortality'. . . .

---

[1] My reading of *Troilus and Criseyde* has been influenced by the work of Charles Muscatine, *Chaucer and the French Tradition, a Study in Style and Meaning* (Berkeley, 1957).

[2] All references in my text to the poetry of Chaucer are taken from *The Works of Geoffrey Chaucer*, edited by F. N. Robinson, second edition (Boston, Mass., 1957).

'The mortal nature is seeking as far as is possible to be everlasting and immortal: and this is only to be attained by generation, because generation always leaves behind a new and different existence in the place of the old'.[1]

This is the fecund power of nature which Lucretius hymns in his *De Rerum Natura*, the power he calls *Venus Genetrix*. The Renaissance reader would also have found the principle expressed in Ovid, notably in the popular *Metamorphoses*. The *Metamorphoses* emerged from the Middle Ages into the Renaissance not entirely freed of heavy Christian moral glosses, but at least it was seen somewhat more clearly for what it is, an epic of natural love and change. For example, Arthur Golding, who produced the English translation used by Sidney's generation, confines his noting of moral exempla in the tales to a long preliminary 'Epistle'.[2] In the 'Preface to the Reader' which follows, Golding states his desire not to offend 'the simple sort', but ends with a humanist's warning to the moralists:

> If any stomacke be so weake as that it cannot brooke,
> The lively setting forth of things described in this booke,
> I give him counsell too absteine untill he bee more strong,
> And for too use Ulysses feat ageinst the Meremayds song.
> Or if he needes will heere and see and wilfully agree
> (Through cause misconstrued) untoo vice allured for too bee:
> Then let him also marke the peine that doth therof ensue,
> And hold himself content with that that too his fault is due.
>
> (215–22)

Ovid's message in the philosophical climax of the work, the discourse of Pythagoras, does not finally seem uncongenial to Golding:

[1] *Dialogues of Plato*, translated by Benjamin Jowett, in *Great Books of the Western World*, Vol. VII (Chicago, 1952), p. 165. Text references will be to this edition unless otherwise indicated.

[2] Golding's translation of the *Metamorphoses* was published in 1567 and was dedicated to Sidney's uncle, the Earl of Leicester. Jean Robertson notes, in the Introduction to her edition of *The Countess of Pembroke's Arcadia* (*The Old Arcadia*) (Oxford, 1973), p. xxviin., 'for the bulk of his numerous similes and metaphors from classical mythology in the *Old Arcadia* Sidney went to Ovid's *Metamorphoses*, sometimes in Golding's translation'. All passages from the *Metamorphoses* in my text will be taken from Golding's translation, in the edition *Shakespeare's Ovid*, edited by W. H. D. Rouse (New York, 1966). My interpretation of the *Metamorphoses* as an epic of earthly love and change is indebted to Brooks Otis, *Ovid as an Epic Poet* (Cambridge, 1966).

All things doo chaunge. But nothing sure dooth perrish.
   This same spright
Dooth fleete, and fisking heere and there dooth swiftly take
   his flyght
From one place too another place, and entreth every wyght,
Removing out of man too beast, and out of beast too man.
But yit it never perrisheth not never perrish can.
                                        (*Metamorphoses*, XV. 183–7)

A third group of materials on love presents ancient and medieval ideas as they were recombined in new ways for the Renaissance. Dante spiritualized his passion in the *Divine Comedy* and made his beloved seem part Madonna, part Platonic World-Soul. Petrarch in his *Rime* gave a more tensely human version of the same high emotion. Lastly the Neo-Platonic theory of love was developed by the Florentine scholar Marsilio Ficino (1433–99) and was popularized in innumerable poems, paintings, and prose dialogues on love. In his famous *Commentary on the Symposium*, Ficino uses Plato's own distinction between two Venuses, a heavenly one and an earthly or human one, and the two kinds of love which accompany them. But Ficino adds grandeur. He raises heavenly love from Plato's idea of an intelligent and tender relationship between males to the sphere of beatific rapture. In doing so he also raises earthly love to a greater dignity. He makes it a twin (*geminae Veneres*) to the other love, he gives it a share in divine power, and he postulates the existence of a still lower kind of love, the bestial, which, in contrast to the human, has no redeeming divinity at all. The two acceptable types of love Ficino describes thus:

Venus is two-fold. . . . The first, by innate love is stimulated to know the beauty of God; the second, by its love, to procreate the same beauty in bodies. The former Venus first embraces the Glory of God in herself, and then translates it to the second Venus. This latter Venus translates sparks of that divine glory into earthly matter.

*   *   *

There is a love in each case: in the former, it is the desire of contemplating Beauty; and in the latter, the desire of propagating it; both loves are honorable and praise worthy, for each is concerned with the divine image.[1]

---

[1] Marsilio Ficino, '*Commentary on Plato's Symposium*, the text and a translation, with an introduction, by Sears R. Jayne', *The University of Missouri Studies*, XIX. i (Columbia, Mo., 1944), 142.

Although the more contemplative love is considered higher, the propagative love is not therefore deprived of importance. Ficino himself praised the second Venus, in his letter entitled *Prospera in fato*, as a 'nymph of heavenly origin, beloved by God on high before all others'; and he urged the youthful recipient of the letter to take her as his bride.[1] The young correspondent of Ficino was Lorenzo de' Pierfrancesco Medici, a cousin of the Magnificent, and the patron for whom Botticelli executed his companion paintings of the twin Venuses. This famous pair have long been known as *The Birth of Venus* and *Primavera*. But in recent years the pioneering work of E. H. Gombrich and Erwin Panofsky has amassed convincing evidence to suggest that Botticelli's subject-matter may actually have been Neo-Platonic: 'The Advent of the Celestial Venus', in the painting where the naked Venus rises on a shell from the sea, and 'The Realm of the Natural Venus', in the painting where the central female figure, richly clothed and possibly gravid, stands on the earth with the Horae of Spring and the Graces on either side.[2] Another famous work of the period by Titian, a painting traditionally entitled *Sacred and Profane Love*, also uses a naked and a clothed woman to suggest heavenly and earthly love, respectively. Panofsky prefers as the title for this painting Ficino's phrase *Geminae Veneres*. Panofsky points out that, unlike the connotations of 'sacred' and 'profane', the original Ficinian conception of two Venuses meant 'not . . . a contrast between good and evil, but . . . one principle in two modes of existence and two grades of perfection'.[3]

One critic concludes, prior to a study of love themes in Sidney, that human love was 'morally suspect' in the Renaissance.[4] In light of the information above, it seems to me that this conclusion does not do justice to the range of opinions on the subject at the time. In particular, it ignores the most humane and generous point of view—the one evidenced by Ficino himself—that could

---

[1] Translation from the Latin by Erwin Panofsky, *Renaissance and Renascences*, p. 195.

[2] See E. H. Gombrich, 'Botticelli's Mythologies: A Study in the Neoplatonic Symbolism of His Circle', *Journal of the Warburg and Courtauld Institutes*, VII (1945), 7–60 and also Panofsky, *Renaissance and Renascences*, pp. 191–200.

[3] *Studies in Iconology: Humanistic Themes in the Art of the Renaissance* (New York, 1962), pp. 151–2.

[4] Mark Rose, *Heroic Love: Studies in Sidney and Spenser* (Cambridge, Mass., 1968), p. 34.

affirm the moral good in human love without losing sight of its fundamental difference from heavenly love.

From the Academy of Ficino, from the Neo-Platonic mythologies of the painters, the theory of love came home to the drawing-rooms of ladies—and to its widest popularity—with the publication of the many Renaissance dialogues on love. One of the best known of these in England was Castiglione's *Book of the Courtier*, translated from the original Italian by Sir Thomas Hoby in 1561. In the Neo-Platonic discourse by Pietro Bembo which ends that work, the earthly love of a woman is permitted to the courtier in his youthful years; but it is for the 'Courtier not yong' to leave bodies behind and meet soul to soul with his beloved, to 'be ravished through heavenly love to the beholding of heavenly beautie'.[1] Castiglione chooses for the presentation of his ideas on love a completely different forum from Ficino's meeting of like-minded idealists. It is a forum which qualifies and humanizes instead of simply affirming philosophical speculation. Bembo's speech opens to a direct challenge from an older courtier, Master Morello: '(Me think) the possessing of this beautie which he prayseth so much, without the bodie, is a dreame'. And Bembo closes, having completely left behind argument and reasoning, with a rapturous exhortation and prayer:

Let us climbe up the staires, which at the lowermost steppe have the shadow of sensuall beautie, to the high mansion place where the heavenly, amiable and right beautie dwelleth, which lyeth hidden in the innermost secretes of God. . . .[2]

The 'holy furie of love' having passed, Lady Emilia, though deeply moved, nevertheless indulges her characteristic humour. She

tooke him by the plaite of his garment, and plucking him a little said.

Take heede (maister Peter) that these thoughts make not your soule also to forsake the bodie.

Madam, answered maister Peter, it should not be the first miracle that love hath wrought in me.

Unlike Ficino, Castiglione returns us from the high and lonely

---

[1] Quotations from Hoby's translation of the *Book of the Courtier* in *Three Renaissance Classics*, pp. 606, 607.

[2] *Book of the Courtier*, pp. 597, 613.

vision of the prophet to the jokes and compliments of the courtier.[1]

These were the attitudes to love which formed the background to Sidney's ideas.[2] We have already noted the acceptance of human experience which figured in Sidney's definition of self-knowledge. We have also found evidence of his religious intuition about the preservation of beauty in the world. Add to these the simple fact of Sidney's youth, and we should be prepared for an attitude towards love which is as friendly to the worldly twin as to her heavenly sister.

In saying this, I do not forget that Sidney translated the religious poetry of du Bartas and the theological essay of Duplessis-Mornay, *De la verité de la religion Chrestienne*, and that he versified the first forty-three Psalms. The evidence is indisputable that Sidney acknowledged the superiority of whatever was Heaven's own. In the *Defence* he longs for Englishmen to write religious poetry:

Other sort of poetry almost have we none, but that lyrical kind of songs and sonnets: which, Lord, if He gave us so good minds, how well it might be employed, and with how heavenly fruit, both private and

---

[1] *Book of the Courtier*, p. 615. Two studies have likened Castiglione's practice in this scene directly to Sidney's poetry. See Kalstone, p. 122: 'Astrophel's is the kind of human response [in *Astrophil and Stella*, No. 71] . . . that is felt by Signora Emilia after Pietro Bembo's rapt discourse on Platonic love at the end of *The Courtier*'. Also see Rudenstine, p. 30: 'Sidney's heroes [in the *Old Arcadia*], like Bembo, are continually plucked by the garment and brought back to earth, either by the narrator, by events, or by their own unmanageable desires'.

[2] Despite his negative conclusion about love mentioned above, Mark Rose remarks in his essay on the importance which it had in Renaissance literature: 'To the matter of the classical epic the Renaissance added a new subject, love. Vergil had sung of arms and the man, but Ariosto announces that his song is to be "of Dames, of Knights, of armes, of loves delight" ' (p. 2). Tasso defended the choice of love as an epic theme in his *Discources on the Heroic Poem* (1594, translated by Allan H. Gilbert in *Literary Criticism: Plato to Dryden* [New York, 1940], p. 485):

It cannot be denied that love is a passion suitable to heroes. . . . If love is not merely a passion and a movement of the sensitive appetite but also a noble habit of the will, as Saint Thomas thought, love will be praiseworthy in heroes and consequently in the heroic poem. The ancients did not know this love, or did not wish to describe it in heroes. But if they did not honor love as a human virtue, they adored it as divine; therefore they should have esteemed no other virtue more fitting to heroes.

Among Elizabethan poets specifically, Spenser, in his *Four Hymns*, gives each type of love and its accompanying type of beauty a separate and honorable place in the hierarchy of love which mounts 'up to the heavens' height'. The Garden of Adonis in Book III of *The Faerie Queene* is an even more powerful exposition by Spenser of the importance of earthly love.

public, in singing the praises of the immortal beauty: the immortal goodness of that God who giveth us hands to write and wits to conceive; of which we might well want words, but never matter; of which we could turn our eyes to nothing, but we should ever have new-budding occasions (p. 116).

But despite his pious wish, Sidney's own talent for poetry, like that of his countrymen, ran another way. All that survives and all that we know of as original by him (not a translation of the work of others) honours Heaven only indirectly, and comes 'under the banner of unresistible love' (*Defence*, pp. 116–17).

Furthermore, in the catalogue of types of poets and poetry which opens the *Defence*, Sidney specifically leaves to the Biblical prophets the imitation in poetry 'of that unspeakable and ever-lasting beauty to be seen by the eyes of the mind, only cleared by faith' (*Defence*, p. 77). The task of 'right poets' (*Defence*, p. 80) like himself is set on a different plane. They go 'hand in hand with nature' and 'make the too much loved earth more lovely' (*Defence*, p. 78). Thus, as I see it, the focus of Sidney's 'golden world' of poetry is the realm of the natural, not the celestial Venus.[1] The

---

[1] The question of the extent of Sidney's idealism in poetry is, of course, a complex one about which there is considerable disagreement and little hope of arriving at a definitive answer. I have chosen to emphasize in my argument the tie to nature which can be found to be part of Sidney's conception of the 'golden world', as created by 'right poets' (*Defence*, pp. 78, 80). For although Sidney does mention the word *idea* in its Platonic sense when it suits his immediate purpose in the *Defence* (p. 79), more often Sidney seems to me to depend on Aristotelian precepts for his arguments, thus accepting in poetry, as Aristotle does in the general functions of the mind, a basic link between creative thought and its surroundings in nature. This link is present, Sidney states in the *Defence*, even for the metaphysician: 'though it be in the second and abstract notions, and therefore be counted supernatural, yet doth he indeed build upon the depth of nature' (*Defence*, p. 78). Two critics recently have expressed views about Sidney opposite to my own. Walter R. Davis in *Idea and Act in Elizabethan Fiction* (Princeton, N.J., 1969), p. 30, remarks about the meaning of the *Defence*: 'The object of poetic imitation does not exist in nature at all, but only in the mind of the poet. Poetry becomes, for Sidney, the animation of a Platonic Idea....' Similarly Forrest G. Robinson argues in *The Shape of Things Known: Sidney's Apology in Its Philosophical Tradition* (Cambridge, Mass., 1972), p. 132, that 'the poet derives his materials, not from his experiences in the phenomenal world, but from an internally viewed universe of more ideal, more general truths'. I find more convincing the combination of idealism and naturalism implicit in Northrop Frye's statement in *Anatomy of Criticism* (Princeton, N.J., 1957), p. 59, that Sidney 'makes it clear that this golden world is not something separated from nature but is "in effect a second nature": a unification of fact, or example, with model, or precept'. Harry Berger, Jr. also follows that line of thinking in 'The Renaissance Imagination: Second World and Green World', *The Centennial Review*, IX. i (Winter 1965), 36–78. Although he makes use of Sidney's term 'golden world' to refer

fertile invention of the poet, who Sidney says, 'doth grow in effect another nature' (*Defence*, p. 78), and the eloquence of the lover, as in Pyrocles' glowing praise of Arcadia below, pay tribute to the same animating and generative spirit in the earth:

Do you not see how everything conspires together to make this place a heavenly dwelling? Do you not see the grass, how in colour they excel the emeralds, everyone striving to pass his fellow—and yet they are all kept in a equal height? And see you not the rest of all these beautiful flowers, each of which would require a man's wit to know, and his life to express? Do not these stately trees seem to maintain their flourishing old age with the only happiness of their seat, being clothed with a continual spring because no beauty here should ever fade? Doth not the air breathe health, which the birds, delightful both to the ear and eye, do daily solemnize with the sweet consent of their voices? Is not every echo here a perfect music? And these fresh and delightful brooks, how slowly they slide away, as loath to leave the company of so many things united in perfection! And with how sweet a murmur they lament their forced departure! Certainly, certainly, cousin, it must needs be that some goddess this desert belongs unto, who is the soul of this soil; for neither is any less than a goddess worthy to be shrined in such a heap of pleasures, nor any less than a goddess could have made it so perfect a model of the heavenly dwellings.[1]

The *Old Arcadia* must be the proving-ground for any idea which aspires to a larger usefulness in illuminating Sidney's poetry. The primary reason is that this is the only work which we can be sure Sidney carried to his intended conclusion. The *New Arcadia* breaks off in mid-sentence; and there is disagreement about the arrangement of poems within *Certain Sonnets* and even within *Astrophil and Stella*, though the order of the sonnet sequence is constant in the most substantive manuscripts. But the *Old Arcadia*, in all nine extant manuscripts, is complete as it stands; thus the ideas which Sidney wished to embody in it are, presumably, identifiable in their complete form. A second reason for concentrating on the *Old Arcadia*, particularly in order to examine

exclusively to creations of an absolutely ideal character, set in contrast to reality, Berger's other term 'second world' or 'heterocosm', which he uses for mental constructs that hold the ideal and real in closer connection, actually suits better the kind of 'golden world' which Sidney himself created, especially in his *Arcadia*.

[1] *The Countess of Pembroke's Arcadia* (*The Old Arcadia*), edited by Jean Robertson (Oxford, 1973), p. 15. Other references in the text to the prose of the *Old Arcadia* will be to this edition. The 'glow' of Pyrocles' description should be regarded with a humorous eye, in the same way that Sidney regards the 'superlatives' of the poets in the *Defence* (p. 121).

Sidney's conception of love as it developed from the early to the late poetry, is that the Arcadian lovers, in the original story and in the later revision, actually claimed most of Sidney's attention as a poet.

Another reason for interest is that critics disagree about the nature of the feelings of Pyrocles and Musidorus. Some believe that the love of the princes in Arcadia is different from the frankly sexual love of Astrophil, is morally more acceptable than Astrophil's love and thus is capable of a happier resolution. One critic argues that the marriage of the princes to the women they desire gives them the moral sanction which Astrophil lacks. Others argue that the good in the princes' love lies in its implications of a disembodied heavenly perfection like that envisioned by Bembo in the *Book of the Courtier*. Still others find, in the trial of the lovers which dominates the last 'Act' or Book of the *Arcadia*, support for the idea that Sidney finally condemns love.[1] I think, however, that Sidney wrote about the same kind of love between men and women throughout his poetry; and I think that there is evidence in the *Old Arcadia* of a more affirmative view of that earthly kind of love than any of these critics allows.

The 'goddess' whose influence Pyrocles feels at the opening of the *Old Arcadia* (see the passage above) appears soon afterwards embodied in 'the ornament of the earth, young Philoclea' (*Old Arcadia*, Bk. I, p. 37). Her dress, like the rich robes of Titian's and Botticelli's earthly Venus, provokes rather than restrains the sensual imagination: '. . . her body covered with a light taffeta garment, so cut as the wrought smock came through it in many

---

[1] Marriage is the theme of Rose's study, *Heroic Love*; and the higher passion is the theme of Davis's 'Map of Arcadia' as well as the section on Sidney in his other study, *Idea and Act*. All three studies base their arguments on the hybrid 1593 *Arcadia*, where the completed portion of the *New Arcadia* has been combined artificially with the last three books of the *Old Arcadia*. I have referred earlier (see Introduction, p. 3n.) to the drawbacks of this critical procedure. On the other side are two critics who concentrate on the *Old Arcadia* to support their negative views on love. See Richard A. Lanham, 'The *Old Arcadia*', in *Sidney's Arcadia* (New Haven, Conn., 1965), p. 316: 'It is Euarchus who spells out the reader's second thoughts about the adventures in Arcadia'. Lanham insists that even after the

fairy tale ending . . . has married the princely couples and forgiven the Duchess and Duke, the reader cannot help recalling Euarchus' speech. The Duke's murder, he had said, was not the central issue. Justice was demanded for ravishing the princesses. Not private accommodation but justice. (p. 317)

See also Franco Marenco, *Arcadia Puritana: L'uso della tradizione nella prima Arcadia di Sir Philip Sidney* (Bari, 1968).

places (enough to have made a very restrained imagination have thought what was under it) . . .' (p. 37). She draws the lover into a 'contemplation' (p. 38) of her beauty which ends, not in a Neo-Platonic rapture, but in a bed of earthly sexual joy and finally, beyond marriage, in the promise of generation, in the hope of a child to come.

But the solemnities of these marriages, with the Arcadian pastorals full of many comical adventures happening to those rural lovers, the strange story of the fair queen Artaxia of Persia and Erona of Lydia, with the prince Plangus's wonderful chances, whom the latter had sent to Pyrocles, and the extreme affection Amasis, king of Egypt, bare unto the former, the shepherdish loves of Menalcas with Kalodoulus's daughter, and the poor hopes of the poor Philisides in the pursuit of his affections, the strange continuance of Klaius's and Strephon's desire, *lastly the son of Pyrocles named Pyrophilus, and Melidora the fair daughter of Pamela by Musidorus, who even at their birth entered into admirable fortunes,* may awake some other spirit to exercise his pen in that wherewith mine is already dulled.

(Final paragraph of the *Old Arcadia*, emphasis mine)

It is not only in this final passage that the experience of Musidorus in love parallels that of Pyrocles. What Pyrocles demands to know at the beginning: 'If we love virtue, in whom shall we love it but in virtuous creatures?' (p. 22), Musidorus proclaims at the end as the fruit of knowledge in 'those manlike courages that by experience know how subject the virtuous minds are to love a most virtuous creature' (p. 402). Just as, from the first, Pyrocles reacts on an earthly plane to love, by wanting 'fully to prove myself a man in this enterprise' (pp. 22–3), so Musidorus defends to the last his wish 'to seek the satisfaction of honourable desires' (p. 402) with Pamela. Like Chaucer's Troilus, Musidorus begins by scorning the love of women; thus his precipitate fall ('He was wounded with more sudden violence of love than ever Pyrocles was' [p. 41]) is a great proof, as Pyrocles notes, of the power of 'the goddess of those woods . . . to transform everybody' (pp. 41–2).

Chaucer points his lesson about Troilus towards the irresistible force of earthly love:

> Forthy ensample taketh of this man,
> Ye wise, proude, and worthi folkes alle,
> To scornen Love, which that so soone kan

The fredom of youre hertes to hym thralle;
For evere it was, and evere it shal byfalle,
That Love is he that alle thing may bynde,
For may no man fordon the lawe of kynde.

(Troilus and Criseyde, I. 232–8)

Sidney's theme is the same. But he also introduces, through the disguises of the princes, a second theme of love's transforming power. This last has roots in the *Metamorphoses* of Ovid, as well as in the *Golden Ass* of Apuleius (where the theme has both comic and mystical overtones) and in the Circe myth derived from Homer (where the transforming power of sexual love is seen as purely destructive and evil). The theme was taken up in the Renaissance by many writers. We can find it in Erasmus's *Praise of Folly*, in Spenser's *Faerie Queene* (in a positive way Britomart is transformed by human love; in a negative way Grill is transformed by bestial love), and in *A Midsummer Night's Dream*, to name only one of several plays where Shakespeare suggests it.

In the *Old Arcadia* Musidorus acknowledges that love's metamorphoses may not necessarily be evil. But he warns his friend that, on earth, love changes men into fools:

For, indeed, the true love hath that excellent nature in it, that it doth transform the very essence of the lover into the thing loved, uniting and, as it were, incorporating it with a secret and inward working. And herein do these kinds of love imitate the excellent; for, as the love of heaven makes one heavenly, the love of virtue, virtuous, so doth the love of the world make one become worldly. And this effeminate love of a woman doth so womanize a man that, if you yield to it, it will not only make you a famous Amazon, but a launder, a distaff-spinner, or whatsoever other vile occupation their idle heads can imagine and their weak hands perform.

(Old Arcadia, Bk. I, p. 20)

Pyrocles' reply is a charming and clever verbal parry. But I think that the humorous tone of the close prevents the inference which some critics have made that the young man has a serious 'plan for a trip up the Platonic ladder' of love.[1]

Even that heavenly love you speak of is accompanied in some hearts with hopes, griefs, longings, and despairs. And in that heavenly love, since there are two parts (the one, the love itself; the other, the excellency of the thing loved), I (not able at the first leap to frame both in myself)

---

[1] Davis, 'Map of Arcadia', p. 71.

do now, like a diligent workman, make ready the chief instrument and first part of that great work, which is love itself. Which, when I have a while practised in this sort, then you shall see me turn it to greater matters. And thus gently you may, if it please you, think of me. Neither doubt you, because I wear a woman's apparel, I will be the more womanish; since, I assure you, for all my apparel, there is nothing I desire more than fully to prove myself a man in this enterprise.

(pp. 22–3)

These discourses (and our varying interpretations of them) notwithstanding, both the young princes fall in love and disguise themselves. Indeed, like Bottom, they are 'translated', although they wear the 'ass's head' of earthly love with infinitely more grace. Their experience follows a dictum of Folly that even the god Jupiter himself cannot escape:

But the selfe Iupiter, father of the Goddes, and kynge of kynges, who with his onely becke, can shake all heauen, must laie downe his threforked thunder, . . . yea and lyke a plaier must disguise hym selfe into an other personage, in case he woulde . . . gette children.[1]

Their transformation costs the princes some humorously exaggerated sighs:

'O my Dorus, my Dorus', said Cleophila, 'who would ever have thought so good a schoolmaster as you were to me could for lack of living have been driven to shepherdry?'
'Even the same', said Dorus, 'that would have thought so true a chaste boy as you were could have become a counterfeit courtesan.'

(*Old Arcadia*, Bk. III, pp. 168–9)

Moreover, before they reach their journey's end, the metamorphosis of love almost costs them their lives. 'Never had I shepherd to my nephew, nor never had woman to my son', says Euarchus as he proceeds to order their execution (pp. 411–12). Musidorus has argued that 'our doing in the extremest interpretation is but a human error' (p. 402). Euarchus, however, speaking for 'the never-changing justice' (p. 407), comes to his verdict against the lovers by means of reasoning which neatly echoes that used by Musidorus himself in the beginning of the story:

That sweet and heavenly uniting of the minds, which properly is called love, hath no other knot but virtue; and therfore if it be a right love, it can never slide into any action that is not virtuous. (p. 407)

---

[1] *Praise of Folly*, p. 14.

Commentators on the *Arcadia* have often been confused by the trial of the princes (see, for example, Ringler's Commentary on the *Old Arcadia* Poems, pp. 378–9, where he calls this 'the most unsatisfactory part of the *Old Arcadia*'). But those who think, like Ringler, that Sidney meant to put his heroes on trial for a 'crime' extraneous to the main action and theme of love greatly underrate his mastery. Euarchus quickly disposes of the possible guilt of the princes in murdering Basilius. He quite explicitly hangs his whole judgement of them on the second accusation, that they are the lovers of Basilius's daughters:

They deny the murder of the duke, and against mighty presumptions bring forth some probable answers, which they do principally fortify with the duchess's acknowledging herself only culpable. Certainly, as in equality of conjectures we are not to take hold of the worst, but rather to be glad we may find any hope that mankind is not grown monstrous (being undoubtedly less evil a guilty man should escape than a guiltless perish), *so if in the rest they be spotless, then is this no further to be remembered.* (p. 405, emphasis mine)

Of course, they are not spotless; indeed, they cannot be. As Chaucer says, 'May no man fordon the lawe of kynde' (*Troilus and Criseyde*, I. 238). The princes stand accused of the one spot which no human being can avoid. Accused with them, and the first to be condemned for the human spot of love, is that lovable creature, Sidney's open favourite among the ladies in the book, Philoclea. Found guilty of being 'not altogether faultless', she is penalized with a perpetually enforced chastity (p. 380). Her mother follows, an 'excellent lady . . . having not in her own knowledge ever spotted her soul with any wilful vice but her inordinate love of Cleophila' (p. 384). Although her shameful passion remains hidden, she is sentenced to be buried alive for causing the death of Basilius. Next Pyrocles defends himself against the charge of higher crimes, but love he cannot deny:

For my own respect, if I thought in wisdom I had deserved death, I would not desire life; for I know nature will condemn me to die, though you do not, and longer I would not wish to draw this breath than I may keep myself unspotted of any horrible crime. Only I cannot, nor ever will, deny the love of Philoclea, whose violence wrought violent effects in me. (p. 395)

Last Musidorus gives his plea, conceding that love is 'a human error' but asking that Euarchus 'like a wise father turn even the fault of your children to any good that may come of it, since that is the fruit of wisdom and the end of all judgements' (pp. 402–3). The law remains, however; the law must be enforced; and Euarchus, with reason to guide him, enforces it. Pyrocles will be thrown to his death from a tower; Musidorus will be beheaded. Then the revelation comes which draws the judge himself under a more basic law than that of Arcadia, what Chaucer calls 'the law of kynde'. It is his own son and nephew whom Euarchus has condemned to death. He loves them, and thus he too suffers for the touch of humanity in his heroic composition. As he orders justice to go forward, Euarchus is both an admirable and a pitiable figure: 'With that, though he would have refrained them, a man might perceive the tears drop down his long white beard . . .' (p. 412).

By making the trial focus on love, Sidney put Euarchus in the delicate position of passing a condemning verdict on the main action of the *Old Arcadia*, and then having his verdict summarily overthrown. These events have been interpreted either as Sidney's rejection of a too-harsh judge, or as Sidney's heart-felt condemnation of earthly love, spoken through Euarchus, followed by an obligatory happy ending borrowed from the romance tradition. It is useful to consider, before accepting either conclusion, that Sidney also borrowed the idea for the trial itself from an ancient romance, Heliodorus's *An Aethiopian History*. A brief comparison of Sidney's treatment with his source will indicate the deliberateness with which Sidney tied the trial to love and will also reveal Sidney's determination, in the process, not to undermine either the dignity of Euarchus, who must sit in judgement on love, or the heroism of the lovers, who defend it.

In Heliodorus, the trial scene is merely the last bead attached to the string of unrelated adventures in which his lovers participate. Theagenes and Chariclea are condemned to death because they happen to be captives of a foreign war, and thus the law requires their sacrifice. Sidney made a major shift in his trial scene to make love itself the central reason for condemning the lovers to death, but he carefully left out the test of virginity which is important in Heliodorus and which would have been an easy device at hand if Sidney had seriously wished to shame Philoclea and Pyrocles and be a scourge to earthly love. On the judge's side, Sidney quite clearly suppressed several ideas prominent in Heliodorus which, if used, would have weakened the authority of

Euarchus. First, Heliodorus indicates that the law under which his lovers are to die is an unjust and unnecessary law. Sidney could easily have carried this over, especially in the case of Philoclea, but he chose not to. Second, the king–judge in Heliodorus is urged by no less a figure than his high priest to follow the more lenient spirit, not just the letter, of the law. In contrast, Euarchus stands on his own between Philanax, the most powerful Arcadian noble, who urges extreme punishment against the princes, and the princes themselves, who plead for mercy from the weak and doubtful position of accused persons. Third, Sidney omits the the strongest argument used in Heliodorus by the child whose father has condemned her to death: 'Neyther this lawe, nor the lawe of Nature will, that you kill your owne children'.[1] Musidorus and Pyrocles, in a parallel situation, argue against the verdict of their kinsman for reasons of politics, not higher morality (Musidorus states that by killing Pyrocles, Euarchus would deny the rights of the Macedonians to their heir; Pyrocles reverses the argument in defence of Musidorus as the legitimate hope of the Thessalian people). Finally, in Heliodorus, the crowd of onlookers plays a much larger role in the judgement. At first, it is they who desire the human sacrifice, not the king or the high priest; later they are given the right to decide if Chariclea must die. The Arcadian throng has no such power to influence the outcome. In sum, Sidney departed from his source in ways which assure that the choice of life or death is Euarchus's alone, that the legality and morality of the case are unquestioned, and that the general issues at debate are clear. Human love is on one side, law and reason are on the other.

The *Old Arcadia* opens with a debate between two powerful elements in man. Musidorus asserts, 'But the head gives you direction.' Pyrocles replies, 'And the heart gives me life' (p. 23). Seen in these terms, the trial is a final great confrontation between Head and Heart which not only perfects the structural symmetry of the story but also contributes to the over-all thematic statement. The Head directs that the Heart must die, only to discover that it must destroy itself in order to destroy its antagonist. This clash of equally strong forces is also shown in an earlier poem from the *Old Arcadia* eclogues, the 'Skirmish betwixt Reason and Passion'

---

[1] Heliodorus, *An Aethopian History*, translation by Thomas Underdowne (before 1587), The Abbey Classics, No. XXIII (London, 1925), p. 261.

(*Old Arcadia*, No. 27, in Eclogues II). In the end the conflicting elements in man give way to the outside force of Heaven.

Reason.	Yet *Passion*, yeeld at length to *Reason's* stroke.
Passion.	What shall we winne by taking *Reason's* yoke?
R.	The joyes you have shall be made permanent.
P.	But so we shall with griefe learne to repent.
R.	Repent indeed, but that shall be your blisse.
P.	How know we that, since present joyes we misse?
R.	You know it not: of *Reason* therefore know it.
P.	No *Reason* yet had ever skill to show it.
R.P.	Then let us both to heavenly rules give place,
	Which *Passions* kill, and *Reason* do deface.

(ll. 33–42)

Sidney's resolution of this allegory by invoking heavenly rules is not unlike Chaucer's choice to remove Troilus up to Heaven at the end of *Troilus and Criseyde*. Looking down from on high at 'this litel spot of erthe' (*Troilus and Criseyde*, V. 1815), Troilus is cured of his human weakness in love.

Sidney gives his narrative a different ending, however, one which I would call more 'Renaissance' in spirit. Both Sidney and Chaucer believed that earthly love, being earthly, is of necessity marked by the eternal blemish of the Fall. But the trial in the *Old Arcadia* gives emphasis to that idea without recourse to Heaven. Human reason on its own, in the person of Euarchus, questions love and points out the 'litel spot of erthe' in even the most heroical human lovers.[1] When that has been done, and when Euarchus himself has been implicated in the universal human plight, then the trial, it seems to me, has served Sidney's purpose.[2] It is not part of his purpose for the Head actually to destroy the Heart. And to prevent that happening Sidney introduces, not a *deus ex machina*

---

[1] I should point out that the word 'spot' is used in Sidney's trial in a different sense from Chaucer's usage; whereas Chaucer creates an image out of the narrative action, Sidney expresses his theme by means of a repeated metaphor. But the general moral concept in both cases is the same.

[2] Spenser's Masque of Cupid in Book III of *The Faerie Queene* seems to me analogous in intent. It displays the dangers of earthly love, but Amoret is not condemned for risking exposure to those dangers by her loving. The two slight wounds which Britomart suffers also show that she, like Sidney's heroes, is 'spotted' by human love, but that fact does not make her less fit to carry the high standard of Chastity.

to set things right, but instead a fool: 'As this pitiful matter was entering into, those that were next the duke's body might hear from under the velvet wherewith he was covered a great voice of groaning . . . the duke lived' (p. 415).

Throughout the *Old Arcadia* Basilius has played the clown. His egregious foolishness in love is set in high comic relief against the subtler foolishness of the younger lovers. In the scene of his waking, too, this clownishness is demonstrated in his loud groans and his continuing insistence that Cleophila must be a woman. Thus the action which Basilius takes, his reversal of the original verdict of the trial, cannot realistically be regarded as the triumph of a superior human reason over Euarchus's.[1] Rather it must be taken as an affirmation of higher principles than even the wisest man could have approached by human reason alone. Basilius's judgement partakes of the greater wisdom allowed to Renaissance fools.

Considering all had fallen out by the highest providence, and withal weighing in all these matters his own fault had been the greatest, the first thing he did was with all honourable pomp to send for Gynecia . . . to recount before all the people the excellent virtue was in her. . . .

Then with princely entertainment to Euarchus, and many kind words to Pyrocles (whom still he dearly loved, though in a more virtuous kind), the marriage was concluded . . . betwixt these peerless princes and princesses. . . . (pp. 416–17)

Only the fool can admit so readily the supra-rational workings of Providence, and can give way so humbly to his consciousness of personal fault. Basilius implies in effect what Sidney puts into the mouth of another character in the Eclogues of the *Old Arcadia*:

[1] According to the formula for comedy described by Northrop Frye in his *Anatomy of Criticism* and, more briefly, in his article 'The Argument of Comedy', reprinted in *Shakespeare: Modern Essays in Criticism*, edited by Leonard F. Dean (New York, 1961), Euarchus belongs, as does Basilius, to the category of comic figure called the 'blocking character'. Both the duke and the king in the *Old Arcadia* (Gynecia also to a lesser extent) have a part to play in trying to keep the heroes away from their loves. But where Frye states that at the end of comedy the blocking character is typically exposed, defeated, and shown to be absurd, we see something different in Sidney's treatment of Euarchus. The variation may stem from the respect for authority which Frye also notes is a typical feature of Renaissance literature. There is always, he says (*Anatomy of Criticism*, p. 58), 'something about it of the court gazing upon its sovereign'. Euarchus is indeed overruled like the blocking character which Frye describes (*Anatomy of Criticism*, p. 171), but by using another blocking character to overrule him, this time clearly a foolish one, Sidney allows Euarchus to retain his heroic stature.

Lett our unpartiall eyes a litle watche
Our owne demeane, and soone we wondre shall
That huntinge faultes, our selves we did not catch.
Into our mindes let us a little fall,
And we shall find more spottes than Leopard's skinne.
Then who makes us such judges over all?

(*Old Arcadia*, No. 10, in Eclogues I ll. 91–6)

Only a fool, not the responsible magistrate, can afford to acknowledge his part in fallen human nature. And only the fool, finally,
can create social harmony out of others' folly. Basilius does this
first by being blindly simple-minded about his wife's desire to
cuckold him; but after all, as Folly herself says, 'How muche
better shall he finde it to be deceiued so, than thoroughe ielousie
to frette hym selfe, and set all thynges on a rore.'[1] Second,
Basilius is mercifully open-hearted in giving to each other the
young whom Nature has urged to obey 'the lawe of kynde'.

What Troilus learns to see from the Eighth Sphere about the
inevitable imperfection of love in the world is a lesson which
Sidney also teaches in the trial scene of the *Old Arcadia*. With
Basilius's intervention the Head is not definitively refuted; the
Heart is pardoned but not absolved of its human spot. Nevertheless, the conflict between them is effectively stilled without the
necessity, as in Chaucer's medieval *envoi*, of the world and man
fading utterly away before the transcendent love of Heaven.
Earthly love, immanent and eternal in nature, has been Sidney's
subject throughout; and that is what he affirms at the end. Wise
men and heroes may feel its power and may dispute about it, even
to the point of punishing each other. But the mighty force of
generation by which they are affected in fact encompasses far
more than themselves or the whole race. For that reason, I think,
Sidney, like Shakespeare at a similar moment, leaves it to the fool to
recognize of the great and unknowable spirit that, indeed, 'it hath
no bottom'.[2] Where the wisest man would have made a tragedy,
the fool affirms love and life and brings joy, 'inestimable joy',
Sidney notes (p. 417), even to Euarchus himself.

---

[1] *Praise of Folly*, p. 28.

[2] All quotations from Shakespeare in my text and notes are taken from *The
Complete Works*, edited by Alfred Harbage (Baltimore, 1969). Here I quote Bottom's
speech from *A Midsummer Night's Dream*, IV.i. 208–13:

The eye of man hath not heard, the ear of man hath not seen, man's hand is not able to taste, his tongue to conceive, nor his heart to report what my dream was. I will get Peter Quince to write a ballet of this dream. It shall be called 'Bottom's Dream,' because it hath no bottom. . . .

That it should be given to the fool only, not the wise man, to touch upon the essential mystery of the irrational, is an idea which has important Christian connotations. A root-source is St. Paul, I Cor. 2. 9–10, 14:

9 But as it is written: The eye hath not seene, & the eare hath not heard, neither haue entred into the heart of man, the thynges which God hath prepared for them that loue hym.

10 But God hath revealed thē unto us by his spirite: For the spirite searcheth all thinges, yea the deepe thinges of God . . . .

14 But the naturall man perceaueth not the thynges of ye spirite of God, for they are foolyshenesse unto hym. . . .

(Bishops' Bible, 1568. This wording would probably have been familiar to Sidney. An earlier translation also current in the Elizabethan period, the Great Bible, refers in verse 10 'the bottom of gods secretes. . . .')

Erasmus, like Shakespeare later, echoed the biblical passage as he described the highest form of folly:

For this vndoubtedly is euin the very gwerdone that the Prophete promyseth, Saiyng, *was neuer mans eie sawe, nor eare heard, nor thought of hert yet compassed, what, and how great felicitee god hath prepared vnto suche as dooe loue him.* And this is Mary Magdalens porcion, whiche by chaunge of life shall not be plucked awaie, but rather be more perfitely confyrmed.

(*Praise of Folly*, pp. 127–8)

For the Renaissance background to the idea I am indebted to Walter Kaiser, Lectures on Shakespeare at Harvard University, Autumn, 1973.

CHAPTER II

Sidney's Conception of Poetry

THE CLOSING moments of human foolishness in the *Old Arcadia* are linked by their theme of earthly love to the actions which precede them. But the structural link between scenes is a curiously lengthy and detailed digression about Gynecia's potion. At one level Sidney has placed the digression skillfully, in that the leisurely telling of the tale smooths over what might have been a too-sudden leap in the main plot from sorrow to joy, from the verdict of the trial to the final happy release.[1] In addition the substance of the digression itself suggests more subtle uses. It has about it the air of a valediction to the audience Sidney has long held enthralled. More important it introduces, albeit casually, some deeper ideas of Sidney about the nature and purpose of his art. For that reason, at the risk of giving too great prominence to a minor passage, I shall give the digression in full as a preface to my discussion of Sidney's idea of poetry:

... the duke lived. Which how it fell out in few words shall be declared.

So it was that the drink he had received was neither (as Gynecia first imagined) a love potion nor (as it was after thought) a deadly poison, but a drink made by notable art, and as it was thought not without natural magic, to procure for thirty hours such a deadly sleep as should oppress all show of life. The cause of the making of this drink had first been that a princess of Cyprus, grandmother to Gynecia, being notably learned (and yet not able with all her learning to answer the objections of Cupid), did furiously love a young nobleman of her father's court, who fearing the king's rage, and not once daring either to attempt or accept so high a place, she made that sleeping drink, and found means

---

[1] William L. Godshalk, in *Sidney and Shakespeare: Some Central Concepts* (Harvard Doctoral Dissertation, 1964), notices Sidney's skill with the digression, but censures Sidney's 'moral ambiguity':

Although Pyrocles and Musidorus have sinned, they are pardoned. By launching into an explanation of the sleeping draught and recounting the distribution of rewards, Sidney covers the moral ambiguity of the conclusion. Though they have, perhaps, learned from their experience, the princes have sinned with absolute impunity. (p. 76)

by a trusty servant of hers (who of purpose invited him to his chamber) to procure him, that suspected no such thing, to receive it. Which done, he no way able to resist, was secretly carried by him into a pleasant chamber in the midst of a garden she had of purpose provided for this enterprise, where that space of time pleasing herself with seeing and cherishing of him, when the time came of the drink's end of working (and he more astonished than if he had fallen from the clouds), she bade him choose either then to marry her, and to promise to fly away with her in a bark she had made ready, or else she would presently cry out, and show in what place he was, with oath he was come thither to ravish her. The nobleman in these straits, her beauty prevailed; he married her and escaped the realm with her, and after many strange adventures were reconciled to the king, her father, after whose death they reigned. But she, gratefully remembering the service that drink had done her, preserved in a bottle (made by singular art long to keep it without perishing) great quantity of it, with the foretold inscription. Which wrong interpreted by her daughter-in-law, the queen of Cyprus, was given by her to Gynecia at the time of her marriage; and the drink, finding an old body of Basilius, had kept him some hours longer in the trance than it would have done a younger.

(*Old Arcadia*, Bk. V, pp. 415–16)

Here at the penultimate moment of the *Old Arcadia* Sidney has framed a narrative excursion which, as it leads the reader away from the trial, recapitulates in embryo the main events of the rest of the story. We hear once again of the serious young person overcome by passion, the obstacles to love, the conquest of those obstacles, the elopement of the lovers, and their final reconciliation with their royal parent. Sidney also glances humorously at the ageing, would-be lovers in the main plot: the mistaken adulteress Gynecia and Basilius, the infirm victim of her desires, who has tried to fulfil foolish desires of his own. By its love theme the digression looks backward to the main plot and also forward, lending an air of inevitability to the coming reconciliation of parents and children and the affirmation of love. The digression implies at the same time that the longer tale of love in Arcadia has been but one more version of an ancient human story which echoes eternally from generation to generation.

The central motif of the tale, however, has a striking resemblance to *A Defence of Poetry*. The potion with its irresistible effect echoes the 'medicine of cherries' in the *Defence*, the simile which is used by Sidney to express the irresistible effect of poetry:

For even those hard-hearted evil men who think virtue a school name, and know no other good but *indulgere genio*, and therefore despise the austere admonitions of the philosopher, and feel not the inward reason they stand upon, yet will be content to be delighted—which is all the good-fellow poet seemeth to promise—and so steal to see the form of goodness (which seen they cannot but love) ere themselves be aware, as if they took a medicine of cherries.

(Defence, p. 93)[1]

The parallel seems to me significant. The main action of the *Old Arcadia* is clearly drawing to a close at the point where the digression occurs, and those who have been prevailed upon by Sidney's own 'notable art, and . . . natural magic' to while away a good many hours in Arcadia will soon be freed from the poet's spell. Coming where it does, Sidney's careful explanation about the potion provides a commentary on the nature of that spell: its purpose is not to arouse lust or to infect with evil, though the lustful or the ignorant may thus mistake it. Its power, instead, is to disarm those who would resist beauty and to ravish them away from ordinary cares into the presence of beauty, which seen they must choose, like the nobleman, to love. The enchantment of the *Old Arcadia*, Sidney thus assures his readers at parting, has been a benign one.

I believe that Sidney had control of these implications, but the delicacy with which the larger ideas make themselves felt is integral to the charming effect of the passage. The little story is comparable, both in its suggestions about poetry and in the lightness of touch with which they are made, to the epilogue of *A Midsummer Night's Dream*. There Shakespeare chooses the trickster Puck as spokesman (one is reminded of Sidney's 'good-fellow poet'). It is he who comes, with apologies, with assurances and with the humorous suggestion of playing still another trick, to release the audience from the spell of the play. And in this case it is a spell through which, again as in the *Old Arcadia*, we have been moved to see the tricks and transformations of earthly love as being foolish, but finally indispensable to human happiness:

---

[1] There is a direct verbal parallel to the *Old Arcadia* in this passage from the *Defence*. Timautus, in the *Old Arcadia*, is described like the 'hard-hearted evil men' in the essay: 'As for virtue, he counted it but a school name' (*Old Arcadia*, Bk. IV, p. 322).

> If we shadows have offended,
> Think but this, and all is mended—
> That you have but slumb'red here
> While these visions did appear.
> And this weak and idle theme,
> No more yielding but a dream. . . .
>
> (V. i. 412–17)

Through the potion of the *Old Arcadia* earthly beauty prevails, but goodness is said to prevail through the 'medicine of cherries' in the *Defence*. This seeming inconsistency between the two works points to a central critical problem about Sidney's conception of poetry. Sidney's one surviving theoretical discussion on poetry—the *Defence*—seems to demand from poetry a moral didacticism which his own work does not supply. Madeleine Doran, writing about the *Defence*, points to the implied contradiction:

A moralistic aesthetic is apt to regard the romance as either trifling or morally dangerous and is bound to reduce the love sonnet and the pure lyric to lady trifles and immoment toys. Both Sidney and Puttenham are a little deprecatory of the English 'lyrical kind of songs and sonnets'.[1]

Yet the romance, the love sonnet, and the pure lyric are precisely the literary forms in which Sidney chose to write.

The contradiction is a seeming, not a real one, in my opinion. For I have already cited (Chapter I, pp. 11–12) two important passages by Sidney where earthly beauty and heavenly goodness are closely related. These are his argument against atheism in the *New Arcadia* and his words at death. In both places 'this goodly bodie' of the physical world (*New Arcadia*, Bk. III, p. 408) betokens for Sidney the benevolence of God.

By assuming that a distinction does exist between goodness, as extolled in the *Defence*, and beauty, as extolled in the poetry, some critics have been led to conclude that Sidney wanted to reform his poetry at the end and bring it closer to the requirements of the *Defence* by writing the *New Arcadia*. But if we look at the moral growth of Pyrocles and Musidorus in the *Arcadia*, we see that theirs is not the development along strictly didactic lines—from ignorance to knowledge or from sin to salvation—

[1] Madeleine Doran, *Endeavors of Art: A Study of Form in Elizabethan Drama* (Madison, Wis., 1964), p. 88.

on which some critics insist.[1] The princes undergo a subtler moral transition to 'well-doing' from 'well-knowing only', the same sort of transition which Sidney describes as necessary in the *Defence*. The essay makes clear, as we have noted earlier, that human beings—even the best-intentioned and most learned ones —must adjust to 'the balance of experience' (*Defence*, p. 82). Far from showing an intention to change this pattern in the *New Arcadia*, Sidney reinforces his point. For he has added a line in the revision which underlines what Musidorus learns from falling in love: 'I find indeed, that all is but lip-wisdome, which wants experience' (*New Arcadia* only, Bk. I, p. 113).

Accompanying the idea that the *New Arcadia* represents an attempt by Sidney to reform his poetry along the lines of the *Defence* has been the assumption that 'not the *Old Arcadia*, but the *New* belongs to the same period of composition as the *Defence of Poesie*'.[2] All evidence for dating the *Defence*, however, points the opposite way. The *Old Arcadia*, not the *New*, is contemporary with *A Defence of Poetry*. Both seem to have been written around the year 1580. Thus it is very likely that affinities of idea exist between the essay and the earlier version of the Arcadian story.[3]

It is misleading, however, to regard *A Defence of Poetry* as an entirely straightforward exposition of Sidney's theory of poetry which can be applied point by point in comparison with his poetic practice. We have already remarked the philosophical relationship between Sidney's praise of poets and the paradoxical attitudes of Castiglione towards courtiers and Erasmus to his praise of folly. On a formal level as well, Sidney's essay can be understood as participating in the ancient and traditional modes of

[1] Davis in 'Map of Arcadia' and Danby in *Elizabethan and Jacobean Poets* contend that the princes learn to repudiate sinful thoughts of suicide and advance from sexual to heavenly love. The idea of placing suicide at the thematic centre of the *Arcadia* has been countered with convincing arguments by Richard Lanham in 'The *Old Arcadia*', and by Paul David Green in '*Long Lent Loathed Light*': *A Study of Suicide in Three English Nondramatic Writers of the Sixteenth Century* (Harvard Doctoral Dissertation, 1971). Reuben A. Brower, in *Hero and Saint: Shakespeare and the Graeco-Roman Heroic Tradition* (New York, 1971), supplies additional evidence of 'the uncertainty in Stoic thought and in Elizabethan drama as to the rightness or wrongness of suicide, despite the Church's clear judgement' (p. 27).

[2] Myrick, p. 299.

[3] The evidence for dating the *Defence* as contemporaneous with the *Old Arcadia* is given at length on pp. 59–63 of *Sidney's Miscellaneous Prose*. The existence of the verbal parallel to which I drew attention above should also be adduced as evidence for proximity of dating of the two works.

paradox which reappeared and flourished in the Renaissance.[1] One of those was the rhetorical paradox, 'the formal defence . . . of an unexpected, unworthy, or indefensible subject'.[2] At the opening of *A Defence of Poetry* the unworthy and the unexpected unite in Sidney's subject. On the one hand the praise of poetry will be treated in the same spirit as Pugliano's outlandish praise of horsemanship ('if I had not been a piece of a logician before I came to him, I think he would have persuaded me to have wished myself a horse', p. 73). On the other hand it is unexpected that 'poor poetry' should need defending:

And yet I must say that, as I have more just cause [than Pugliano] to make a pitiful defence of poor poetry, which from almost the highest estimation of learning is fallen to be the laughing-stock of children, so have I need to bring some more available proofs: since the former [horsemanship] is by no man barred of his deserved credit, the silly latter hath had even the names of philosophers used to the defacing of it, with great danger of civil war among the Muses.

(*Defence*, pp. 73–4)

The essay also embodies a paradox of self-reference, which hinges on the speaker being a member of the group he speaks about. In the *Defence* it is Sidney the poet who affirms that poets never lie, or rather (even more paradoxically) that poets never claim to tell the truth and therefore cannot be said to lie (*Defence*, p. 102).[3]

---

[1] Rosalie Colie, in *Paradoxia Epidemica*, gives some general reasons for the flourishing of the form:

Quite clearly, paradoxes are phenomena by no means peculiar to the historical period called the Renaissance, but occur in any period or place where intellectual speculation goes on. They tend to constellate, however, in a period, like the Renaissance, of intense intellectual activity, with many different ideas and systems in competition with one another.

She names two possible reasons specific to the Renaissance.

One is the humanist return to ancient texts as models for both life and art. The classical paradox lay ready to hand, easily imitable. . . . The other is the mastery, by the humanists themselves, of the arts of the trivium, which permitted them the linguistic acrobatics required by paradoxy. (p. 33)

[2] Colie, p. 3. She mentions as examples of the form Synesius's praise of baldness, Lucian's praise of the fly, and in the Renaissance, Erasmus's *Praise of Folly* and Ortensio Lando's *Paradossi*—which praises the virtues of debt, of exile, and of other dishonourable or disagreeable conditions (p. 4). In his correspondence, Sidney himself holds forth with equal ease and relish on such diverse subjects as the defence of his own laziness (Sidney to Hubert Languet, 1 Mar. 1578), the defence of the practice of usury among the Genoese (Languet to Sidney, 7 May 1574), and the perfect right of Welshmen to pride themselves on their thieving forebears (Sidney to Languet, 11 Feb. 1574).

[3] Colie, p. 6, gives the model for this type of paradox: 'Epimenides the Cretan said, "All Cretans are liars."'

Thus while the essay makes serious statements, it has other not so serious purposes as well.[1]

What is serious in the *Defence* must also be regarded as related to the particular circumstances that gave rise to the essay. It was not simply a free expression of Sidney's thoughts on poetry. Because puritan moralizing was the source of the attack on poetry which Sidney sought to counter, it is logical that, as Madeleine Doran points out, 'the poets and lovers of poetry therefore were bound to conduct their defence on the ground chosen by the attackers'.[2] This may account for the special emphasis of the *Defence* on the didactic property of poetry.

Moreover, the didactic itself seems to have had a broader meaning in Renaissance poetic theory than we have yet allowed. Rosemond Tuve comes to that conclusion in the course of examining the impact of Ramist logic on Elizabethan poetic imagery:

The poet's 'teaching' does not equate with 'exhorting to moral elevation' in Elizabethan theory or Elizabethan practice. . . . Didactic imagery might quite well assist a poet to argue cogently against accepted moral attitudes. The stress on the didactic amounts to making it a desideratum that images be functional. The image it would exclude is not the one which exhibited no designs toward the moral elevation of the reader, but rather the one which was only in the poem because it happened to occur to the author.[3]

All the reasons cited above should make us wary of extrapolating too widely from the *Defence* as a yardstick for Sidney's poetry, especially as regards its moral tone. Looking in the other direction, from the poetry to the essay, however, we may note a place in the *Old Arcadia* where Sidney's moral tone is obvious. That is in the dialogue of Plangus and Boulon (*Old Arcadia*, No. 30, from the Eclogues to Book Two). The poem repays examination in detail because the moralizing is progressively softened by an awareness of and sympathy for human weakness. Here is the serious side of Sidney's consciousness of human folly,

[1] The traditional purposes of paradox are, according to Colie, 'to show off the skill of an orator and to arouse the admiration of an audience, both at the outlandishness of the subject and the technical brilliance of the rhetorician' (p. 3).

[2] Doran, p. 86.

[3] Rosemond Tuve, 'Imagery and Logic: Ramus and Metaphysical Poetics', in *Renaissance Essays from the Journal of the History of Ideas*, p. 295. See also Rosemond Tuve, *Elizabethan and Metaphysical Imagery* (Chicago, 1947).

and it leads away from, rather than towards a poetry of rigid moral didacticism which some readers of the *Defence* have expected Sidney to produce.

In the dialogue one speaker (Plangus) despairs over the suffering of his imprisoned lover, while the other speaker (Boulon) tries to console him. Boulon begins by warning Plangus sharply against despair and by offering the traditional Stoic–Christian answers to human suffering:

> O man, take heed, how thou the Gods do move
>   To causefull wrath, which thou canst not resist.
>   Blasphemous words the speaker vaine do prove.
> Alas while we are wrapt in foggie mist
>   Of our selfe-love (so passions do deceave)
>   We thinke they hurt, when most they do assist.
>   (*Old Arcadia*, No. 30, ll. 65–70)

But later Boulon's compassion leads him to moderate his tone.

> Thy wailing words do much my spirits move,
>   They uttred are in such a feeling fashion,
>   That sorrowe's worke against my will I prove.
> Me-thinkes I am partaker of thy passion. . . .
>   (ll. 125–8)

Finally his sympathy for Plangus's sorrow grows into a general lament that ends the poem.

> Woe to poore man: ech outward thing annoyes him
>   In divers kinds; yet as he were not filled,
>   He heapes in inward griefe, that most destroyes him.
> Thus is our thought with paine for thistles tilled:
>   Thus be our noblest parts dryed up with sorrow:
>   Thus is our mind with too much minding spilled.
> One day layes up stuffe of griefe for the morrow:
>   And whose good happ, doth leave him unprovided,
>   Condoling cause of friendship he will borrow. . . .
>   (ll. 170–8)

It is a similar attitude in the *Defence* which qualifies all the high claims—moral and otherwise—that Sidney makes for poetry. For example, when he arrives at the idea that the poet can bring 'things forth surpassing her [Nature's] doings' (*Defence*, p. 79), Sidney goes only that far but no further in following the argument of his source, the *Poetices* of Scaliger. Whereas Scaliger goes on to conclude that the poet 'in this process even makes himself almost into another god', Sidney prefers to remind the reader 'of that first accursed fall of Adam'.[1] So too, in his discussion of the 'moving' power of poetry, Sidney puts as much stress on the weakness of men ('most of which are childish in the best things, till they be cradled in their graves'—p. 92) as on the strength of poetry. The following passage shows a typical balance of human capacity with incapacity:

Nay truly, learned men have learnedly thought that where once reason hath so much overmastered passion as that the mind hath a free desire to do well, the inward light each mind hath in itself is as good as a philosopher's book . . . But to be moved to do that which we know, or to be moved with desire to know, *hoc opus, hic labor est.*

(*Defence*, p. 91)[2]

Precisely because of his sense of human weakness, then, the 'moving' power of poetry is as important to Sidney as its 'teaching' power, even more important: 'And that moving is of a higher degree than teaching, it may by this appear, that it is well nigh both the cause and effect of teaching. For who will be taught, if he be not moved with desire to be taught?' (*Defence*, p. 91). This crucial process of 'moving' is accomplished by what Sidney calls 'delight'. I give his definition of the term in full both because of its importance to the *Defence* and because of its possible application to the *Old Arcadia*:

the whole tract of a comedy should be full of delight, as the tragedy should be still maintained in a well-raised admiration.

But our comedians think there is no delight without laughter; which is very wrong, for though laughter may come with delight, yet cometh

---

[1] Scaliger, *Poetices*, I. i. 5, as quoted in the edition of *An Apology for Poetry* by Geoffrey Shepherd (London, 1965), p. 155.

[2] A recent book *Sidney's Two Arcadias: Pattern and Proceeding*, by Jon S. Lawry (Ithaca, N.Y., 1972), has failed to take into consideration precisely this un-idealistic aspect of the *Defence*. As a result Lawry imputes to Sidney a totally positive, indeed a quasi-religious view of poetry whereby the neo-classical 'speaking picture' of the essay comes to sound more like an 'epiphany' of James Joyce's theories ('a speaking picture is in a sense incarnative, allowing the word to be made flesh. . . .' p. 4). I would argue that Sidney makes clear in the *Defence* that poetry is one thing and religion is something else. Except in a few cases, like David's, where the poet is also a religious seer or *vates*, the two do not mix. Certainly Sidney would never have agreed that poetry could substitute for Christian grace, as Lawry would have it, by enabling fallen man almost directly 'to recover his original high estate' (p. i). No human endeavour, in Sidney's view, could adequately perform that function.

it not of delight, as though delight should be the cause of laughter; but well may one thing breed both together. Nay, rather in themselves they have, as it were, a kind of contrariety: for delight we scarcely do but in things that have a conveniency to ourselves or to the general nature; laughter almost ever cometh of things most disproportioned to ourselves and nature. Delight hath a joy in it, either permanent or present. Laughter hath only a scornful tickling.

For example, we are ravished with delight to see a fair woman, and yet are far from being moved to laughter; we laugh at deformed creatures, wherein certainly we cannot delight. . . .

Yet deny I not but that they may go well together. For as in Alexander's picture well set out we delight without laughter, and in twenty mad antics we laugh without delight; so in Hercules, painted with his great beard and furious countenance, in a woman's attire, spinning at Omphale's commandment, it breedeth both delight and laughter: for the representing of so strange a power in love procureth delight, and the scornfulness of the action stirreth laughter. But I speak to this purpose, that all the end of the comical part be not upon such scornful matters as stir laughter only, but, mixed with it, that delightful teaching which is the end of poesy. . . . For what is it to make folks gape at a wretched beggar and a beggarly clown; or, against law of hospitality, to jest at strangers, because they speak not English so well as we do? . . . But rather, a busy loving courtier and a heartless threatening Thraso; a self-wise-seeming schoolmaster; an awry-transformed traveller. These, if we saw walk in stage names, which we play naturally, therein were delightful laughter, and teaching delightfulness. . . .

(*Defence*, pp. 115–16)

There are pitfalls in assuming too high a degree of comparability between the *Defence* and Sidney's poetry, even poetry of the same period like the *Old Arcadia*. Nevertheless, Sidney's distinctions in the passage above help to illuminate the various moods of his story. In the part of the plot acted out by the heroic characters (the princes and princesses, Basilius, Gynecia, and Euarchus) delight is the dominant mood, coupled with that 'delightful laughter' which, Sidney shows, accompanies the realization that we share in the general human folly, as when we see those characters on stage which, he says, 'we play naturally'. To the broader characterizations of the courtier, the bully, the schoolmaster, and the affected traveller mentioned in the *Defence*, the *Old Arcadia* adds its subtler portrayal of 'these fantastical mind-infected people that children and musicians call lovers' (as Musidorus describes them, *Old Arcadia*, Bk. I, p. 17).

'Scornful laughter', mentioned with greater reservations in the passage above, is used in the *Old Arcadia* against the low-born characters and, at times, against Basilius. Some critics also see an implied condemnation of the 'scornfulness' of Pyrocles' action in the image Sidney uses in the passage from the *Defence* of 'Hercules, painted with his great beard and furious countenance, in a woman's attire'. But the joke here rests on Hercules being the famous strong-man out of popular drama, not a lovely boy like Pyrocles. The transformation of sex, which Sidney describes in the *Old Arcadia* without a trace of scorn and with great enthusiasm for each detail of dress, actually affects the reader more in the first way Sidney mentions above, 'the representing of so strange a power in love procureth delight'.[1] Indeed, when Sidney does evoke the image of 'Hercules in a play' early in the *Old Arcadia*, he uses it to describe Dametas, who 'came swearing to the place where Cleophila was, with a voice like him that plays Hercules in a play and, God knows, never had Hercules' fancy in his head' (*Old Arcadia*, Bk. I, p. 31). In contrast, when Sidney refers to Pyrocles, it is in terms of the more graceful Ovidian stories. For example, Musidorus observes admiringly, as he looks at the new-made Amazon:

Sweet cousin, since you are framed of such a loving mettle, I pray you, take heed of looking yourself in a glass lest Narcissus's fortune fall unto you. For my part, I promise you, if I were not fully resolved never to submit my heart to these fancies, I were like enough while I dressed you to become a young Pygmalion.

(*Old Arcadia*, Bk. I, p. 27)

The last image is repeated, also in a delightful rather than a scornful context, at the moment when Philoclea discovers that Cleophila is a man:

The joy which wrought into Pygmalion's mind while he found his beloved image wax little and little both softer and warmer in his

[1] Most notably Mark Rose has branded Pyrocles' disguise as 'ridiculous', both in his book *Heroic Love* (pp. 50–1) and in the article 'Sidney's Womanish Man', *Review of English Studies* N.S. XV (1964), 353–63. Sidney, as if he had been alert to precisely this danger of misinterpretation about Pyrocles' action, added to the costume of the Amazon in the *New Arcadia* an emblematic jewel with the device, 'A *Hercules* made in little fourme, but a distaffe set within his hand as he once was by *Ompholes* commaundement with a worde in Greeke, but thus to be interpreted, *Never more valiant*' (*New Arcadia*, Bk. I, pp. 75–6).

folded arms, till at length it accomplished his gladness with a perfect woman's shape, still beautified with the former perfections, was even such as, by each degree of Cleophila's words, stealingly entered into Philoclea's soul, till her pleasure was fully made up with the manifesting of his being, which was such as in hope did overcome hope.

(*Old Arcadia*, Bk. II, p. 120)

Sidney mentions delight in the *Defence* primarily as the emotion which poetry must stir in the reader if it is to succeed in moving him. But it can be further inferred from the essay that delight is the feeling which moves the poet himself to write. Most of Sidney's attention in the *Defence* is directed towards the feelings of the reader, not the poet. But when he mentions David, Sidney does give his version of what the Psalmist felt: '. . . almost he showeth himself a passionate lover of that unspeakable and ever-lasting beauty to be seen by the eyes of the mind, only cleared by faith. . . .' (*Defence*, p. 77). It is the special subject-matter of David —his imitation of 'the unconceivable excellencies of God' (*Defence*, p. 80)—not any difference in his response to that subject-matter, which causes him to be placed in a separate category (*vates*, or prophet) from Sidney's makers or 'right poets' (p. 80). These last, instead of seeing and loving the immortal beauty, rather show themselves lovers of the 'too much loved earth' (*Defence*, p. 78). But the response to beauty from both types of poets must be the same. Thus the prophet's passionate feeling, imputed to the maker in the domain of earthly beauty, becomes Sidney's joyful and even lover-like feeling of delight. Indeed, Sidney exemplifies delight in a way that suggests strongly that the poet-maker and the lover may converge. For we are all, Sidney states, 'ravished with delight to see a fair woman . . .' (*Defence*, p. 115).

If the poet shares with the lover delight at the perception of earthly beauty, he also shares the lover's desire to propagate that beauty. In the presentation of poetry in the *Defence*, as in the presentation of love in the *Old Arcadia*, Sidney focuses his attention not on private Neo-Platonic raptures, but on the generative principle. Where his earthly lovers aim to propagate beauty in bodies, Sidney's poet aims to propagate the feeling of delight in the minds of his readers. Sidney even argues lightheartedly (following Plato himself, among others) that poetry can outdo nature in the work of generation. For poetry functions not only to make a Cyrus, which had been but a particular excellency as nature might have done, but to bestow a Cyrus upon the world to make many Cyruses, if they will learn aright why and how that maker made him.

(Defence, p. 79)[1]

Thus Sidney's conceptions of love and poetry can be seen to draw towards one another. The vital link between them is the concept of delight, coupling a joy in human and natural things ('for delight we scarcely do but in things that have a conveniency to ourselves or to the general nature'—*Defence*, p. 115) with a gentle sense of comedy.[2] If we return to our starting-point in this chapter, the digression on the potion in the *Old Arcadia*, we can see that the intentions of the lover in making her spellbinding draught parallel the intentions of the poet as set out in *A Defence of Poetry*. Later on, in Sidney's Astrophil, the motives of poet and lover are even more inextricably mixed:

> Loving in truth, and faine in verse my love to show,
> That the deare She might take some pleasure of my paine:
> Pleasure might cause her reade, reading might make her know,
> Knowledge might pitie winne, and pitie grace obtaine. . . .
> *(Astrophil and Stella*, No. 1)

To understand Sidney's conception of poetry we must, finally, look at the elements of conventional poetic theory which Sidney rejected, as well as those which he seems to have espoused. Prominent among the former is the idea of the *furor poeticus* or divine fury. Sidney does not seem to have been attracted to the

---

[1] See Plato's *Symposium* for the parallel argument that love and poetry have similar procreative functions (Jowett translation, p. 166—the words are spoken by Diotima):

Those who are pregnant in the body only betake themselves to women and beget children—this is the character of their love. . . . But souls which are pregnant—for there certainly are men who are more creative in their souls than in their bodies—conceive that which is proper for the soul to conceive or contain. And what are these conceptions?—wisdom and virtue in general. And such creators are poets and all artists who are deserving of the name inventor. . . . Who when he thinks of Homer and Hesiod and other great poets would not rather have their children than ordinary human ones? Who would not emulate them in the creation of children such as theirs which have preserved their memory and given them everlasting glory?

[2] Davis in *Idea and Act* also takes note of the way, in Sidney's *Defence*, that poetry draws close to love through the working of delight; but Davis's thoroughgoing Platonism makes his presentation of the idea different from my own:

Poetry is, therefore, like love in its being and operation. It exists, like love, as intermediary between the concretely actual and the Idea; it acts, like love, to draw men from the actual to the Idea. It is, in short, the mediator of two worlds. (p. 41)

popular theory, which held generally that poets are singled out for direct celestial inspiration. In the *Defence* Sidney uses it merely to crown his argument that Plato, the originator of the idea, 'attributeth unto poesy more than myself do, namely, to be a very inspiring of a divine force, far above men's wit . . .' (p. 109). At the end of the essay, a brief ironic glance at the belief that poets 'are so beloved of the gods that whatsoever they write proceeds of a divine fury' is included in Sidney's final sally of ironic praise (p. 121). Sidney's own rather different assumptions about the relationship between divine inspiration, human wit, and poetry are expressed in a passage I have cited earlier:

> Neither let it be deemed too saucy a comparison to balance the highest point of man's wit with the efficacy of nature; but rather give right honour to the heavenly Maker of that maker, who having made man to His own likeness, set him beyond and over all the works of that second nature: which in nothing he showeth so much as in poetry, when with the force of a divine breath he bringeth things forth surpassing her doings—with no small arguments to the credulous of that first accursed fall of Adam, since our erected wit maketh us know what perfection is, and yet our infected will keepeth us from reaching unto it.
>
> (*Defence*, p. 79)

This statement does not raise the poet above other men. The moment of direct inspiration from God was the Creation, when man's wit in general was formed and endowed with its wondrous creative and imitative powers. The phrase, 'with the force of a divine breath', attributes to the poet–maker a special creative gift among human beings for producing imitations from nature and endowing them with seeming life, but not a super-human contact with divinity.[1]

Another idea which is conspicuously absent from Sidney's statements about his art is the ancient grand belief of poets,

---

[1] Doran (p. 57) takes this passage as evidence that Sidney was 'touched by the inspirational doctrine of poetry set forth in the *Ion*, the *Phaedrus*, and the *Laws*'. But indeed the measure of Sidney's avoidance of that doctrine is to be seen by comparison with the much more extreme 'raptures' of Drayton (in his poem to Henry Reynolds, 'of Poets and Poesie'), whom Doran cites in the same passage as one of the Elizabethan poets that 'likewise respond sympathetically to the doctrine':

> Neat Marlowe, bathed in the Thespian springs,
> Had in him those brave translunary things
> That the first poets had; his raptures were
> All air and fire, which made his verses clear,
> For that fine madness still he did retain
> Which rightly should possess a poet's brain.

'Exegi monumentum aere perennius.'[1] This involves a double claim to immortality, not only for the poetry, but for the object of its praises. Like the *furor poeticus*, the idea becomes the target of Sidney's irony about poets, 'believe themselves, when they tell you they will make you immortal by their verses' (*Defence*, p. 121). Sidney's attitude in this should be compared with Spenser's and Shakespeare's. Spenser, unlike Sidney, expresses faith in the deathless power of poetry:

> Loe I haue made a Calender for euery yeare,
> That steele in strength, and time in durance shall outweare:
> And if I marked well the starres reuolution,
> It shall continewe till the worlds dissolution.[2]

Shakespeare, a dozen or so years later, had an equal assurance about his work:

> Not marble nor the gilded monuments
> Of princes shall outlive this pow'rful rime. . . .
>
> (*Sonnets*, No. 55)

One looks in vain for such an assertion by Sidney. At one point in *Astrophil and Stella* he does play with the possibility of poetical fame, 'Stella thinke not that I by verse seeke fame' (No. 90). But his approach to praising Stella here and throughout the sonnet sequence opposes any claim that poetry could confer immortal renown on her. Rather, she is the source of whatever value the poetry itself may contain:

> For nothing from my wit or will doth flow,
> Since all my words thy beauty doth endite,
> And love doth hold my hand, and makes me write.

It is not only the interest in immortality which is lacking in Sidney's poetry, but also the consciousness of mortality. There are menaces to love in the *Old Arcadia*, but rapacious Time is not one of them. The wish, indeed the necessity in Arcadia is instead (as Sidney puts it in the revised version), 'to give more feathers to the winges of Time' (*New Arcadia*, Bk. III, p. 360). *Certain Sonnets* likewise, has few references, amid frequent outcries of

[1] Horace, *Odes*, Book III, Ode 30 (from Horace, *Odes and Epodes*, *The Loeb Classical Library* [Cambridge, Mass., 1960]).

[2] All text references to the poetry and letters of Edmund Spenser will be taken from *The Poetical Works of Edmund Spenser*, edited by J. C. Smith and E. De Selincourt (London, 1924). I quote from here p. 467, the Epilogue to *The Shepheardes Calender*.

unhappy love, to the fact that time will run out for the lover, even fewer references to the *carpe diem* convention that time will surely run out for the cold and refusing lady.[1]

In *Astrophil and Stella* there is a similar carelessness of time. Throughout the sonnet sequence, the fact that Stella will grow old is never mentioned. *Carpe diem* is not among the many forms of persuasion which Astrophil urges upon her with passionate ingenuity. The reference in the Fourth Song to 'Niggard Time' means the giver of opportunity:

[1] A single, rather tentative statement of the *carpe diem* theme in *Certain Sonnets* is all that I can find:

> If either you would change your cruell hart,
> Or cruell (still) time did your beautie staine:
> If from my soul this love would once depart,
> Or for my love some love I might obtaine,
> Then might I hope a change or ease of minde,
> By your good helpe, or in my selfe to finde.
>
> *(Certain Sonnets, No. 19)*

Unlike the poems in the rest of the series, the two sonnets with which Sidney closes, and especially the last, 'Leave me ô Love, which reachest but to dust', depend on the reminder of time and its end. In the last sonnet this theme is introduced by the 'dust' of the first line and it is carried on by line ten, 'this small course which birth drawes out to death' *(Certain Sonnets, No. 32)*. I have noted earlier in discussing Greville's views about Sidney how rare such sentiments are in Sidney's poetry. That fact is worth emphasizing again. Indeed, an argument can be made that Greville himself may have influenced the unusual choice of theme—for Sidney, not for Greville—in the two final sonnets of *Certain Sonnets*. According to Greville's account in the *Life of Sidney*, as well as Sidney's own testimony in his 'Disprayse of a Courtly Life' *(Other Poems, No. 7)*, the two friends and another, Edward Dyer, had a custom of making poems in each other's company, sometimes on common or answering themes. *Certain Sonnets* preserves one known example of this practice, the companion poems No. 16a, by Dyer, and No. 16, by Sidney, both of which use an image about a satyr in order to differentiate each writer's attitude towards love. In the case of 'Leave me ô Love, which reachest but to dust', there is at least an intriguing likeness of phrasing between Sidney's opening and Greville's close in *Caelica*, No. LXXI:

> . . . I no more will stirre this earthly dust,
> Wherein I lose my name, to take on lust.

The most recent biographer of Greville, Ronald A. Rebholz, in *The Life of Fulke Greville, First Lord Brooke* (Oxford, 1971), corroborates my argument in so far as he concludes (Appendix I, p. 327) that Greville wrote the first seventy-six *Caelica* poems as well as *Caelica*, No. LXXXIII before Sidney died. In this Rebholz agrees with Bullough, the editor of Greville's *Poems and Dramas*. J. M. Purcell gives a detailed list of parallelisms between Greville's work and Sidney's in 'Sidney's *Astrophil and Stella* and Greville's *Caelica*', *Publications of the Modern Language Association*, L (1935), 413–22. In this Purcell inaccurately treats *Certain Sonnets*, Nos. 31 and 32 as the final poems in *Astrophil and Stella*, but nevertheless shows their comparability to Greville's themes. Purcell concludes, 'There are sufficient parallels to imply consultation . . . the parallels would certainly be fewer were they the result of chance' (p. 422).

> Niggard Time threats, if we misse
> This large offer of our blisse,
> Long stay ere he graunt the same. . . .
>
> (ll. 31–3)

Furthermore, there is not the faintest intimation, even in the sonnets where Stella is sick (Nos. 101, 102), that she will die. Thus there is no call for the theme of Spenser in 'One day I wrote her name upon the strand' (*Amoretti*, No. 75) and Shakespeare in 'Like as the waves make towards the pebbled shore' (*Sonnets*, No. 60) that the poet's verse will eternalize the frail human beauty of his beloved.[1]

It can be proved that, outside the world of his poetry, Sidney was fully conscious of time. In the letter he wrote to Edward Denny in May of 1580, at the same period when he was engaged in writing the *Old Arcadia*, the following passage occurs:

Resolve thus $\frac{t}{y}$ when so ever you may iustly say to your selfe you loose your tyme, you doe indeed loose so much of your life; since of lyfe (though the materiall description of it, be the body & soule) the consideration and markinge of it stands only in tyme.

(Sidney to Denny, 22 May 1580)

A poem from the Eclogues of the *Old Arcadia* accords with this view, for in a country disguise it gives an angry portrayal of time wasted at court:

---

[1] David Kalstone, in his book *Sidney's Poetry*, is also struck by the lack of sense of time in *Astrophil and Stella*, particularly in comparison to Sidney's model, the love poems of Petrarch:

By presenting love against an extended backdrop of time, Petrarch can convince us of its refining power and its stimulus to the imagination; he can make evaluations that convey some air of order and certainty. Sidney's sonnets noticeably lack a sense of time and the bearing of time upon love, a characteristic that distinguishes them from the sonnets of Shakespeare and the other Elizabethans. He chooses to ride on the dial's point of the moment and to dramatize the demands of appetite on the world of the ideal. (p. 122)

The difference of Sidney's attitude from Petrarch's can be seen especially clearly in *Astrophil and Stella*, No. 71, where, Kalstone and others agree, Sidney has followed a single, identifiable Petrarchan model, *Rime*, No. 248. In Petrarch's poem the harmonious relationship of beauty and virtue in Laura comes to remind the poet–lover of her mortality ('Cosa bella mortal, passa, e non dura'). In Sidney's work Stella's perfections bespeak a similar ordered relationship between virtue and beauty, which is broken not by the reminder of time and death, but by the lover's relentless physical desire ('"But ah", Desire still cries, "give me some food"'). For a more extended comparison of the two poems see Kalstone, pp. 117–24.

As for the rest, howe shepeheardes spend their daies,
At blowe point, hotcocles, or els at keeles
While, 'Let us passe our time' each shepeheard saies.
So small accompt of time the shepeheard feeles
And doth not feele, that life is nought but time
And when that time is paste, death holdes his heeles.

(*Old Arcadia*, No. 10, ll. 46–51)

But that consciousness on Sidney's part is largely suppressed in the rest of the *Arcadia* and the rest of the poetry. Sidney's lovers, like Shakespeare's courtiers in the Forest of Arden, 'fleet the time carelessly as they did in the golden world'.[1]

The differences I have indicated between Sidney's attitude towards poetry and that of other great Elizabethan poets should not be taken as a sign of his lesser achievement, but of his unique place in this high company. Sidney did not share the professional pride of his fellows. The view of Sidney as a dilettante has frequently been misused either as a means to disparage him, or as a clog to hinder anything but mindless wonder at his gifts.[2] Nevertheless I think it is accurate to say, without prejudice to Sidney's seriousness, his poetic genius, or his considerable craftsmanship, that he made poetry to pass time, without any pretension to conquering it. He drew back quite deliberately from accepting the poetic gift as a mantle conferring on him special powers. This refusal did not prevent Sidney from exercizing his talent brilliantly. But the omission from his work of the conventional poetic aspiration to immortality does have the effect of reinforcing the idea to which I have returned several times already, that of the earthliness of Sidney's creative vision. Neither love nor poetry, which comes close to love in Sidney's theorizing, is raised by him to a super-human power.

[1] *As You Like It*, I. i. 110–111.

[2] The consequences of this view of Sidney have been presented and successfully refuted by Myrick in his book *Sir Philip Sidney as a Literary Craftsman*.

CHAPTER III

Play and the Courtly Maker

IN THE preceding chapters I have discussed the ideas of love and poetry in Sidney's works, but it is also necessary to turn outwards from Sidney's thought and art to get a perspective on the society in which he lived. Sidney's poetry, more than the work of any other Elizabethan, demands attention for its persistent tone of personal revelation. But it is important to understand the social spirit in which those revelations were made, and the related spirit in which they would have been received by the audience towards whom Sidney aimed his works.

Two concepts will assist that understanding. One is a general view of Renaissance society—a view first formulated by Johan Huizinga—which focuses on a social spirit of play and which emphasizes the aspect of games in Renaissance life. The second is a concept of a particular social setting for poetry, poetry both of the late Middle Ages and of the Renaissance, as reflected in the contemporary term 'courtly making'. This term is clearly related to the broad concept of poetry as 'making' with which we began our study of Sidney. But courtly making can be much more narrowly defined, and here it will have a distinct and special meaning and use.

Sidney's private life, and especially his love for Penelope Rich, has been the subject of a more widespread and durable interest by the general public than his poetry itself has been. The popular assumption, fed by often superficial portraits of 'immortal Sidney', is that Sidney lived out his brief life with total romantic sincerity.[1] That view, however, is at odds with what historians know of the sophistication and self-awareness of Renaissance man. Jacob Burckhardt, Erwin Panofsky, and Johan Huizinga have all three described this state of self-awareness as a definitive characteristic of the generalized Renaissance personality.[2] It is

[1] Emma M. Denkinger, *Immortal Sidney* (New York, 1931).

[2] Burckhardt opens his *Civilization of the Renaissance in Italy* (translated by S. G. C. Middlemore, New York, 1935) by describing the new-found political self-awareness

Huizinga who has provided the terms of reference most appropriate for studying Sidney. In his book *Homo Ludens*, Huizinga writes of the Renaissance spirit as playful, treating life as a game.

If ever an élite, fully conscious of its own merits, sought to segregate itself from the vulgar herd and live life as a game of artistic perfection, that élite was the circle of choice Renaissance spirits. We must emphasize yet again that play does not exclude seriousness. The spirit of the Renaissance was very far from being frivolous. The game of living

of the Renaissance Italians, their deliberate attempt to make the state into 'a work of art' (p. 22). Erwin Panofsky, in trying to differentiate the Renaissance from periodic 'Renascences' of the Middle Ages, fastens on the same qualities of 'reflection and calculation' which Burckhardt finds characteristic of the Renaissance mind (Burckhardt, p. 22). But Panofsky phrases his own discussion of them in terms of costuming, rather than art:

'A girl of eighteen', it has been said, 'dressed up in the clothes which her grandmother wore when a girl of eighteen, may look more like her grandmother as she was then than her grandmother herself looks now; but she will not feel or act as her grandmother did half a century ago'. However, if this girl adopts her grandmother's clothes for good and wears them all the time in the conviction that they are more becoming and appropriate than those she used to wear before, she will find it impossible not to adapt her movements, her manners, her speech, and her susceptibilities to her remodeled appearance. She will undergo an inner metamorphosis which, while not transforming her into a duplicate of her grandmother (which no one has claimed to be true of the Renaissance in relation to classical antiquity), will make her 'feel and act' quite differently from the way she did as long as she believed in slacks and polo coats . . . . *Thus the very self-awareness of the Renaissance would have to be accepted as an objective and distinctive 'innovation' even if it could be shown to have been a kind of self-deception.*

(*Renaissance and Renascences*, pp. 36–8, emphasis mine)

In 'Et in Arcadia Ego' (*Meaning in the Visual Arts* [Harmondsworth, Middlesex, 1970], pp. 348–9), Panofsky gives an example of this self-'costuming' which is of particular interest to students of Sidney and of the Arcadian tradition:

Like the whole classical sphere, of which it had become an integral part, Arcady became an object of that nostalgia which distinguishes the real Renaissance from all those pseudo- or proto-Renaissances that had taken place during the Middle Ages . . . . At the height of the Quatrocento an attempt was made to bridge the gap between the present and the past by means of an allegorical fiction. Lorenzo the Magnificent and Politian metaphorically identified the Medici villa at Fiesole with Arcady and their own circle with the Arcadian shepherds . . . .

There is evidence that the same sort of metaphorical identification was made, at least after Sidney's death, between Arcadia and England, with the dead Sidney as the 'fairest shepherd of our green' (George Peele, *Polyhymnia*). Spenser carries through that idea in *Astrophel*, his pastoral elegy to Sidney; and a poem which accompanied it, an elegy by the Countess of Pembroke, is also 'costumed' as the lay of the doleful shepherdess 'Chlorinda'. Roger Howell, in *Sir Philip Sidney: The Shepherd Knight* (London, 1968), makes a case for the usefulness of the fiction of Sidney as the 'shepherd knight' in a national effort to 'build up in the terms of chivalrous romance the political and theological position of Protestant England' (p. 8). In this scheme Sidney was invested after his death with the symbolism both of Christian humility and of heroic action.

life in imitation of Antiquity was pursued in holy earnest . . . . And yet the whole mental attitude of the Renaissance was one of play. This striving, at once sophisticated and spontaneous, for beauty and nobility of form is an instance of culture at play.[1]

By describing the spirit of the Renaissance in terms of the larger concept of 'Homo Ludens', or the spirit of play present in every human society, Huizinga opens the possibility of discovering links between the especially heightened self-awareness of the period and older cultural games of the medieval past. More important, Huizinga's concept of play also allows psychological complexity. It is not simply a consciously-indulged pretence or a form of nostalgia. A game, Huizinga points out, does not exclude real feeling. In fact it can elicit and sustain intense emotions. One can believe, even passionately, in the game being played, and yet know at the same time that one is 'only playing'.

Two examples from the life of Queen Elizabeth convey the variety, the widespread use, and the almost instinctive observance of games in Renaissance England. Both examples depend on the fact that Elizabeth, as the Virgin Queen of Protestantism, came to be identified symbolically with the Virgin Mary.[2] It is reason-

---

[1] *Homo Ludens*, p. 180. Huizinga finds two powerful authorities for the attitude of play in Western culture. One is the Biblical passage I have quoted earlier about the seeming foolishness of God's wisdom (I Cor. 2. 9–10, 14), the other is the following passage from Plato:

God alone is worthy of supreme seriousness, but man is made God's plaything, and that is the best part of him. Therefore every man and woman should live life accordingly, and play the noblest games and be of another mind from what they are at present . . . . What, then, is the right way of living? Life must be lived as play, playing certain games, making sacrifices, singing and dancing, and then a man will be able to propitiate the gods, and defend himself against his enemies, and win in the contest.

(*Laws*, vii. 803, Huizinga's translation in *Homo Ludens*, pp. 18–19)

It is this aspect of Elizabethan social life which Anthony Esler has noted unfavourably in *The Aspiring Mind of the Elizabethan Younger Generation* (Durham, N.C., 1966), p. 115: 'All these Elizabethans had a remarkable facility for swathing and muffling facts in pink clouds of fiction. They clothed their lives in lovely little Arabian Nights' entertainments which served to soften the rough edge of reality whenever it forced itself upon their consciousness'. His point of view is extended to a criticism of Sidney: 'His life and his writings were permeated with "that element of unreality, or deliberate make-believe" of his time and class.'

[2] The 'play' of the Renaissance was not limited, as this example shows, strictly to 'the game of living life in imitation of Antiquity' (Huizinga, *Homo Ludens*, p. 180). But the research of Frances A. Yates in 'Queen Elizabeth as Astrea', *Journal of the Warburg and Courtauld Institutes*, X (1947), 27–82, does indicate that the symbolism

able to suppose that this identification both arose spontaneously among the English and was encouraged consciously by the Queen and her policy-makers. My first example of 'play' on the theme comes from the end of a pageant which Sidney himself wrote, *The Lady of May*. It was performed for the Queen either in May 1578 or in May 1579 at Wanstead, the estate of Sidney's uncle Robert Dudley, the Earl of Leicester. The religious symbolism referring to the Queen is in this instance merely the vehicle for a courtly compliment from the host to his lady-sovereign as she was presented with a gift of agate beads. After the main action of the pageant was over, the pedantic country schoolmaster of the play stepped forward with these additional lines:

Sic est, so it is, that in this our city we have a certain neighbour, they call him Master Robert of Wanstead. He is counted an honest man, and one that loves us doctified men *pro vita*; and when he comes to his aedicle he distributes *oves, boves et pecora campi* largely among the *populorum*. But so stays the case, that he is foully commaculated with the papistical enormity, *O heu Aedipus Aecastor*. The *bonus vir* is a huge *catholicam*, wherewith my conscience being replenished, could no longer refrain it from you, *proba dominus doctor, probo inveni*. I have found *unum par*, a pair, *papisticorum bedorus*, of Papistian beads, *cum quis*, with the

which Elizabeth attracted throughout her reign—Astrea, Diana, Cynthia, Belphoebe, the English Vestal Virgin, as well as the Virgin Mary—can all be connected through classical sources. For example, in the *Fourth Eclogue* of Virgil, the prophecy of the return of Astrea had long been regarded as a reference to the Virgin Mary (Yates, p. 32). In another instance of 'play', one concerning the Earl of Leicester, however, the Christian symbolism seems to have sprung up not from any such learned considerations, but simply from the longing of the people of the low Countries to find a 'saviour'. Sidney wrote to his uncle that 'your Lordeshippes comming . . . is heer longed for as Messias is of the Jews . . .' (Sidney to Leicester, 22 Nov. 1585, Letter No. LXVI in Sir Philip Sidney, *The Defence of Poesie, Political Discources, Correspondence, Translation*, edited by Albert Feuillerat, *The Prose Works of Sir Philip Sidney*, Vol. III [Cambridge, 1923]). Without any direct connection to Sidney, nevertheless his remark is echoed (in a Christian context) in the pageantry which greeted Leicester's arrival at Flushing in early 1586. I quote from the account given in David Bergeron, *English Civic Pageantry, 1558–1642* (London, 1971), p. 52:

The first show, presented on the water, was a fascinating enactment of a Biblical scene with allegorical overtones for that contemporary moment. The earl was confronted with certain fishermen representing Peter, James, and John; 'by them Christ walking on the water, who commanded them to cast out their nets the second time (according to that, of saint Matthew) they drew in abundance. . . .' This striking tableau, without any analogous parallel in English pageantry, doubtless alludes to the 'casting of the nets to France, from whence they had returned empty-handed, and the second casting towards England which had brought forth this "miraculous draught" of Leicester and his mighty army'. Such an interpretation corresponds with the religious fervour that made out of the whole expedition a type of holy war.

which, *omnium dierum*, every day, next after his *pater noster* he *semper* suits 'and Elizabeth', as many lines as there be beads on this string.[1]

The charge of recusancy made here about Leicester, the leader of the most staunchly Protestant faction at court, and stated in Rhombus's fractured Latin is patently comic. The actual source of the Queen's displeasure towards Leicester in the years 1578–9 was not his religious, but his amorous inconstancy. If the assurance of Leicester's devotion expressed above was intended to answer any specific charge at all, it probably attempted to counter the Queen's growing anger and jealousy at the slowly emerging facts of Leicester's love affair with the Countess of Essex and (in September 1578) his secret marriage to her.[2]

But the threat of recusancy elsewhere among Elizabeth's courtiers and in the kingdom at large was real and serious. During the late summer of 1578 the Queen went on progress through Suffolk and Norfolk, an area of lingering Catholic allegiance. A contemporary letter records an event which took place at the house of one recusant gentleman in Suffolk, and which provides the second, very different example of a 'game' played on the same religious theme:

This Rookewoode is a Papyste of kynde, newly crept out of his late Wardeshipp. Her Ma^{ty}, by some meanes I know not, was lodged at his house, Ewston, farre unmeet for her Highnes, but fitter for the blacke garde. . . . And, to dissyffer the Gent. to the full; a peyce of plaite being missed in the Coorte, and serched for in his hay house, in the hay rycke such an immaydge of o^{r} Lady was ther fownd, as for greatnes, for gayness, and woorkemanshipp, I did never see a matche; and, after a sort of cuntree daunces ended, in her Ma^{ty}'s sighte the idoll was sett behinde the people, who avoyeded: She rather seemed a beast, raysed upon a sudden from Hell by conjewringe, than the Picture for whome it hadd bene so often and longe abused. Her Ma^{ty} com'anded it to the

---

[1] *The Lady of May*, in *Sidney's Miscellaneous Prose*, p. 31. Text references will be to this edition.

[2] The Spanish spy at the Elizabethan court, Bernadino de Mendoza, reported that on 28 April 1578 some unspecified rumour about Leicester had been circulated to the Queen which caused her to cancel all her meetings for the day (one meeting had been scheduled with Mendoza himself) and to rush to Leicester's house for an explanation. From *Calendar of Letters and State Papers Relating to English Affairs, Preserved Principally in the Archives at Simancas*, edited by Martin A. S. Hume (London, 1894), II. 581. Henceforward I will refer to this work as *State Papers, Spain. State Papers, Spain* and several histories of the period agree that by the summer of 1579 the Queen had definitely been told of Leicester's marriage.

fyer, wch in her sight by the cuntrie folks was quickly done, to her content, and unspeakable joy of every one but some one or two who had sucked of the idoll's poysoned mylke.

> (Letter of Richard Topclyffe to the
> Earl of Shrewsbury, 30 Aug. 1578)[1]

This remarkable scene was not rehearsed, though Topclyffe's Protestant commentary adds to its quality of staginess. Yet spontaneously the crowd consented to play a game of choosing the true Virgin and repudiating the false one. The unplanned action here has affinities to much of the planned pageantry of the period, where good and evil were often juxtaposed in order to emphasize the preferred choice of the good.[2] For example, one of the *tableaux* which greeted the Queen's entrance into London in 1559, during the first year of her reign, displayed two hills, one barren, 'Ruinosa Respublica', the other green, 'Respublica bene instituta', with a cave between them. As the royal entourage approached, two figures, an old man representing Time, leading a young maid representing his daughter Truth (and carrying an English Bible), emerged from the cave to state the importance of the choice which—in this case—it was necessary for the Queen to make:

> Now since the Time again his daughter Truth hath brought,
> We trust O worthy quene, thou wilt this truth embrace.
> And since thou understandst the good estate and nought
> We trust welth thou wilt plant, and barrennes displace.[3]

Like the *tableau*, Sidney's *Lady of May* is built around a choice which the Queen must make between two suitors of the May Lady. In the Suffolk 'play' the pattern is simply reversed. The country people, in order to prove their loyalty, must make the

---

[1] Letter in John Nichols, *The Progresses and Public Processions of Queen Elizabeth*, (New York, 1966), II. 216–17.

[2] In literature of the period, this particular motif is repeated in the juxtaposition of the false and true Florimell, *The Faerie Queene*, V. iii. 24:

> Then did he set her by that snowy one
>   Like the true saint beside the image set,
>   Of both their beauties to make paragone,
>   And triall, whether should the honor get.
>   Streight way so soone as both together met,
>   Th' enchaunted Damzell vanisht into nought:
>   Her snowy substance melted as with heat,
>   Ne of that goodly hew remayned ought,
> But th' emptie girdle, which about her wast was wrought.

[3] Bergeron, p. 48.

Queen herself their choice. They, of course, rise to the occasion and fulfill its implicit dramatic requirements. On the other side of the 'game', Elizabeth herself may have invested real emotion in the symbolic identification with the Virgin, so much so that she was personally affronted by this appearance of her rival. The possibility is suggested by the unusually sharp and public irritation she is reported to have expressed, as the same progress continued, on her entrance into nearby Norwich. When some children said, 'God save the Queen', she turned to them and replied, 'Speak up; I know you do not love me here'.[1]

Sidney himself, besides writing *The Lady of May*, participated actively in games of another sort which were enjoyed by Elizabeth and her court. These were the neo-chivalric tournaments and tilts. One element of contemporary interest in such events lay in watching the action and judging the skill of the combatants at managing weaponry and horses. Sidney refers to this sporting aspect of tournaments in his letter to his brother Robert of 18 October 1580 and in *Astrophil and Stella*, Nos. 41 and 53.[2] In addition there were the attractions of watching the colourful and rich costuming and of deciphering the mottoes and devices of individuals. An examination of some mottoes and devices which were used by Sidney in tournaments will reinforce the general point I would make about the Renaissance attitude to life as a game: it involved both genuine feeling and self-conscious,

---

[1] The Queen's words were reported by Mendoza to the King of Spain, *State Papers, Spain*, II. 611. In Nichols (II. 129), we have the report of the progress: 'On Sunday, the 10th [of August 1578], the Queen was entertained at Euston Hall, near Thetford, by Mr. Rookwood who was afterwards but ill requited for his hospitality'. The Norwich entry took place six days later, on Saturday, 16 August 1578 (Nichols, II. 137).

[2] Sidney to Robert Sidney, 18 October 1580:

When you play at weapons, I would have you get thick caps and brasers, and play out your play lustily, for indeed ticks and dalliances are nothing in earnest, for the time of the one and the other greatly differs, and use as well the blows as the thrust: it is good in itself, and besides exerciseth your breath and strength, and will make you a strong man at the tourney and barriers.

From *The Correspondence of Sir Philip Sidney and Hubert Languet*, selections edited and translated by Steuart A. Pears (London, 1845), p. 202. The original English has been modernized. *Astrophil and Stella*, No. 41 begins:

> Having this day my horse, my hand, my launce
> Guided so well, that I obtain'd the prize....

Astrophil and Stella, No. 53 opens:

> In Martiall sports I had my cunning tride,
> And yet to breake more staves did me addresse....

socially-accepted display. Neither aspect should be forgotten in assessing Sidney's behaviour. For example, the Elizabethan historian William Camden recorded that

Sir Philip Sidney, who was a long time Heir apparent to the Earl of Leicester, after the said Earl had a Son born to him, used at the next Tilt-day following 'Speravi' dashed through, to shew his hope therin was dashed.[1]

On the one hand the motto signifies, by Sidney's public show of interest, a compliment to Leicester as a new father. On the other hand the event did indeed dash real hopes, particularly financial and marital ones, for Sidney. Ringler dates the birth of Leicester's son around July 1581.[2] In December of the same year a letter from Sidney to Sir Francis Walsingham indicates that Sidney had by then begun marriage negotiations for Walsingham's only daughter, a match which, historians agree, was lower down the social scale than those previously proposed for Sidney. It is also clear from the letter that Sidney needed money. The oblique and witty voice of the *Defence* is heard once more in the passage where Sidney asks his prospective father-in-law, in effect, to pay the postage:

I will be bold to add heerwith the beseeching yow to favor this bearer, that he mai have som consideration for the packet he brought, becawse belonging to my brother Robert, a yonger brother of so yongeli a fortuned famili as the Sidneis, I am sure at least have very vehement conjectures that he is more stored with discowrces then monei.
(Sidney to Walsingham, 17 Dec. 1581)[3]

A motto which Sidney used more frequently and which, indeed, was carried as his official 'word' in his funeral procession, is 'Vix Ea Nostra Voco'. The phrase comes from Ovid's *Metamorphoses*, Book XIII, the famous scene where Ulysses debates with Ajax over which of them deserves to have the arms of the dead Achilles. Of course, Sidney took for himself words spoken by the greater

---

[1] William Camden, *Remains Concerning Britain—1605* (London, 1870), p. 384. Camden also lists another device of Sidney, a thoroughly conventional one, on p. 374: 'Sir Philip Sidney, to note that he persisted always one, depainted out the Caspian Sea surrounded with his shores, which neither ebbeth nor floweth, and over it, "Sine refluxu"'. Frances A. Yates, in 'Elizabethan Chivalry: The Romance of the Accession Day Tilts', *Journal of the Warburg and Courtauld Institutes*, XX (1957), 16, notes several tilts which had a sustained story. In one of them, *The Four Foster Children of Desire*, Sidney was a participant, and may even have been the author.

[2] Ringler, p. 441.

[3] Letter No. LI in the Feuillerat edition of Sidney's correspondence.

hero Ulysses, a choice which, in a later chapter, I shall relate to
Sidney's eventual choice to become a poet. For my present purpose, however, it is enough to note the context of the words, as
translated by Golding:

> For as for stocke and auncetors, and other such like things
> Whereof ourselves no fownders are, I scarcely [vix] dare
>   them [ea] graunt [voco]
> Too bee our owne [nostra].
>   (*Metamorphoses*, XIII. 173–5)

John Buxton has explained that, by taking the motto, Sidney
'proclaimed that proud as he was of the nobility of his descent,
he preferred to it the fame won by his own exertions'.[1] This
sounds like no more than a Renaissance cliché, but, as with so
many aspects of Sidney's life, the cliché intersects with a deeply
personal sentiment. From childhood Sidney had had impressed
upon him the importance of his mother's powerful brothers, the
Earl of Leicester and the Earl of Warwick, to both of whom
Sidney was prospective heir. Even though Sidney's father himself
had a respectable pedigree, nevertheless the deference of the father
to his wife's relations is obvious from a letter which he wrote to
Sidney when the boy was twelve years old:

Remember, my son, the noble blood you are descended of by your
mother's side; and think that only by virtuous life and good action you
may be an ornament to that illustrious family. Otherwise, through vice
and sloth, you may be counted *labes generis*, one of the greatest curses
that can happen to man.

                              (Sir Henry Sidney to Philip Sidney, 1566)[2]

When in 1572 Sidney travelled to Europe to complete his education, the fame of his family had preceded him. At Paris he was
made a baron and a Gentleman of the French king's bedchamber,
not only, according to the official record, because of his personal
qualities, but also 'considerans combien est grande la maison de
Sydenay en Angleterre'.[3] The fact that a tension had already
developed in Sidney's mind between the sense of family and the

---

[1] John Buxton, *Sir Philip Sidney and the English Renaissance* (London, 1965), p. 149.

[2] Letter in Wallace, pp. 68–9. Mona Wilson, in *Sir Philip Sidney* (New York, 1932),
p. 17, mentions the fact that Sir Henry Sidney's own pedigree was largely invented.

[3] Official record given in James M. Osborn, *Young Philip Sidney, 1572–1577* (New
Haven, Conn., 1972), p. 54. Sidney's friends in Europe often wrote to him as 'Baron'
or 'Comte' Sidney.

desire to be accepted for himself is shown by the assurances of personal interest which his friend Hubert Languet felt compelled to make early in their correspondence:

Remember that I fully respect and admire the brilliance of your lineage and all the other gifts with which nature and fortune have so kindly and generously endowed you. But remember also that as a friend my only regard is for the excelling spirit, the love of virtue, and the great integrity which you so radiantly display. For should I encounter a young man of no means whatever who resembled you in manner and spirit, most certainly I should make him my adopted son and heir to all I possess. Nor would I consider it my business to inquire after his family.
(Hubert Languet to Philip Sidney, 18 Dec. 1573)[1]

When Sidney returned from the continent it was again 'that friendly foe,/Great expectation' (*Astrophil and Stella*, No. 21), as well as his own interest in humanist learning, which helped to make him much sought-after as a patron. By 1580 when the *Defence* was written, the list of dedications to Sidney was already long; and it included—besides the dedication to Gosson's *School of Abuse* which may have called forth the *Defence* itself—the dedication to *The Shepheardes Calender*.[2] This last, it seems, was actually meant for Leicester himself. Spenser lowered his sights to choose Sidney because 'me seemeth the work too base for his excellent Lordship' (Letter of Spenser to Harvey, 16 Oct. 1579).[3] A few years earlier Sidney had corresponded directly with Théophile de Banos about another dedication, the one for de Banos's edition of Ramus's *Commentaries*. A portion of de Banos's reply makes clear that the issue was not only Sidney's personal modesty, but also his touchiness about the mention of his powerful relations:

As for your request to change the dedication: although it is impossible to do a complete job, as two thousand copies of the *Commentaries* have already been printed, yet Wechel and I will see to it that, at my expense, your wish may, if possible, be fulfilled at least in the other copies. Admonished by the letter you wrote me last July, I did indeed leave out many praises of your nobility, so as to comply with your wish. The

---

[1] Osborn's translation of the original Latin of the letter, p. 119.

[2] A list of works dedicated to Sidney is given by Berta Siebeck, *Das Bild Sir Philip Sidneys*, Schriften der Deutschen Shakespeare-Gesellschaft, Neue Folge, III (Weimar, 1939). This list is supplemented by William H. Bond, *The Reputation and Influence of Sir Philip Sidney* (Harvard Doctoral Dissertation, 1941).

[3] Smith and De Selincourt edition of Spenser, p. 635.

words I did use, however, were not published at my own impulse, but
on the advice of Master Languet, who considered that nothing more
modest could be said than to mention that noble gentleman, Philip
Sidney, as belonging to the illustrious family of the Earls of Warwick.

(de Banos to Sidney, 19 Mar. 1576)[1]

The meaning of 'Vix Ea Nostra Voco' as a motto for Sidney
is enriched by this evidence that real tension existed in Sidney's
mind between being 'the son of a family' (as Languet frequently
puts it in their correspondence) and wishing to excel on his own
merits. But Sidney did not reject his family. Instead, we will see
later, he tried to cultivate his personal gifts in order to serve his
family better in their interests at court.

Another device besides 'Vix Ea Nostra Voco' which Sidney
used in the play of tournaments and military display deserves
careful attention here. It is a device, 'Spotted to Be Known',
which Sidney both wore in real life and mentioned in the *New
Arcadia* as belonging to Philisides, his anagram for himself. This
constitutes, in fact, the single reference to Philisides which Sidney
allowed in the revision. The character (who in the *Old Arcadia*
plays a much different role) appears only in Book Two of the *New
Arcadia*, as a participant in the Iberian tournament:

... Against him came forth an *Iberian* whose manner of entring was,
with bagpipes in steed of trumpets; a shepheards boy before him for a
Page, and by him a dosen apparelled like shepherds for the fashion,
though rich in stuffe, who caried his launces, which though strong to
give a launcely blow indeed, yet so were they couloured with hooks
neere the mourn, that they pretily represeted shephooks. His own
furniture was drest over with wooll, so enriched with Jewels artificially
placed, that one would have thought it a mariage betweene the lowest
and the highest. His *Impresa* was a sheepe marked with pitch, with this
word *Spotted to be knowne*. And because I may tell you out his conceipt
(though that were not done, till the running for that time was ended)
before the Ladies departed from the windowes, among them there was
one (they say) that was the *Star*, wherby his course was only directed.
The shepherds attending upō PHILISIDES went amōg thē, & sāg an
eclogue. ...

(*New Arcadia*, Bk. II, pp. 284–5)

Abraham Fraunce, in a manuscript treatise *Symbolicae Philosophiae
liber quartus et ultimus de Symbolis absolutis*, supplies a description of

---

[1] Osborn translation from Latin, pp. 416–17.

the personal device which Sidney tried to recall in the passage above. It was a sheep marked with *stars*, not simply daubed with pitch, and it carried the same motto as Philisides' device, *Macular modo noscar*.[1] The actual presence of stars on the sheep clears up what is confusing about Sidney's explanation of Philisides' 'conceipt'. Sidney himself has assumed that the spots are also stars, for he states that the device means, 'there was one (they say) that was the *Star*, wherby his course was only directed'. The spots or stars are the sign by which the lover is known. In the trial scene of the *Old Arcadia* Sidney makes significant use of the theme that human love is 'spotted'. The device of the tournament restates this literary theme with the added overtone of a compliment; the spots of love are also precious marks of distinction for the lover.

There is further evidence that stars were an important element of the personal symbolism which Sidney developed fairly late in his career for show in tournaments and finally in battle. A unique pictorial record which survives of Sidney's funeral shows that the gloves and helmet of his armour were both engraved with stars. Moreover, a guidon from his battle array which was carried in the funeral procession also plays on the star-theme. It represents a fish looking up at the stars, with the motto, 'Pulchrum propter se'.[2]

Sidney's most famous 'star'—a key to which these other symbols are presumably related—is Stella in the sonnet sequence. Literary and historical evidence suggests that she represents a real emotional attachment which Sidney felt for Penelope Rich, an attachment which troubled him even on his deathbed.[3] But in

---

[1] Reported by D. Coulman in 'Spotted to Be Known', *Journal of the Warburg and Courtauld Institutes*, XX (1957), 179.

[2] See Thomas Lant, *The Funeral of Sir Philip Sidney* (London, 1587). In addition, the Oxford book of elegies to Sidney, *Exequiae* (1587), has an elegy to Sidney which refers to him as 'Stellati Pastoris', and another elegist, Francis Mason, states that Sidney's shield was *Stellatus clypeus* (Buxton, p. 176). Buxton takes these as references directly to the poetry, and he expresses surprise that *Astrophil and Stella* could have been so widely known so soon after Sidney's death; but the stars might also refer to the personal symbolism which Sidney had used publicly before his death.

[3] Ringler gives a summary of the evidence that Stella was really Penelope Rich and that Sidney was in love with her (pp. 435–6). Corroborating this evidence is Gifford's account, wherein Sidney is quoted as saying on his deathbed:

'I had this night a trouble in my mind: for searching myself, methought I had not a full and sure hold in Christ. After I had continued in this perplexity a while, observe how strangely God did deliver me—for indeed it was a strange deliverance that I had! There came to my remembrance a vanity wherein I had taken delight, whereof I had not rid myself. It was my Lady Rich. But I rid myself of it, and presently my joy and comfort returned'. *(Sidney's Miscellaneous Prose*, p. 169)

tournaments, as in the poetry, Sidney was capable of putting that deep attachment quite consciously on display.

Turning to the poetry, it should be understood that the use of the word *star* for a beloved woman was conventional long before the Renaissance. For example, Ringler notes that an Elizabethan reader had scribbled these lines from the *Greek Anthology* opposite the Philisides passage about the star: 'My star (Stella meus), while you look at the stars would that I myself might be the sky that I might gaze at you with many eyes' (*Greek Anthology*, vii. 669).[1] The place of the star in the repertoire of poets must have been confirmed in 1572 when a new star appeared for several months in the constellation of Cassiopeia. The most common way of describing this phenomenon, in the Renaissance and also in present-day histories of astronomy, is poetically suggestive: 'It was brighter than any other star; it equalled Venus in brilliancy. . . .'[2] That much-publicized fact may have influenced Spenser in his elegy to Sidney at the point when he describes Stella (whom he associates with Sidney's widow). For he seems to allude to the famous 'Nova Stella' of the recent past:

> Stella the faire, the fairest star in skie,
> As faire as Venus or the fairest faire. . . .
>   (*Astrophel*, ll. 55–6)[3]

J. Robertson, in 'Sir Philip Sidney and Lady Penelope Rich', *Review of English Studies*, New Series XV (1964), 296–7, compares the two extant manuscripts of Gifford's account and decides that the mention of Lady Rich is probably not an unauthorized interpolation. For of the two manuscripts, the one (Cotton Vitellius C. 17, fols. 382–7) which does not have this passage has instead an awkward phrasing, 'whereof I had not rid my selfe, I rid my s. . . .' This seems to have been caused by the deliberate excision of Lady Rich's name, which appears in the other, presumably earlier, Juel-Jensen manuscript.

[1] Ringler, p. 492.

[2] A. Pannekoek, *A History of Astronomy* (New York, 1961), p. 207. See also Giorgio Abetti, *The History of Astronomy* (New York, 1952), p. 84: 'In November, 1572, there appeared in the constellation Cassiopeia, a new, very luminous star, which equaled Venus at her greatest brightness.'

[3] The rapid fading of the star provided another kind of symbol to the Elizabethans. To Thomas Moffet, Sidney's physician and writer of the biography of Sidney entitled *Nobilis or A View of the Life and Death of a Sidney*, the recent manifestation of mortality and change in the heavens was linked in meaning to the untimely death of Sidney:

But in truth let us be mindful, little men, of what worth we are. Are we seasonably born? We die unseasonably. Do we expect health? We feel disease grow stronger. Is hope daily increased? On the very spot it is let slip, and sometimes expires with him who hopes. Everywhere on earth life is lived under the law of mortality, and the

Sidney himself, before he wrote of Stella, was no stranger to the well-worn image of stars as ladies' eyes. It appears in one of his early poems about Mira, the unkind mistress of Philisides (*Old Arcadia*, No. 62, but according to Ringler all poems about Mira actually pre-date *The Old Arcadia*). There Sidney praises the 'eben browes' of the lady and 'the Starres, those spheares conteene' (*Old Arcadia*, No. 62, ll. 9, 15). An interesting change was made in this imagery when Sidney revised the poem extensively late in 1581. 'Eben' (ebony) was replaced by 'even' for the eyebrows, seemingly on purpose so that the colour black could be trans-ferred directly to the lady's eyes: 'the blacke starres those Spheares containe'.[1] If we look at the prose text of the *Old Arcadia*, we will see that Philoclea is described in all manuscripts, early and late, as having black eyes.[2] Yet it was not until a year after Sidney had completed the *Old Arcadia*, at the very time when Stella was be-ginning to form in his imagination, that he merged Philoclea's black eyes with Mira's stars as he revised the earlier poem. It should be clear that, although the same imagery reappears with new vigour in a sonnet like *Astrophil and Stella*, No. 7 ('When Nature made her chiefe worke, *Stella's* eyes') and with new love-liness in a sonnet like *Astrophil and Stella*, No. 48 ('Soule's joy, bend not those morning starres from me'), it was neither new, nor even new to Sidney.

The discussion above suggests that a relationship of themes and imagery exists between Sidney's poetry and the semi-literary emblems which he invented for the game of Elizabethan chivalry.

---

fabric of heaven and the stars is not so fixed but that they are changed in a con-tinuous course, and at the time when they are said to be very large then they are sometimes least visible.

Thus there was hope for Sidney as long as there was life; but the hope which in the first week of his treatment afforded signs of health, in the following forsook his body.

(*Nobilis*, translated by Virgil B. Heltzel and Hoyt H. Hudson [San Marino, Calif., 1940], p. 91.)

[1] The change to black stars appears in the *St* and *Bo* manuscripts of the *Old Arcadia* only. In his summary of the manuscript evidence on p. 370, Ringler dates these two manuscripts (both transcripts of Sidney's *fourth* revision of the *Old Arcadia*) as late 1581 or early 1582, because the *Bo* manuscript is on paper with the same watermark as a letter of Sidney's dated December 1581. The *Bo* manuscript has *ebeene* for the lady's brows, but *St*, the more accurate of the two manuscripts, has *eben* corrected to *even*.

[2] *Old Arcadia*, Bk. I, p. 37 (same in all manuscripts), about Philoclea: '. . . with the sweet cast of her black eye which seemed to make a contention whether that in perfect blackness, or her skin in perfect whiteness, were the most excellent . . .'.

It should also suggest the more intriguing idea that the poetry itself has game-like qualities. Not all poetry of the period has the special combination we have seen above, of autobiographical realism displayed in a context which calls attention to sophistication as well as sincerity. But Sidney's poetry does; and it does so, I think, because Sidney belonged to that special group of poets known as the 'courtly makers'. It was an Elizabethan contemporary, George Puttenham, in *The Arte of English Poesie* (1589), who named Sidney among the 'crew of Courtly makers Noble men and Gentlemen of her Maiesties owne seruauntes, who haue written excellently well as it would appeare if their doings could be found out and made publicke with the rest . . .'. The special designation 'courtly maker' had been used by Puttenham immediately before to describe the 'company of courtly makers', led by Sir Thomas Wyatt and the Earl of Surrey, which was active in literature at the close of King Henry's reign. In neither passage does the phrase imply any derogation of these poets' artistic skill. On the contrary, it seems to have been easy for Puttenham to assume that the court, the centre for so much else of significance in national life, should also be a centre for those 'who haue written excellently well'. In fact, he goes on to say that 'others haue also written with much facillitie, but more commendably perchance if they had not written so much nor so popularly'.[1] Beyond the idea, however, that the courtly makers were associated with the court and declined to publish their work, it is difficult to understand from Puttenham's use of the term what it may apply.

Puttenham's classification of Sidney has drawn little critical attention recently, probably because critics wish to avoid the implication that Sidney was an amateur. In the past, that idea, as I stated in Chapter II above, has led directly to a great deal of confused thinking about the worth of Sidney's poetry. But there have been several serious modern inquiries into the meaning of Puttenham's phrase with regard to earlier Tudor poets. These studies have developed a useful body of facts and theory about the predominant form of the literary practice which Puttenham described as courtly making—the lyric; about the predominant subject-matter—love; and about the poets' range of voices, poses, and literary devices. They have also revealed valuable information

[1] George Puttenham, *The Arte of English Poesie*, 1589 edition, reissued in the English Linguistics series, 1500–1800, No. CX (Menston, Eng., 1968), pp. 49, 48, 51.

about the courtly society which produced the courtly makers, and which the courtly makers served in turn by their verse.[1] In the light of this research we should be willing to give, and can afford to give, serious consideration to the idea of Sidney as a courtly maker.

The ties between Sidney's writing of poetry and his association with the court are very strong indeed. All the available evidence suggests that he only began to write poetry after he was established as a courtier, not while he was a student or a traveller abroad. It has been traditional to suppose that Sidney, on his arrival in France in 1572, sought out Ronsard, de Baif, du Bartas, and possibly Tasso.[2] But Ringler finds no evidence for those suppositions; and James Osborn, whose book *Young Philip Sidney, 1572–77* offers a detailed account of that particular period of Sidney's life, concurs.[3] Furthermore, Osborn's evidence, drawn mainly from Sidney's extensive correspondence, shows that the young man's dominant interests were not poetry, but politics and history. When Sidney did make the acquaintance of two Italian poets—Cesare Pavese and Cesare Carrafa—it was not as poets that Sidney seems to have cultivated their friendship, but as sources of information about Italian politics and current events.[4] The earliest mention of Sidney's interest in poetry came in 1577, when Sidney returned to Europe, after two years at the English court, on an embassy from Queen Elizabeth. A poem written at that time by the German poet Melissus (Paul Schede) refers to 'Sydnee Musarum inclite cultibus'. This may, in fact, be a reference to Sidney only as a patron or a lover of poetry, not as himself a poet.[5] But that is not the case with a second reference to Sidney's writing in 1579, in a Latin poem to Sidney by Daniel Rogers. Rogers enumerates the charms of the ladies of Queen Elizabeth's court, including Sidney's mother, sister, aunts, 'second mothers', and other friends. Then he adds (as J. A. van Dorsten translates the passage),

---

[1] I am especially indebted to Raymond Southall, *The Courtly Makers*, and to John Stevens, *Music and Poetry in the Early Tudor Court*.

[2] See Buxton, *Sir Philip Sidney and the English Renaissance*, pp. 47–8.

[3] Ringler, p. xxii and Osborn, p. 53.

[4] Osborn, pp. 376, 386–7.

[5] Buxton, p. 91, takes the statement simply as a reference to Sidney's 'reputation as a patron'; van Dorsten, in *Poets, Patrons, and Professors*, p. 51, argues the opposite.

My Muse has often urged me to speak of them, but sounds halt in my mouth, and fade. Worthy they are, I think, to be celebrated by the voice of Phoebus, or of you, Sidney, or of you, Dyer. For yours is not a body without a heart, nor were you only born in an illustrious family.

Jupiter has inspired you with a rare genius, the eloquence of Suada has taught your tongue. Whether you wish to speak out in Latin, or prefer the accents of Gallia, or rather express your feeling in Italian speech, nobody could do it more gracefully or better than you. But when your passion seizes our arts, then how abundant are the streams in which your wit flows forth.[1]

It is noteworthy that Rogers assumes Sidney's poetic output is limited to the courtly praise of ladies. When Rogers comes to extolling Sidney's 'pious' interests, it is more than a hundred lines further on in the poem, and the idea is phrased in terms of Sidney's only discussing such subjects. If Sidney had been writing poetry about them, Rogers would certainly have alluded to the fact here:

Nor are you without a faithful and happy circle of companions in whom, in close friendship, there abounds a pious love. In divine virtue Dyer, keeper of judgement, storer of wit, excells. Next comes Fulke whom you have known since the earliest days of manhood, Fulke, dear offspring of the House of Greville. With them you discuss great points of law, God, or moral good, when time permits these pious studies.[2]

Thus it was probably not religious poetry like that of du Bartas which first formed a model for Sidney's verse, but light love lyrics like those of Sidney's friend Edward Dyer, for example. Dyer had been a courtier since around 1565 and had been writing poetry at least that long.[3] In addition, we know that another fellow-

---

[1] *Poets, Patrons and Professors*, p. 63.

[2] Van Dorsten translation, *Poets, Patrons and Professors*, p. 66.

[3] Ralph M. Sargent, in *At the Court of Queen Elizabeth: The Life and Lyrics of Sir Edward Dyer* (London, 1935), p. 11, credits Dyer with being the first Elizabethan courtly maker. He states further,

As the first and eldest lyricist, through both his person and his songs Edward Dyer must be credited with the laurels of a moving spirit in the development which made poetry so popular an ornamentation of Elizabeth's court. In the years immediately following, after he had entered Court life, many other courtiers turned to the lyric for expression: the Earl of Oxford, Sir Philip Sidney, Fulke Greville, Sir Walter Raleigh, the Earl of Essex. Significantly, with the exception of Oxford, all were personal friends of Dyer, and knew and admired his verse. (p. 11)

Ringler, p. xxxvi, lists as other influences on Sidney's verse the poetry of Ovid, Virgil, Horace, Petrarch, Sannazaro, and Montemayor.

courtier Thomas Drant (who died in April 1578) was an early influence on Sidney, specifically on his writing poetry in classical metres. The Spenser-Harvey correspondence of 1580, wherein this last fact is revealed, also carries another direct reference to Sidney as a practising poet. Harvey, like Rogers, mentions Sidney as a poet in company with Dyer; and his adjectives about their work once again evoke the writing of lyrics: '. . . some delicate, and choyce elegant Poesie of good *M. Sidneys*, or *M. Dyers*, (ouer very *Castor*, and *Pollux* for such and many greater matters) . . .'. These are not poets with serious ambitions to 'overgo' Ariosto, as Harvey's friend Spenser was hoping to do even at that early date (Harvey to Spenser, May 1580).[1] Rather they are writers of a different kind of poetry suitable to their main social role as courtiers. Like Wyatt and Surrey before them, they are courtly makers.

The earliest known work by Sidney is *The Lady of May*, written expressly to divert the Queen on progress. There is a further possibility that Sidney also composed another pageant in 1581 for court performance, the tourney-play *The Foster Children of Desire*.[2] As for his other creative endeavours, Sidney did not publish any of them, but rather, again like Wyatt and Surrey, circulated hand-written copies of selected pieces among his friends.[3] Indeed the *Defence* offers a humorous apology for this practice among the better sort of English poets:

For now, as if all the Muses were got with child to bring forth bastard poets, without any commission they do post over the banks of Helicon, till they make the readers more weary than post-horses; while, in the meantime, they

Queis meliore luto finxit praecordia Titan [Juvenal, *Satires*, xvi. 35]

---

[1] Smith and De Selincourt edition of Spenser, pp. 626, 628.

[2] See Ringler, p. 518, where he summarizes the evidence which led him to include two poems from the pageant in his edition designated as 'possibly by Sidney'.

[3] For example, one copy of *Certain Sonnets*, No. 30 has written on it, 'A Dytte mad by Sʳ phillip sydnye gevene me Att pvttenye In svrrye Decembris xᵒ Annᵒ 1584' (Ringler, p. 555). The sheet of paper appears in a collection of verses made by Edward Bannister, a Catholic recusant who lived near Sidney at Barn Elms, the home of Sidney's father-in-law Sir Francis Walsingham. Also Ringler finds (p. 557) that several versions of poems from *Certain Sonnets* 'must derive from a body of texts that circulated in the manuscript miscellanies of the 1580's and 1590's'. These collections of verses are similar to the Devonshire manuscript of early Tudor courtly poetry mentioned by Southall and Stevens.

are better content to suppress the outflowings of their wit, than, by publishing them, to be accounted knights of the same order.

(*Defence*, p. 111)[1]

[1] Another similarity between Sidney's poetry and that of his predecessors is also worth mentioning in our attempt to give evidence that Sidney was a courtly maker. Sidney's lyrics, like the 'balets' of Wyatt and the early Tudor courtly makers, are closely associated with music. In fact the association is so close that questions inevitably arise about the extent of Sidney's accomplishments as a musician and the predominance of music or poetry in inspiring him to write. *The Lady of May* and the *Old Arcadia* both have stage directions calling for musical instruments (cornets, recorders, rebecks, harps, lyras, and lutes) to accompany various poems. In *Certain Sonnets* there are references of a conventional type to the poet 'singing' of love. But in addition eight of the poems (*Certain Sonnets*, Nos. 3, 4, 6, 7, 23, 24, 26, 27) carry indications of actual tunes (not composed by Sidney) to which the verses written by Sidney were presumably meant to be sung. One poem, *Certain Sonnets*, No. 24 (to the tune of 'The Smokes of Melancholy'), seems to scan in iambics with the pause of a whole foot (/∪) on the single-syllable word 'pangs' in line two. The extra beat would have been supplied by the accompanying music:

Who hath ever felt the change of love,	5a iambic
And knowne those pangs that the losers prove	5a iambic
May paint my face without seeing mee	5b iambic
And write the state how my fancies bee,	5b iambic
The lothsome buds growne on sorrow's tree.	5b iambic

In *Astrophil and Stella*, besides the eleven poems specifically designated as 'Songs', there are several casual allusions, like this one in sonnet No. 57, to musical performances of the poetry:

> She heard my plaints, and did not only heare,
> But them (so sweete is she) most sweetly sing.

Furthermore it should be remembered that one of Sidney's purposes in undertaking to versify the *Psalms* was a musical one, that they could be more easily set to music and sung. Like Sidney, Wyatt and Surrey both were drawn to attempt the same task late in their lives. Finally in this connection with music, it is significant that one of only two extant references by Sidney to his own poetry in a private letter is the special reminder he sent to Edward Denny in the letter of 22 May 1580: 'remember w[t] your good voyce, to singe my songes, for they will one well become an other'. The questions which this information raises about Sidney's knowledge of music are the same sorts of questions which John Stevens attempted to answer for the earlier courtly makers in *Music and Poetry in the Early Tudor Court*. I think that Stevens's conclusion about the earlier poets holds true for Sidney: 'The only strong link between poets and composers was their mutual interest in popular song. Whatever the mainspring of the early Tudor lyric, it was not, as I see it, music' (p. 139). Although Sidney was obviously very interested in music, his lack of real knowledge of the subject is reflected in the letter to his brother Robert of 18 October 1580: 'Now, sweet brother, take a delight to keep and increase your music, you will not believe what a want I find of it in my melancholy times' (Pears, p. 202). For further discussion of the relationship between Sidney's poetry and music, see Frank J. Fabry, 'Sidney's Poetry and Italian Song-Form', *English Literary Renaissance*, III. ii (Spring 1973), 232–48.

John Stevens makes a useful connection between courtly making as a concept of socially-orientated poetry and the larger concept of games which we have examined in the society to which Sidney belonged. Stevens argues that the actual distinguishing characteristic of the courtly makers is that they wrote poetry as part of a game—the aristocratic game of courtly love. In the passage below from his book *Music and Poetry in the Early Tudor Court*, there is a clear resemblance between what Stevens remarks about early Tudor courtly life and what we have already remarked in the Elizabethan court culture surrounding Sidney, as well as in Sidney's own actions and poetry. In this formulation the concepts and practice of courtly love and courtly making emerge from the same social spirit of play, the same balance of sincerity and self-awareness that we have seen at work before.

Wyatt's balets were written for occasions when the presence of ladies was more important than the presence of music. The balets belong to a tradition of *vers de société* which can be traced back at least a hundred and fifty years. This tradition is inseparably bound up with courtly love. The 'courtly makers' were the 'courtly-love makers' before they were anything else. Perhaps also the 'courtly love-makers', though this does not necessarily follow . . . . One basic false assumption has vitiated much critical comment on the literature of courtly love in the later Middle Ages; it is the idea that courtly love was either 'literary' or 'actual'. The conclusion reached is that as it was, manifestly, seldom 'actual', a matter of historical fact, it must therefore have been purely 'literary'. . . . The point is that literature was not only literature but very much more. . . .

'Ritual' is a possible word with which to describe the 'middle space' of courtly love, a space of attitude and behaviour, words and actions, included neither under actual *amours* nor under literature. But the word I prefer and shall use is 'game'—a good Middle English term with a wealth of association: fun; a diversion; amorous play; a contest; an intrigue; the chase; the quarry. All these related meanings are apt when we are trying to reconstruct the social fiction which was courtly love in action.[1]

---

[1] Stevens, pp. 150–51. Stevens (p. 153) acknowledges the influence of Huizinga's *Waning of the Middle Ages* (London, 1927), but states that Huizinga's other book *Homo Ludens* did not become available until after he had formed his own conclusions about games and courtly making. The idea of the 'game of love' should be differentiated from David Lloyd Stevenson's idea of the 'love-game comedy', in *The Love-Game Comedy* (Morningside Heights, N.Y., 1946). Stevenson makes a sharp distinction between the Renaissance and the Middle Ages in the attitude to love, and he only allows the term 'love-game' for certain comedies by Shakespeare. For

As this passage strongly implies, the 'game of love' was not invented by the Renaissance, but like the play of chivalry, was
inherited from the Middle Ages. In Sidney's milieu, as in Wyatt's
and in Chaucer's, love was the socially desirable outlet for the
poet, and poetry was the socially acceptable outlet for the lover.
For example, in *The Knight's Tale* there is a festive gathering at
the palace of Theseus. Among pastimes like dancing and singing
Chaucer also mentions 'who moost felyngly speketh of love'.[1] A
note by Ringler on *Astrophil and Stella* is illuminated by reference
to a similar sort of social setting for poetry of love as well as for
talk of love:

As soon as the sonnets began to circulate after Sidney's death, a number
of contemporaries identified Stella as Lady Rich, and in five of the
seven books dedicated to her, between 1594 and 1606, the authors went
out of their way to associate her with Astrophil, which shows that she
was pleased with and accepted the identification.[2]

Despite the fact that Penelope Rich was married—and also became
the mistress of another man, Charles Blount, in 1588—she did
not object to being associated openly at the same time with a
brilliant series of poems by a third wooer who was known to have
had the power to speak 'moost felyngly' of love.

example, *As You Like It* is a 'love-game comedy', but *A Midsummer Night's Dream*
is not. Danby's idea of 'Great House' literature, which he propounds in *Elizabethan
and Jacobean Poets*, also sounds similar to courtly making; but actually Danby's term
is merely an impressionistic one (Sidney, as a 'Great House' poet, is compared to
Shakespeare, the writer of the 'open air'—pp. 16–17). Danby does not seek to
identify a literary practice of a social group, but to convey the atmosphere of the
work of an individual. One last comparison should be noted between Stevens and
Southall in *The Courtly Makers*. The following quotation from Southall will indicate
the way in which he diverges from Stevens's interest in identifying the conventions
of the game of love. Southall has a much greater interest in the psychological
realism behind the early Tudor lyric:

The first impression which such poetry is bound to make is of the highly conventional character of the sentiment. . . . But once the conventions have been assimilated
what appears is a new and important 'voice' plaintively expressing a trepidation and
insecurity which gives to the complaint a new and personally direct urgency. It is
here, when the psychological dimensions of some early-Tudor Court poems are
considered, that it becomes necessary to suppose that one is confronting a personality. . . . (p. 67)

Southall's greater concern with the historical and psychological circumstances of
the early Tudor lyric makes his work not the less stimulating, but less useful for my
particular purpose of crossing historical lines to place Sidney among the courtly
makers.

[1] *The Knight's Tale*, l. 2203, Fragment I(A) of *The Canterbury Tales* in the Robinson
edition. This reference came to my attention through Stevens, p. 159.

[2] Ringler, p. 436.

On Sidney's side of the love affair, as it is reflected in *Astrophil and Stella*, the same social element is visible. Self-display, and even an aspect of contest between courtier-poets, coexists with Sidney's expression of deep personal feelings. Critics have often noted, for example, the autobiographical and topical allusions in Sonnet No. 30 to 'my father' and to the current political situation of 1582, the conceit of Sonnet No. 65 using the Sidney coat of arms ('Thou bear'st the arrow, I the arrow head'), the reference in Sonnet No. 13 to the Devereux heraldry ('[Stella's] face he [Cupid] makes his shield,/Where roses gueuls are borne in silver field'), and several puns throughout the sonnet sequence on the name of Lord Rich (see *Astrophil and Stella*, No. 24, 35, 37).[1] Although no evidence survives that Sidney actually performed or circulated the poems during his lifetime, these allusions were obviously conceived not merely to pique the interest of a curious posterity, but to entertain some knowing, and thus readily appreciative, Elizabethan company.

Evidence does remain to suggest that a playful rivalry may have existed between Sidney and Greville as to who could write 'moost felyngly' of love, in particular about the circumstances of Sidney's emotional entanglement. What Astrophil calls once 'the tale of me' (*Astrophil and Stella*, No. 45) may indeed reflect the fact that Sidney's story of Astrophil and Stella is a fictionalized account of real events which Greville also takes his turn at telling in a pair of poems about the lovers Philocell (like the name Astrophil, it is suggestive of *Philip* Sidney) and Caelica (Greville's whole heaven of 'stars').

Caelica, No. LXXIV, like its companion poem No. LXXV, is in the same distinctive trochaic metre as Sidney's Eighth Song from *Astrophil and Stella*.[2] In fact, the opening lines of all three

---

[1] Charles Lamb was particularly struck by this aspect of Sidney's sonnets. Comparing Sidney's *Astrophil* poems to Milton's sonnets, Lamb states, 'They savour of the Courtier, it must be allowed, and not of the Commonwealthsman' ('Some Sonnets of Sir Philip Sidney', in *Works*, edited by Thomas Hutchinson [Oxford, 1924], p. 737). Later in the same essay, Lamb notes of the sonnets, 'They are full, material, circumstantiated. Time and place appropriates every one of them. . . . An historical thread runs through them, which almost affixes a date to them; marks the *when* and *where* they were written' (p. 743).

[2] Purcell, in his comparison of *Astrophil and Stella* with *Caelica*, matches Sidney's Eighth Song with *Caelica*, No. LXXV only, and sets *Astrophil and Stella*, No. 87 alongside *Caelica*, No. LXXIV.

poems seem to echo each other. Here is the opening of the song from *Astrophil and Stella*:

> In a grove most rich of shade,
> Where birds wanton musicke made,
> May then yong his pide weedes showing,
> New perfumed with flowers fresh growing,
> *Astrophil* with *Stella* sweete,
> Did for mutuall comfort meete . . . .
>
> (Eighth Song, ll. 1–6)

Greville's opening of *Caelica*, No. LXXIV answers Sidney almost directly with a darker view of human love, cut off from nature's freshness.

> In the window of a Graunge,
> Whence men's prospects cannot range
> Ouer groues, and flowers growing,
> Natures wealth, and pleasure showing;
> But on graues where shepheards lye,
> That by loue or sickness die;
> In that window saw I sit,
> *Caelica* adorning it . . . . (ll. 1–8)

Caelica, No. LXXV returns to the outdoor setting of Sidney's song; but like Greville's companion poem, it separates the human lovers from the verdant and sensual scene in which they are placed, and through which they bear their human burdens of sorrow on the one hand and disdain on the other.

> In the time when herbs and flowers,
> Springing out of melting powers,
> Teach the earth heate and raine
> Doe make *Cupid* liue againe:
> Late when *Sol*, like great hearts, showes
> Largest as he lowest goes,
> *Caelica* with *Philocell*
> In fellowship together fell . . . . (ll. 1–8)

The bleak and unsentimental view of human love, characteristic of Greville from the start of the poems, continues in both versions of the lovers' meeting and parting. The same event, in Sidney's telling, is full of the sweetness and pain of real mutual affection, frustrated by the 'Tyran honour' (Eighth Song, l. 95) of the lady. The greatest difference from Sidney is that Greville makes it clear that love exists in the passionate imagination of Philocell

much more than in reality. Philocell is also more reticent than
Astrophil in forcing his attentions on his beloved.

> So diuers wayes his heart doth moue,
> That his tongue cannot speake of loue.
> Onely in himself he sayes,
> How fatall are blind *Cupids* waies ....
> (*Caelica*, No. LXXIV, ll. 51–4)

> He good Shepherd loueth well,
> But *Caelica* scorn'd *Philocell*
> Through enamel'd Meades they went,
> Quiet she, he passion rent.
> (*Caelica*, No. LXXV, ll. 19–22)

In fact, Greville's message in both works is a call to Philocell to
be bolder in his advances to Caelica:

> But silent Loue is simple wooing,
> Euen Destiny would haue vs doing.
> Boldnesse neuer yet was chidden,
> Till by Loue it be forbidden ....
> (*Caelica*, No. LXXIV, ll. 57–60)

> *Philocell* that onely felt
> Destinies which *Cupid* dealt;
> No lawes but Loue-lawes obeying,
> Thought that Gods were wonne with praying.
> (*Caelica*, No. LXXV, ll. 107–10)

Of course, it is not possible to discover which version, Sidney's
or Greville's, is closer to the facts of Sidney's relationship with
Penelope Rich.[1] But it is certain that Greville, at least when he

---

[1] Indeed, both J. G. Nichols and Rosalie Colie argue that seeking those facts
behind the poems is not important:

I see Astrophil, then, as a dramatic character, in the sense that he likes to dramatize
himself and his feelings, and also in the sense that he should not necessarily, or
lightly, be identified with his creator. (Nichols, *The Poetry of Sir Philip Sidney: An
Interpretation in the Context of His Life and Times*, p. 77.)

However privately Sidney looked in his heart and wrote ... the lyric 'I' is Astrophil
rather than P. Sidney, Kt., son and son-in-law of great men and heir to broad estates.
No one nowadays takes biography seriously as the sole, or even the major, clue to
literary imagination: the poet writing lyric verse has license to present himself however he will, to distort his own personality and feelings however he wishes to make
his poetic point. For, even supposing the poet were totally 'sincere', his sincerity
is, to other men, unverifiable. (Colie, *Paradoxia Epidemica*, p. 360)

wrote his second Philocell poem, had an audience of 'many ladies', perhaps with one special lady among them, in mind. For he closes *Caelica*, No. LXXV by posing to that audience a series of *demandes d'amour*, than which nothing could be more traditional in the courtly game of love:

> Shepheardesses, if it proue,
> *Philocell* she once did loue,
> Can kind doubt of true affection
> Merit such a sharpe correction?
> When men see you fall away,
> Must they winke to see no day?
> It is worse in him that speaketh,
> Than in her that friendship breaketh?
> Shepheardesses, when you change,
> Is your ficklenesse so strange?
> Are you thus impatient still?
> Is your honour slaue to will?
> They to whom you guiltie be,
> Must they not your errour see?
> May true Martyrs at the fire
> Not so much as life desire?
>
> (*Caelica*, No. LXXV, ll. 181–96)

Sidney himself uses the *demande d'amour*, with graceful indirectness, in his sonnet to the Moon:

> Then ev'n of fellowship, ô Moone, tell me
> Is constant *Love* deem'd there but want of wit?
> Are Beauties there as proud as here they be?
> Do they above love to be lov'd, and yet
> Those Lovers scorne whom that *Love* doth possesse?
> Do they call *Vertue* there ungratefulness?
>
> (*Astrophil and Stella*, No. 31)

Besides involving these obviously public gestures about the private emotion of love, the poetry of courtly making also expresses the often contradictory moods which were encompassed within the game that was built and maintained by aristocratic society in the Middle Ages and Renaissance around the basic sexual relationship between man and woman. For example, in

Since some of the facts exist, however, and others were clearly supposed to be inferred from the poetry, their presence in the background can only heighten the reader's enjoyment of the paradox that 'I am not I' in Sidney's lyrics, a paradox to which Colie draws attention in her chapter on *Astrophil and Stella* (see especially p. 95).

Astrophil and Stella the romantic tenderness of the Eighth Song
may be compared with the broad sexual innuendoes of Sonnet
No. 76:

> But lo, while I do speake, it groweth noone with me,
> Her flamie glistring lights increase with time and place;
> My heart cries 'ah', it burnes, mine eyes now dazled be:
> No wind, no shade can coole, what helpe then in my case,
>   But with short breath, long lookes, staid feet and
>   walking hed,
> Pray that my sunne go downe with meeker beames to bed.[1]

It should be emphasized that the intent of the poet in a passage
like this was not to shock, but to entertain. Sidney's lines do not
represent a lapse from courtly taste, nor was their appeal as
entertainment meant to be limited to men.

Idealism and cynicism about women constitute another pair of
extremes which was accommodated within the game of love. In the
Fifth Song from *Astrophil and Stella*, Sidney cleverly combines
praise and blame of his lady in a sustained *double entendre*. Only in
the last stanza of the poem does he reveal his game:

> You then ungratefull thiefe, you murdring Tyran you,
> You Rebell run away, to Lord and Lady untrue,
> You witch, you Divill, (alas) you still of me beloved,
> You see what I can say; mend yet your froward mind,
> And such skill in my Muse you reconcil'd shall find,
> That all these cruell words your praises shall be proved.[2]
>
> > (ll. 85–90)

---

[1] See also in this connection *Astrophil and Stella*, No. 77, the stately blazon which
leads up to the conclusion that the minor perfections of Stella are blessing enough,
'Yet ah, my Mayd'n Muse doth blush to tell the best'. The poem which follows in
the sonnet sequence also plays on a sexual pun. Its subject is Astrophil's jealousy of
Stella's husband, and its concluding line is this: 'Is it not evill that such a Devill wants
hornes?' (*Astrophil and Stella*, No. 78). Greville's *Caelica*, No. LVI ends with another
double entendre of the same type, and it carries a veiled reference to Sidney's 'star':

> He that lets his *Cynthia* lye,
> Naked on a bed of play,
> To say prayers ere she dye,
> Teacheth time to runne away:
> Let no Loue-desiring heart,
> In the Starres goe seeke his fate,
> Loue is onely Natures art,
> Wonder hinders Loue and Hate.
> *None can well behold with eyes,*
> *But what underneath him lies.* (ll. 45–54)

[2] The opposite kind of play between cynicism and idealism—that is, praise with
an undertone of blame—can be seen in several poems in the collection of Rossell

The mock blazon of Mopsa in the *Old Arcadia* (No. 3) should also be understood as belonging to a similar convention of counter-games within the game of courtly love. Sidney's comic blazon (written, appropriately enough, in the thumping poulter's measure) may have been intended originally as a companion piece to the idealizing blazon of Mira (*Old Arcadia*, No. 62). Certainly this last poem pre-dates the *Old Arcadia*, and perhaps the other does as well. The idea of matching themes in the two poems is suggested by their parallel opening lines:

> That length of verse can serve brave Mopsa's good to show,
> Whose vertues strange, and beuties such, as no man them
> may know?
>
> (*Old Arcadia*, No. 3)

> What toong can her perfections tell
> In whose each part all pens may dwell?
> (*Old Arcadia*, No. 62)

The matching of praise and irony would be perfectly in keeping with the conventions of courtly making.[1]

Hope Robbins, *Secular Lyrics of the XIVth and XVth Centuries*, 2nd edn. (Oxford, 1955). For example, Robbins, No. 38 has the epigraph, 'of all Creatures women be best:/Cuius contrarium verum est', a text reminiscent of Chauntecleer's 'Mulier est hominis confusio,—/Madame, the sentence of this Latyn is,/"Womman is mannes joye and al his blis"' (*The Nun's Priest's Tale, Canterbury Tales*, B, ll. 4354-6). Robbins, No. 112, 'Punctuation Poem, III', is another example of the same game:

> In women is rest peas and pacience.
> No season. for-soth outht of charite.
> Bothe be nyght & day. thei haue confidence.
> All wey of treasone. Owt of blame thei be.
> No tyme as men say. Mutabilite.
> They haue without nay. but stedfastnes.
> In theym may ye neuer fynde y gesse. Cruelte
> Suche condicons they haue more & lesse.

A similar mood of cynicism, still within the bounds of courtly making, is expressed through Robbins, No. 114, 'When to Trust Women' (the gist of the poem is—never), and again in Donne's much more impressive poem, 'Goe, and catche a falling starre' (*Songs and Sonnets*, No. 1, in Helen Gardner's edition of *The Elegies and The Songs and Sonnets* [Oxford, 1965]).

[1] Even Wyatt has a poem of abuse against a woman:

> Ye old mule that thinck your self so fayre,
> Leve of with craft your beautie to repaire,
> For it is true withoute any fable
> No man setteth more by riding in your saddell;
> To much travaill so do your train apaire,
> Ye old mule! (ll. 1–6)

This is No. XXXV in the Poems from the Egerton Manuscript, in Sir Thomas Wyatt, *Collected Poems of Sir Thomas Wyatt*, edited by Kenneth Muir and Patricia

The *Old Arcadia* has still other signs of the social spirit of courtly making. There is the first-person narrator, with his intermittent gallantries aimed at 'you, fair ladies that vouchsafe to read this' (*Old Arcadia*, Bk. I, p. 27). His presence in the *Old Arcadia* seems to be adapted from the tradition of self-deprecating and semi-flirtatious narrators in Chaucer's *Troilus, Parliament of Fowls*, and his other courtly poems. There is also the deliberate self-display of Philisides as the melancholy lover, which both partakes of a long-standing convention of courtly makers generally, and also reflects the particular influence of Jacopo Sannazaro's *Arcadia* where the author himself appears as Sincero.[1] And finally there are the intriguing private references in the *Old Arcadia* to Strephon and Klaius, Urania, Coredens, Mira, and Agelastus.[2]

Thomson (Liverpool, 1969). The Robbins edition of *Secular Lyrics* shows a great range in the conventional imagery and the tone of poetry about love written in the late Middle Ages. On the one hand there are lines like these:

> your fair here hengyng downe to your knee,
>   with your rollyng eyes whyche ar as glasse clere,
> & your strawbery lyppes as swete as honye,
> with roose red yn your chekes—ye haue no pere!
> (Robbins, No. 130, ll. 13–16)

But seemingly just as admissible in the canon of courtly making were lines like these:

> . . . he that beholdyth you by day and by nyght
> Shal neuer haue cause in hert to be Iocound,
> Rememberyng your grete hede and your forhed round,
>   Wyth Staryng eyen, visage large & huge,
>   And eyþer of youre pappys like a water-bowge.
> (Robbins, No. 209, ll. 17–21)

[1] Philisides' story of his life before entering Arcadia (*Old Arcadia*, Fourth Eclogues, pp. 334–5) is specifically comparable to Chapter 7 of Sannazaro's *Arcadia*, where Sincero tells his own story.

[2] Riddles, anagrams, and other forms of secret reference to persons known by the audience were common in court poetry before Sidney. Robbins, No. 145, 'Joyful Pain, An Anagram', is a fragmentary short poem of this type, as is Wyatt's riddle:

> What wourde is that that chaungeth not,
> Though it be tourned and made in twain?
> It is myn aunswer, god it wot,
> And eke the causer of my payn.
> A love rewardeth with disdain,
> Yet is it loved. What would ye more?
> It is my helth eke and my sore.
> (No. L in Poems from Egerton
MS., Muir–Thomson edition)

As for Sidney, he was careful enough of his reference to Agelastus (*Old Arcadia*, Bk. IV, p. 284) to change his description of the man. In the earliest state of the description we have

Agelastus, one notably noted among them as well for his skill in poetry as for an

We can safely assume that these were designed to reverberate outside the boundaries of the story itself, perhaps in a gathering of 'friends' like those Sidney mentions in the prefatory letter to his sister, 'who will weigh errors in the balance of goodwill' (*Old Arcadia*, Prefatory Letter, p. 3). Indeed one record has survived to show that Sidney read aloud from the *Old Arcadia* as an entertainment for his friend, the exiled Earl of Angus:

> Sir Philip failed not (as often as his affairs would permit him) to visit him, in so much that he did scarce suffer any one day to slip, whereof he did not spend the most part in his company. He was then in travail, or had brought forth rather (though not polished and refined it as now it is) that his so beautiful and universally accepted birth, his *Arcadia*. He delighted much to impart it to Angus, and Angus took as much pleasure to be partaker thereof.[1]

The *New Arcadia* also reflects the existence of the game of love, but not so much in the structural aspects of the book. The loquacious narrator of the *Old Arcadia*, for example, has disappeared; and there is virtually no new poetry to consider. Throughout the revision, however, descriptions of contemporary life have been added. Unlike the comparatively spare narrative of the *Old Arcadia*, the *New Arcadia* opens up to give a much fuller record of the courtly society in which Sidney participated. For instance, we have a picture of the happily married lovers, '*Argalus*

austerely maintained sorrowfulness wherewith he seemed to despise the works of nature. (Cl, As, Da, Ph, Je, Hm MSS.)

When he revised the *Old Arcadia* for the fourth time, however, Sidney changed the passage to

Agelastus, one notably noted among them as well for his skill in poetry as for an austerely maintained sorrowfulness (the cause of which, as it were too long to tell, so yet the effect of an Athenian senator to become an Arcadian shepherd). . . . (St and Bo MSS.)

One is tempted, seeing a line like the following in Book Two, p. 108, 'But alas, sweet Philoclea, how hath my pen forgotten thee, since to thy memory principally all this long matter is intended', to wonder if Sidney had a real person in mind for Philoclea and perhaps Pamela too. The only fact which may support this speculation is that Mary, Sidney's sister, the Countess of Pembroke ('it is done only for you, only to you'—Prefatory Letter to the *Old Arcadia*) was seventeen—the same age as Pamela—in 1579–80.

[1] David Hume of Godscroft, *The History of the Houses of Douglas and Angus* (Edinburgh, 1644), quoted by Robertson, p. xvii. These incidents must have occurred around 1582. Sidney's book would also have been read privately, as by Sidney's younger brother, who was studying on the Continent. Sidney wrote to him, 'My toyfull book[e] I will send with God's helpe by February . . .' (Sidney to Robert Sidney, 18 Oct. 1580, Feuillerat, No. XLII).

at a castle of his owne, sitting in a parler with the faire *Parthenia*, he reading in a booke the stories of *Hercules*, she by him, as to heare him reade . . .' (*New Arcadia*, Bk. III, p. 420). Of course this vignette makes a contribution to Sidney's theme of the heroism of love in the *New Arcadia*. But it also serves more generally— along with the picture we have in Sonnet No. 45 of Astrophil watching Stella shed tears as a sad love tale is read aloud—to reaffirm the fact that courtly society in Sidney's day was not much changed in some ways from what had existed in the late medieval and early Tudor periods. At least, poetry in its social context of courtly making was still, as Chaucer puts it, the servant of the servants of the God of Love.[1]

The Lady of May draws on conventions of the game of love and has, as we remarked at the opening of this chapter, a special play on Leicester's private interests with the Queen. It also plays on an important political issue of the period—all this in a pastoral setting prophetic of the much more substantial work, the *Old Arcadia*, which Sidney was to undertake only a short time later. Thus the little drama deserves attention on several counts.

Medieval and early Tudor literature and pageantry give abundant evidence of the aristocratic pastime of the Court of Love, where love-problems, like legal cases, were propounded and debated. Stevens cites an example of particular interest, 'the occasion described in Boccaccio's Filocolo, when Fiametta is chosen to be queen and arbitress in a love debate and crowned with a garland'.[2] It must have been a similar model of the *Cour Amoureuse* on which Sidney based the structure of *The Lady of May*. In his work, the Queen must be the arbitress between two suitors for the May Lady, and the game is made more complicated by having the two suitors

---

[1] *Troilus and Criseyde*, I. 15: 'For I, that God of Loves servantz serve'. Stevens states further about the connection between love and poetry in aristocratic society (p. 158):

There was perhaps a general expectation of 'dalliance' before, after, and perhaps even during, a reading of a love-poem (the illumination [Corpus Christi College MS. No. 61 of *Troilus and Criseyde*] shows one couple 'commoning' as Chaucer reads). . . .

It was such 'commoning' while reading the romance *Gallehault* in a private place which led to disaster for Dante's lovers Paulo and Francesca (*Inferno*, V. ii. 124–35). Boccaccio made use of that famous incident as a 'gambit' in his own playing of the game of love; for he put the word *Gallehault* as a comic invitation to 'dalliance' at the opening of his book of love-tales, *The Decameron*. Compare Astrophil's amorous interest in writing poetry, especially in the earlier sonnets of Sidney's sequence.

[2] Stevens, p. 166.

carefully matched for their opposite qualities: 'the many great services and many great faults of Therion, or the few small services and no faults of Espilus' (*The Lady of May*, p. 30). The seasonal celebration of May which forms a backdrop to Sidney's pageant (probably chosen out of a consideration for the specific time of the Queen's visit to Wanstead) also has important links with the game of love. Throughout the literature of courtly making, the occasion to 'doon honour to May' is always a significant one for lovers.[1]

Besides its relationship to conventions of the game of love, *The Lady of May* has a special appropriateness to the immediate political situation with which the Elizabethan court was preoccupied at the time of Sidney's writing, because of the imminent decision of the Queen herself to marry. The question of a royal match with the Duke of Anjou (Alençon) was burning in 1578 and especially so in 1579. As reported in a spy communication of 3 May 1579 from the Elizabethan Court to the King of Spain,

> when [the Queen] was leaving to visit a house of Leicester's, six miles off, she took Simier and the ambassador with her, telling them that she would there decide the business definitely. She requested each member of the Council [including Leicester, Sussex, Burghley, Walsingham, and Sidney's father] to give her his opinion in writing, but not one of them would declare himself openly. They merely stated the objections on both sides, which she read privately and alone.
>
> (Bernardino de Mendoza to Philip of Spain, 3 May 1579)

---

[1] *The Knight's Tale*, l. 1047. The presence of foresters in Sidney's May pageant can be connected not only with the traditional presence of Robin Hood at May pageantry (Stevens, p. 186), but also with the 'forester' poems which Stevens points out in early Tudor manuscript collections of courtly poetry. These poems usually have a bawdy undertone ('Foster wyl I be no more; No lenger shote I may' or 'Every bowe for me ys to bygge;/Myne arow ny worne ys;/The glew ys slypt frome the nyk;/When I shud shoote I myse;/Yet have I bene a foster'—Stevens, pp. 214, 222). When, in *The Lady of May*, the mother of the May Lady boldly calls attention to the possible loss of her daughter's 'honesty' (p. 21), she clearly refers to the basic sport of the game of love. It was, perhaps, traditionally indulged more freely in May-time. Sidney certainly associates casual sex with Maying in a later poem (*Other Poems*, No. 4):

> When mery May first early calls the morne,
> With mery maids a Maying they do go,
> Then do they pull from sharpe and niggard thorne
> The plenteous sweets, (can sweets so sharply grow?)
> Then some grene gowns are by the lasses worne
> In chastest plaies, till home they walke a rowe,
>   While daunce about the may-pole is begun,
>   When, if nede were, they could at quintain run. . . .
> (ll. 49–56)

A further letter of 14 May 1579 from the same source offers additional information about the political situation of May 1579:

> I wrote on the 3rd that the Queen had ordered the members of the Council to give her their individual opinions about the marriage with Alençon, which papers she read whilst she was staying in Leicester's house at Wanstead.[1]

The most recent editors of *The Lady of May* have not been able to decide between May 1578 and May 1579 as the date for the first performance of the work.[2] But on the basis of the evidence above from the spy Mendoza's letters, I would say that Sidney's play about love-choices was probably conceived as a delicate accompaniment to the crucial choice—whether or not to marry Anjou—which the Queen had announced she would make at Wanstead in May 1579.

The Lady of May, then, can be likened to the song which, in *The Merchant of Venice*, accompanies Bassanio's all-important choice between the three caskets:

> Tell me where is fancy bred,
> Or in the heart, or in the head?
> How begot, how nourished?
> Reply, reply.
> It is engend'red in the eyes,
> With gazing fed, and fancy dies
> In the cradle where it lies.
> (*Merchant of Venice*, III. ii, 63–9)[3]

Unlike Shakespeare, Sidney did not have complete control over his dramatic situation. For Elizabeth herself was to make the central choice in *The Lady of May*. Nevertheless an argument can be made that, of the two suitors, the forester Therion is favoured by Sidney. Certainly he is the 'greater' man, both in his faults and in his services (*The Lady of May*, p. 30). Moreover, the closing song of the play presents Silvanus, the forest god, as victorious and Pan, the shepherd god, in defeat (p. 30). Elizabeth herself, the text records, designated the other suitor, the shepherd Espilus, as

---

[1] *State Papers, Spain*, II. 669, 674.
[2] *Sidney's Miscellaneous Prose*, p. 13.
[3] Shakespeare seems to have shaped the theme of his song to lead towards the speech of Bassanio which follows it: 'The world is still deceived with ornament' (III. ii. 74). Also *lead*, the substance of the right casket, rhymes with the end-words of the opening lines of the song.

her favourite. This does not negate, however, the theme of the play, or by any means make *The Lady of May* 'a fiasco', as one critic has said.[1] For Sidney's main purpose, it seems to me, is to emphasize the broader theme of choice itself, more than to suggest (as Shakespeare seems to do in his song) a certain way of choosing. A brief look at some other pageants which were written for Queen Elizabeth will show the comparative restraint of *The Lady of May* in its hints.

Thomas Churchyard wrote the pageantry which greeted the Queen's entry into Norwich in 1578. It included—apropos of the marriage question—a 'Shewe of Chastitie', wherein it was announced that 'bycause (said Chastitie) that the Queene had chosen the best life, she gave the Queene Cupid's bow, to learn to shoote at whome she pleased, since none coulde wounde hir Highnesse hart . . .'.[2] Just as openly, George Gascoigne's Kenilworth pageants of 1575 urged the Queen to the opposite course from chastity. Gascoigne prepared a playlet wherein the royal nymph Zabeta (anagram for Elizabeth) was to be convinced that she should follow Juno, not Diana:

> Then geve consent, O Queene, to Juno's just desire,
> Who for your wealth would have you wed, and, for your
> farther hire. . . .

It was Leicester, the host of Kenilworth, whom the goddess had chosen as a husband for her royal nymph:

> Forgeve me, Queene; the words are hers; I come not to
> discusse:
> I am but messenger; but sure she bade me say,
> That where you now in princely port have past one
> pleasant day,
> A world of wealth at wil, you henceforth shall enjoy,
> In weded state, and therewithall holde up from great
> annoy;
> The staffe of your estate; O Queen, o worthy Queen,
> Yet never wight felt perfect blis, but such as wedded bene.[3]

This particular show was evidently not seen by the Queen, for she made an unexpected departure from Kenilworth. At her

---

[1] Stephen Orgel, *The Jonsonian Masque* (Cambridge, Mass., 1965), p. 55. Orgel's discussion of *The Lady of May* is more valuable than his conclusion suggests.

[2] From Churchyard's record of the royal entry, Nichols, II. 189.

[3] 'The Princely Pleasures at Kenelworth, 1575', in Nichols, I. 514–15.

leaving, however, Gascoigne alluded to Zabeta's story in a second poem which explains that many had sued for the hand of the nymph, but she 'so obstinately and cruelly rejected' her suitors that 'yet the tears stande in mine eyes, yea, and my tongue trembleth and faltereth in my mouth, when I begin to declare the distresses wherein some of them doe presently remayne.'[1]

In *The Lady of May* the same general theme of unrequited devotion to the Queen is suggested by a speech of the shepherd Dorcas:

> How many courtiers, think you, I have heard under our field in bushes make their woeful complaints, some of the greatness of their mistress' estate, which dazzled their eyes and yet burned their hearts; some of the extremity of her beauty mixed with extreme cruelty; some of her too much wit, which made all their loving labours folly? O how often have I heard one name sound in many mouths, making our vales witnesses of their doleful agonies! So that with long lost labour, finding their thoughts bare no other wool but despair, of young courtiers they grew old shepherds.
>
> (*Lady of May*, p. 28)

Similarly the forester Rixus goes out of his way to imply adulation of the Queen:

> We have no hopes, but we may quickly go about them, and going about them, we soon obtain them; not like those that, having long followed one (in truth) most excellent chase, do now at length perceive she could never be taken; but that if she stayed at any time near her pursuers, it was never meant to tarry with them, but only to take breath to fly further from them.
>
> (*Lady of May*, p. 29)

The debt of *The Lady of May* to the Kenilworth pageantry may be even more specific, in that the active and passionate Therion of Sidney's play does resemble the Leicester-figure Deep-Desire in Gascoigne's entertainment.[2] But we can only say with certainty

---

[1] Nichols, pp. 518–19.

[2] The direct influence of Gascoigne is suggested by Kimbrough, p. 64. It is probable that Sidney was in the audience of Gascoigne's show, for a letter from Languet to Sidney on 3 Dec. 1575 has this reference to Sidney's activities of the previous summer:

> A full five months have passed since you last wrote. You offer as excuse for your idleness attendance on the progress of the court and your accompanying his Excellency your father. Yet when Caesar wrote his *Commentaries* in camp he was far busier than you.
>
> (Osborn translation, p. 389)

that Gascoigne's work shows conventions of flattery and persuasion upon which Sidney drew with much greater subtlety when he wrote in the same mode on behalf of Leicester in honour of the Queen. The fact that those conventions had been established in Gascoigne's work before the appearance of Anjou as a rival contender for the hand of Elizabeth, and the fact that Sidney made use of them after the disappearance of Leicester's hopes to attain the honour himself, both reinforce the idea that we are dealing here with another aspect of the courtly game.[1]

In the timespan from *The Lady of May* to the *Old Arcadia*, Sidney managed to subsume his lesser talents as a courtly lyricist, an occasional writer of pastoral pageantry, and a would-be 'Prince-pleaser' into the creation of poetry which justifies much more serious consideration.[2] That process of development will be traced in the following chapter.

But there is, I believe, a final point to be made about Sidney as a courtly maker. Stevens gives this description of the game of

---

[1] A further element of the spirit of play besides the courtly one can be seen in *The Lady of May*. That is, the play on an important humanistic theme of the Renaissance. I quote from Stephen Orgel on Sidney's pageant: 'In *The Lady of May*, the validity of the conventional antithesis of pastoral—contemplation versus action—is to be thought through again from the beginning, debated, and judged' (*The Jonsonian Masque*, p. 47). Particularly in the speech of Dorcas and the answer by Rixus, there are echoes of the larger intellectual controversy, Dorcas praising the shepherd's life as being fittest for 'a templer' (*The Lady of May*, p. 28), and Rixus praising forest life for its combination of contemplative quiet with action (p. 29). Yet the presentation of these opposing views in *The Lady of May* must be regarded as playful, as well as serious. Thus I think that Orgel's idea of a flat 'judgement' expressed through the masque is much too heavy and inflexible for Sidney's attitude and for the social circumstances of the masque itself. The entertainment of an educated and courtly audience seems to have been of first importance, not the promulgation of Sidney's settled opinions. Indeed, in another mood in the *Defence*, Sidney simply dismisses the whole debate as an example of the wordy disputes of philosophy, 'excellent in the dangerless Academy of Plato' (p. 84), but less useful than poetry in moving men to well-doing:

Where the philosophers, as they scorn to delight, so must they be content little to move—saving wrangling whether *virtus* be the chief or the only good, whether the contemplative or the active life do excell. . . . (p. 93)

Sidney once remarked of the Italians, 'from a Tapster upwards, they are all discoursers' (Letter of 1579 from Sidney to Robert Sidney, in Philip Sidney, Robert, Late Earl of Essex, and Secretary Davison, *Profitable Instructions; Describing what speciall Observations are to be taken by Travellers in all Nations, States, and Countries, Pleasant and Profitable* [London, 1633]). The implication of 'discoursers', as engaging and skilful—but not totally sincere—practitioners of the art of verbal *duello*, seems to me appropriate for many of Sidney's characters, as well as for their creator.

[2] Quotation from Puttenham, p. 13.

love: 'It taught you how to behave to your peers when you all had time on your hands; not how to do them good, but how to make yourself desirable; how to "commune", especially in mixed company, and how to please'.[1] Yet Baldessar Castiglione, in his *Book of the Courtier*, added to the courtly game precisely that dimension which Stevens finds lacking: 'how to do them good'. And in the *Defence*, although Sidney depends for most of his other arguments on literary theoreticians, it is Castiglione on whom he seems to have drawn for his best-known statement of the poet's purpose:

Now therein of all sciences (I speak still of human, and according to the human conceit) is our poet the monarch. For he doth not only show the way, but giveth so sweet a prospect into the way, as will entice any man to enter into it. Nay, he doth, as if your journey should lie through a fair vineyard, at the first give you a cluster of grapes, that full of that taste, you may long to pass further. He beginneth not with obscure definitions, which must blur the margin with interpretations, and load the memory with doubtfulness; but he cometh to you with words set in delightful proportion, either accompanied with, or prepared for, the well enchanting skill of music; and with a tale forsooth he cometh unto you, with a tale which holdeth children from play, and old men from the chimney corner. And, pretending no more, doth intend the winning of the mind from wickedness to virtue—even as the child is often brought to take most wholesome things by hiding them in such other as have a pleasant taste, which, if one should begin to tell them the nature of *aloes* or *rhubarbarum* they should receive, would sooner take their physic at their ears than at their mouth.

(Defence, pp. 91–2)

The opening motif of the journey, the closing one of the medicine for sick children, the incremental structure of the central sentence ('He beginneth . . . he cometh . . . with a tale forsooth he cometh . . . with a tale . . .'), and above all, Sidney's message here form a strong parallel to the equally well-known passage from the *Book of the Courtier* which tells the way the Courtier may entice his Prince to virtue:

In this wise may hee leade him through the rough way of vertue (as it were) decking it aboute with boughes to shadow it, and strowing it over with sightlye flowers, to ease the griefe of the painefull jorney in him that is but of a weake force. And sometime with musicke, some-time with armes, and horses, sometime with rymes, and meeter,

[1] Stevens, p. 155.

otherwhile with communication of love, and with all those waies that these Lords have spoken of, continually keepe that minde of his occupied in honest pleasure: imprinting notwithstanding therein alwaies beside (as I have saide) in company with these flickering provocations some vertuous condition, and beguiling him with a holesom craft, as the warie Phisitions doe, who many times when they minister to yong and tender children in their sicknesse, a medicine of a bitter taste, annoint the cup about the brimme with some sweete licour.[1]

The closeness of the two passages seems to me a clear sign that Sidney's views about poetry had roots in his courtly values. I have remarked before that Sidney refused to regard the poet's craft as a divine mystery. The social context of courtly making provides a background for that opinion on his part. At one point in the *Defence*, Sidney even gives poets a lesson in art from the everyday practice of courtiers:

Undoubtedly (at least to my opinion undoubtedly), I have found in divers smally learned courtiers a more sound style than in some professors of learning; of which I can guess no other cause, but that the courtier, following that which by practice he findeth fittest to nature, therein (though he know it not) doth according to art, though not by art: where the other, using art to show art, and not to hide art (as in these cases he should do), flieth from nature, and indeed abuseth art.

(*Defence*, p. 118–19)

I have also remarked the absence in Sidney's verse of the conventional poetic aspirations to immortality. If we follow Castiglione's ideas to their logical conclusion, immortality can have little interest for the courtier who has only the limited span of his Prince's life (or a briefer season of power) in which to move him to virtue. The powers of persuasion granted to the courtier, which Sidney merges with the powers of the poet, can make no claim to

---

[1] Hoby's translation, p. 547. The passage has the same similarities to the *Defence* in the original Italian:

In questo modo per la austera strada della virtù potrà condurlo, quasi adornandola di fronde ombrose, e spargendola di vaghi fiori, per temperar la noja del faticoso cammino a chi è di forze debile; ed or con musica, or con arme, e cavalli, or con versi, or con ragionamenti d'amore, e con tutti que' modi che hanno detti questi Signori tener continuamente quell'animo occupato in piacere onesto; imprimendogli però ancora sempre (come ho detto) in compagnia di queste illecebre qualche costume virtuoso; ed ingannandolo con inganno salutifero, come i cauti medici, li quali spesso volendo dar a' fianciulli infermi, e troppo delicati medicina di sapore amaro, circondano l'orifico del vaso di qualche dolce liquore.

Il Libro del Cortegiano del Conte Baldessar Castiglione (Padua, 1766), p. 246.

eternalize either the possessor of those powers or the object of his persuasion.[1]

As the maker and the courtier merge, Sidney, like Castiglione, keeps a balance between his idealistic vision of 'the winning of the mind from wickedness to virtue' and his tender feeling for weak and childish mankind. But in this definition of the poet divinity and immortality have no place. Sidney insists: 'I speak still . . . according to the human conceit'.

In his own poetry Sidney exemplifies what Stevens calls an 'extension out' from the courtly milieu which nourished him and his work. The following statement about Chaucer could apply just as much to Sidney:

The thing that distinguishes his greatest poetry is not the dismissal of the society felt so vividly behind his early work, but the transcendent quality of the art which can now compass so much more than that society demands.[2]

This happens with Sidney in two ways. First he uses and transfuses with new rhetorical energy the courtly 'manner'—that is, the conventional range of courtly lyric and dramatic voices. In that aspect of his development Sidney's greatest achievement is undoubtedly *Astrophil and Stella*. The two *Arcadias*, on the other hand, represent Sidney's highest achievement with the conventional courtly 'matter', sexual love. Sidney treats the theme with a fullness, beauty and deeper significance which only Chaucer, among earlier English courtly makers, rivals in *Troilus and Cryseyde*. Thus the tradition, the social conventions, and the spirit of

---

[1] Colie (p. 92) notes as an example of Sidney's capacity for sustaining brilliant self-contradictions in *Astrophil and Stella*, that he 'reverses the stock theme of the poet's gift of immortality to the beloved, an idea used, to comfort and to threaten, by Petrarca, by Ronsard, by Shakespeare and the rest'. On the other hand, J. G. Nichols (pp. 10–11) attributes the omission of this theme from the poetry to Sidney's social position: 'Maybe this just happens to be one sonnet convention which Sidney forgot to propagate; but it is probably significant that Daniel, Drayton and Shakespeare were writing for patrons—peers perhaps, but not equals'. Nichols's social view of Sidney's poetry is different from the idea of courtly making which I have tried to describe. For I believe that we are dealing in Sidney with a well-established setting for poetry which had its own internal consistency, its own literary and social traditions and forms, and which was not looking outwards—superciliously or otherwise—at groups or classes outside itself. The opposite is strongly implied by Nichols: 'Sidney's social position raised him above the need for patronage and gave his poetry a certain lordly air which might seem offensive to us now if it were not for the pervasive Sidneyan charm' (p. 10).

[2] Stevens, p. 224.

courtly play, instead of confining Sidney's talents, opened possibilities for his poetry to carry still greater 'riches of Knowledge upon the streame of Delight'.[1]

[1] Sidney's description of the 'sportes' of Queen Helen in the *New Arcadia*, Bk. II, p. 283.

CHAPTER IV

The Making of a Poet

AN IMPORTANT period for the growth of Sidney's poetry took place before he wrote any important poetry at all. It was the period between the *Lady of May* and the much more substantial *Old Arcadia* and *Defence of Poetry*, during which time Sidney can justly be said, as he put it, to have 'slipped into the title of a poet' (*Defence*, p. 73). The pose of reluctance in the *Defence* must, of course, be taken lightly. But evidence does survive—particularly in Sidney's extraordinarily well-preserved correspondence—to suggest that Sidney's aims for a vocation were different from the 'unelected vocation' of poetry (*Defence*, p. 73) for which we remember him now. The span of time roughly between 1578 and 1580, when Sidney was moving into, rather than within, the poet's vocation, will be the focus of this chapter. During that period Sidney's expectations for a career of public service came increasingly into conflict with the reality of his minor position and with the narrow vista open on his future. A crisis came in 1580, when Sidney withdrew from court under a cloud of royal disapproval and spent several months at his sister's country estate of Wilton. The fruit of his rustication was the completed *Old Arcadia*.[1] One purpose of my discussion here will be to examine in detail the events and emotions which led Sidney to take up his pen. But my more general purpose will be to relate that historical and personal background to the poetry itself. For in the *Old Arcadia* Sidney's ideals, ambitions, concessions, and frustrations of the immediate moment are all subsumed into something more lasting and more worthy of note than his own private experience.

To begin the inquiry, we should make use of the best window we have on the years up to and including 1580. That window is the correspondence between Sidney and Hubert Languet.[2] The

[1] Robertson, p. xvi: 'The evidence points to the composition of the bulk of the story when he was at Wilton and Ivy Church [a smaller Pembroke family estate nearby] from March to August 1580.'

[2] The seven-year-long exchange of letters (from 22 Sept. 1573 to 28 Oct. 1580) between Sidney and Hubert Languet is an indispensable key to Sidney's private

extant letters amply attest to the fact that Sidney was educated to fill an active role in statesmanship and soldiering, not merely in court and country pastimes. The burden of much of Languet's advice in the early exchanges is reflected in this passage from a 1574 letter:

You must think of your position in life, a position which will not let you grow grey in the study of letters—in fact, the time which remains to you for literary study is very short. So you must see to it that you do not undertake so much at once that one project interferes with another. . . . Keep in mind that the words of the poet apply to you: 'Remember to rule the nations with your sway'. . . .

(Languet to Sidney, 28 Jan. 1574, Osborn, pp. 139–40)

Proof that Sidney himself shared these expectations lies in his own attempt to shape his studies to conform to them. In 1574 he wrote to Languet of his 'burning desire' to study geometry, 'the more so because I have always had the impression that it is closely related to military science'. In the same letter he wrote, 'Of Aristotle's works, I think that one must read his *Politics* in particular' (Sidney to Languet, 4 Feb 1574, Osborn, pp. 142–3). Keeping in mind these early hopes and preparations, we can gauge the disappointment behind the half-humorous question which Sidney posed in 1578 to the mentor of his youth:

To what purpose should our thoughts be directed to various kinds of knowledge, unless room be afforded for putting it into practice, so that public advantage may be the result, which in a corrupt age we cannot hope for?

(Sidney to Languet, 1 Mar. 1578, Pears, p. 143)[1]

thought and feeling. The model for relating the information in the correspondence to a literary analysis is given by Neil L. Rudenstine in his book *Sidney's Poetic Development*; but just as I think that Rudenstine's general theme of unresolved ambivalence in Sidney does not do justice to the complex quality of the poet's imagination, so too I find that Rudenstine's treatment of the letters falls short of rendering the actual complexity, warmth, and interest of Sidney's relationship with Languet. In using the letters, I will depend, wherever possible, on the translations from the original Latin into English made by Steuart A. Pears (*The Correspondence of Sir Philip Sidney and Hubert Languet*) and, more recently, by James M. Osborn (*Young Philip Sidney, 1572–1577*). The translator of each passage will be indicated in the text. Latin letters come from the first edition, *Huberti Langueti, Viri Clarissimi, Epistolae Politicae et Historicae Scriptae Quondam ad Illustrem et Generosum Dominum Philippum Sydnaeum, Equitem Anglum* (Frankfort, 1633). No page references to this edition will be given.

[1] I have noted before about Sidney, however, that the instinct to affirm was as strong as the instinct to question. Thus he wrote to Edward Denny in 1580 about a course of study which Denny had requested to improve his idle times:

Later on Sidney was capable of using the theme of great but un-fulfilled expectations to good effect in *Astrophil and Stella*. There it reinforces the quality of disaster about Astrophil's love (see for example, *Astrophil and Stella*, Nos. 18, 21, 23, 27). The *Defence* also plays on the idea of Sidney's meagre achievements, in the lightly satirical remark near the end of the essay that, if you con-sort with poets, 'your name shall flourish in the printers' shops; . . . you shall be of kin to many a poetical preface' (p. 121). Sidney was clearly conscious of the contrast between the praises and expectations of those who sought his patronage and the 'doubtful stages' (Grenville's phrase, *Life*, p. 53) on which his life was being played out.

The early letters from Languet to Sidney also introduce a very different expectation about the young man's future, one which actually came closer to fulfilment around 1580 than the expecta-tion of Sidney's success ever did. That is the possibility that Sidney might eventually be forced into exile. It is to the credit of Languet as a realist and a genuine friend to Sidney that he did not blindly encourage his youthful and well-born protégé, but prepared him from the beginning for the worst as well as the best that might befall. In those days of widespread religious and civil warfare, the worst was all too likely to happen. Languet was himself a Protestant exile from his native France. He had been in Paris dur-ing the Massacre of St. Bartholomew in 1572 (at which Sidney too had been present) and had narrowly missed being killed by his Catholic countrymen.[1] Many other acquaintances Sidney made on the Continent were also religious exiles, from the Protestant circle he met through Languet to the English Catholics, like Lord Windsor, whom he met at Venice. Thus Languet's infusion of the idea of exile into the advice he gave Sidney in 1574 about choosing friends brings a note of poignant and immediate truth into a passage of otherwise commonplace wisdom:

You should indeed choose your friends primarily in your own country,

I will doe it as well as the hast of your boy, and my litle Judgement will hable me. But first let me reioyse with you, $\frac{t}{y}$ since the unnoble constitution of our tyme, doth keepe us from fitte imployments, yow doe yet keepe your selfe awake, $\frac{t}{w}$ the delight of knowledge; one of the notablest effects of $\frac{t}{y}$, wch makes us differ from beasts. . . . Neither let us leave of, because perchance the right pryce of these things is not had without we shold wishe our selves Asses because some folke knowe not what a man meanes.

(Sidney to Edward Denny, 22 May 1580)

[1] Osborn, p. 71.

so that you may go through life happily with them; if obviously worthy friends should offer themselves in other countries, you should by no means discourage them. Friends of this sort are seldom insincere, since they are not thinking of friendship's advantages. Moreover, they frequently find opportunities to oblige their friends, particularly in this unhappy age when too often we see excellent men exiled from their native land solely because they did not wish to assent to the criminal plans of factious men.

(Languet to Sidney, 5 Feb. 1574, Osborn, p. 145)

In a letter of 18 June 1574, Languet was even more pointed in his application of the idea to Sidney personally:

I advise you to tie the bond of friendship between you and my lord the Count of Hanau as firmly as possible, and to be careful to procure the goodwill of more Germans. . . . I do not wish to prophesy ill for you, but still as I urge these things I have in mind how liable your country is to changes, and when they occur fortune vents her greatest rage against those who are most eminent and distinguished in virtue, ability, and lineage. Accordingly, if either some enemies' unjust power, or some other compulsion, should force you one day to go into exile, nowhere, in my judgement, would a more honourable and secure retreat await you than in Germany.

(Languet to Sidney, Osborn, p. 210)

The subject of Sidney's going into exile does not recur until more than five years later (though the correspondence continues with few gaps). First, in the autumn of 1579, Sidney's quarrel with the Earl of Oxford made leaving England temporarily seem like a sensible course of action to Languet, and evidently to Sidney also. Languet's tone in discussing this plan is unworried, in contrast to his tone a few months later.

If the arrogance and insolence of Oxford have roused you from your trance, he has done you less wrong than they who have hitherto been more indulgent to you. . . . If your absence from home is not inconvenient to your noble Father and your other friends, you will do well, as far as I can judge, to come. I do not reckon as an inconvenience the pain they will feel at your absence by reason of the great love they bear you. For I hope that you will gain experience and information, and return to them so high in reputation, that they will then rejoice at your having left them, and altogether approve your present plan. . . .

Languet to Sidney, 14 Nov. 1579, Pears, p. 168)

On the heels of the Oxford affair, however, a far greater blow to Sidney's prospects came as a result of his *Letter to Queen*

Elizabeth, Touching Her Marriage with Monsieur. Now we find Languet looking at the necessity of exile with a much harder gaze:

The party and influence of Anjou is on the increase here [in the Low Countries], and if you should annoy him by your opposition in England, you will scarcely find a reception here, much less in France. Your religion shuts you out of Spain and Italy, and so Germany would be your only refuge if you were compelled to leave your country.

(Languet to Sidney, 30 Jan. 1580, Pears, p. 170)

The untranslated portion of the letter goes on to offer Sidney somewhat more encouragement:

Si talis mutatio apud vos subsecuta fuerit, ut existimes, tibi non esse honorificum in patria vivere, vel forte à te impetrare non possis, ut ibi vivas, nihil, meo iudicio, voluntario exilio magis honestum, praetexere potes, quam rei militaris studium, cum sis iuvenis et celebs, et non solum privatus, sed etiam filiusfamilias.

(Languet to Sidney, 30 Jan. 1580)

It was on this last assumption—that Sidney was to study the military arts in the Low Countries—that Languet continued to write to his young friend throughout the spring and summer of 1580, up to the final three letters surviving in the correspondence, the letters of 24 September 1580, 22 October 1580, and 28 October 1580. In them, Languet wrote first expressing astonishment and disappointment 'that you find pleasure in your long retirement' (24 Sept. 1580, Pears, p. 182), and then expressing relief and rejoicing 'that you have come forth from that hiding place of yours into open day' [specifically, 'in lucem aulae'] (22 Oct. 1580, Pears, p. 187).

Thus the letters of Languet shed light on the choice which was thrust before Sidney in the year 1579–80. From the correspondence we can also understand the difficulty of the choice for Sidney. He could, it seems, have begun at that point to fulfil his original ambition of becoming a soldier. But leaving England, probably permanently, was the price. To discover how high a price that was for Sidney, and why he refused to pay it, we need only look further at the letters from Languet and others which he received.

From the earliest period of Sidney's journey abroad he had heard directly about the hardships and insecurity attendant upon the lives of exiles. This can reasonably be supposed to have reinforced the reluctance to contemplate his own exile which would be natural in any youth who, like Sidney, had, at first, every assurance of future success in his native country. For example, a letter of 1574 from Languet himself carries an unmistakable tone of discouragement and weariness:

Twenty months ago [in the Massacre of St. Bartholomew] fortune dealt me her cruellest blow in France when she snatched from me in practically a single moment all my friends there; but cruel as this blow was, it could not satisfy her harshness to me, for in Germany she proved most hostile to the men whose virtue and benevolence had made it possible for me to endure the burdens of my long exile with some equanimity.

(Languet to Sidney, 7 May 1574, Osborn, pp. 185–6)

In a letter to Sidney from another exile, Théophile de Banos, we catch a glimpse of a Huguenot trying vainly to return to his family across a continent torn by war. De Banos's homesickness for France is all the more desperate, he tells Sidney, 'For as an exile of Christ I have already tolerated—not to use worse terms—the German way of life for nearly seven years' (De Banos to Sidney, 26 May 1575, translated from Latin, Osborn, p. 320). One more picture is supplied by a letter of 1576 to Sidney from Dr. Andreas Paull in Dresden. This communication also shows, significantly, that one of the few places where the wanderers of Europe looked forward to finding peace was in Sidney's own England:

We are already being treated in such a way that I imagine we will in the end be forced to move. Should anything like that occur, I should certainly not go anywhere else than to your most lovely England which, through the admirable wisdom of its renowned Queen, is far more wisely and successfully governed than any of the other kingdoms of Europe.

(Paull to Sidney, 6 Jan. 1576, Latin original, Osborn, p. 404)

In order to understand the decision Sidney made in 1580, the decision which led to his writing the *Old Arcadia*, we must recognize that he shared, at least in part, Dr. Paull's appreciation of English quiet. He even promoted among his continental friends the idea of their taking refuge in England with him. In 1574 Sidney urged Languet more than once to 'leave that ungrateful soil which you have cultivated now so many years, and reaped no fruit, or almost none; and come to those who love you most truly and are no Laodiceans' (Sidney to Languet, [?18] June 1574, Pears, p. 75). And it was not only Languet whom Sidney invited

to England 'as a safe port from the many storms which have
assailed me' (Languet to Sidney, 4 June 1574, Osborn, p. 202),
but also Claude Aubéry, a French exile in Basle, Dr. Lobbet
from Strasburg, Wolfgang Zündelin, a German Protestant living
in Venice, and Matthäus Wacker, another German Sidney met at
Padua. All were asked at various times by Sidney to join him in
his native country.[1] To the older men and the students of
history, as we have already seen in the case of Languet, the consciousness of the recent bloody past of England made her present
tranquillity seem extremely precarious. Sidney acknowledged to
Languet the possibility of sudden and treacherous shifts in English
politics. But still he argued for Languet to take up residence there:

Be not deterred by the dangers which, it may be, are hanging over my
country; for you who have in your head all the story of all the nations in
the world, are well aware that the only persons who have ever suffered
injury from that quarter are the English nobles themselves.

(Sidney to Languet, [?18] June 1574, Pears, p. 75)

The secret of England's fragile, but still enviable peace was
thought to be, as Dr. Paull implied, the Queen herself. Sidney too
assumed that such a connection existed. It is the subject of one of
the first letters he wrote back to the continent after his return home
to England:

On the last day of May, a fair wind wafted me to this our island nest,
where I found all my family well, and the Queen, though somewhat
advanced in years, yet hitherto vigorous in her health, which (as it is
God's will that our safety should hang on so frail a thread), is with
good reason earnestly commended to the care of Almighty God in the
prayers of our people. She is to us a Meleager's brand; when it perishes,
farewell to all our quietness.

(Sidney to the Count of Hanau, 12 June 1575, from Latin,
Osborn, p. 309)

The feelings exhibited here are not entirely positive. Although
the dominant tone is one of grateful wonder at the 'quietness'
which the Queen has maintained for so long in England, there is
an accompanying uneasiness 'that our safety should hang on so
frail a thread'.

Far more frequently in the letters, however, the Queen's peace
is itself the subject for Sidney's anxiety and impatience. From
both the European point of view (which Sidney had been schooled

[1] Osborn, pp. 223, 237, 293, 428.

by Languet to hold) and the Protestant point of view, England seemed to be risking her autonomy, if not her soul, by her foreign policy of inaction and appeasement of Catholic Spain. Sidney wrote on that theme in 1574:

My dearest Languet, this is certain, that our princes are sleeping too deep a sleep, and I hope that while they are, they will take care not to contract the disease in which the appearance of death is accompanied by death itself. . . . Today I wrote to my uncle, the Earl of Leicester, and told him what great hopes the Spaniards cherish as a result of their victory [the Protestant defeat at Mookerheide in the Low Countries]. Perhaps some good will come of my writing, but if not, so far as I am concerned I would rather be blamed for being too little wise than for being too little patriotic.

(Sidney to Languet, 7 May 1574, Osborn, pp. 178–9)

This mood and its opposite continued to coexist in Sidney's mind during the period of his writing *A Defence of Poetry* and the *Old Arcadia*. The essay has several scoffing remarks about 'idle England, which can now scarce endure the pain of a pen' (*Defence*, p. 111). The *Old Arcadia*, in contrast, opens with unequivocal praise for a quiet land and people:

ARCADIA among all the provinces of Greece was ever had in singular reputation, partly for the sweetness of the air and other natural benefits, but principally for the moderate and well tempered minds of the people who (finding how true a contentation is gotten by following the course of nature, and how the shining title of glory, so much affected by other nations, doth indeed help little to the happiness of life) were the only people which, as by their justice and providence gave neither cause nor hope to their neighbours to annoy them, so were they not stirred with false praise to trouble others' quiet, thinking it a small reward for the wasting of their own lives in ravening that their posterity should long after say they had done so. Even the muses seemed to approve their good determination by choosing that country as their chiefest repairing place. . . .

(*Old Arcadia*, Bk. I, p. 4)

An ambivalent view of English quiet was not peculiar to Sidney, but seems to have been felt by many educated and sensitive people of the age who espoused the cause of militant Protestantism, yet also valued the life of the mind. Languet was wont to scorn English passivity in foreign affairs, but he could recognize and pay tribute to the fact that only in England, among the countries of

Europe, could the precious creative and intellectual activity of humanism continue without the menace of war. Speaking in 1574 of the great religious fire that was burning all Europe, Languet observed to Sidney with some bitterness that, 'You English, like foxes, have slunk out of it, with a woman too for your leader...' (13 May 1574, Pears, p. 63). That tone is heard once again in 1580, in Languet's reminder to Sidney about why the Low Countries have now had to turn to France for aid: 'Those who are idle spectators of other men's dangers, and offer them no help in their need, are unfair if they find fault with them for begging the assistance of others...' (24 Sept. 1580, Pears, p. 186). But a short note written by Languet in August of the same year reveals far different feelings. At a time when Sidney himself, instead of leaving England, was writing the *Old Arcadia*, Languet provides both a cogent reason for, and even an echo of, that appreciation of the only peaceful country which Sidney voices at the beginning of his work. Languet's purpose in the note is to introduce to Sidney a scholar who is fleeing to England from the wars in Europe. His misfortunes, as described by Languet, were probably not unusual in the period.

Qui tibi has meas literas reddet, vir est praeclare doctus, et variarum linguarum cognitione excultus, sed cui suarum facultatum usum ademerunt infelicia haec bella: quorum dum finem per multos annos frustra expectat, ut suorum praediorum proventibus frui possit, absumpsit, quicquid antea comparserat, et quicquid ab amicis sine ipsorum molestia corradere potuit. Iam vero, cum horum malorum finem nullum prospiciat, ac de recuperandis suis facultatibus pene desperet, constituit, vestram beatam Angliam tanquam domicilium quietis et humanitatis adire. . . .

(Languet to Sidney, 3 Aug. 1580)

In 1580 Sidney might have left this 'domicilium quietis et humanitatis' which Languet describes and gone to join the war in the Low Countries. Despite his real and long-standing desire to become a soldier, however, other feelings, just as deeply ingrained, prevented him. An indication of the depth of those feelings is given by a casual discourse Sidney is reported to have uttered in 1577, in Languet's presence, when Sidney was on his brilliant embassy to the Protestant courts of Europe. Explaining, with a delightful show of whimsy, why there are no wolves in England, Sidney bases his reason on the story that English outlaws were once given a choice between going into exile or staying at home to hunt wolves. All the outlaws, Sidney claims, preferred the dangers of that hunting to the penalty of banishment. Indeed, he goes on to say, they sought so narrowly after the animals that the whole breed of wolves was extinguished in the land. And now, he concludes, 'the Banditoes hunting in vaine after that which cannot be found, are forced to abide all their life in exile, which to them is a kind of death.'[1] When, in 1580, Sidney was faced with an analogous choice between remaining in England under a kind of constraint, or suffering 'a kind of death' in exile, he chose the same way the bandits did.[2]

It remains to be shown here that Sidney's decision in turning from politics to poetry was not just a negative one. As a transition to the positive aspect, we may take note of Greville's account, in his *Life of Sidney*, of how he first turned to writing. Greville did so precisely at a time when, like Sidney in 1580, he recognized fully the constraints on noble action which he would encounter if he remained at home. Yet he too dismissed the thought of exile. Significantly, Greville credits Sidney with influencing him to give his thwarted energies an outlet in literature:

[1] P. Camerarius, *The Living Librarie*, translated by John Molle (London, 1621), Bk. II, Ch. 8, p. 99.

[2] Other negative elements were involved in Sidney's decision not to go to the Low Countries. First, the war going on there was a civil war, and therefore not a 'good Warr', to use the distinction Sidney used to his brother Robert (reported by Robert to his father Henry Sidney, 1 Nov. 1580, in Arthur Collins, *Letters and Memorials of State* [London, 1746], p. 286). In a letter of 1576 to Languet, Sidney expressed a preference 'to fight my first campaign' against the Turks, 'rather than involve myself in a civil war' (21 Apr. 1576, Osborn, p. 420). In 1578, Languet suggested a moral problem about Sidney's going to the Low Countries as a private soldier: 'If you kill a man against whom you have no lawful cause of war, you are killing an innocent person' (Languet to Sidney, 22 Oct. 1578, Pears, p. 154). Another factor was that the Queen herself acted as a powerful force to keep her courtiers at home in England, simply by her disapproval and by her influence abroad to prevent Englishmen from being received, or, if they were received, by her power to refuse further aid to the country which received them. Greville tells, in the *Life of Sidney* (pp. 169–70), that he was more than once refused admission to the Queen's presence for months after he returned from unauthorized trips abroad. Something else working against Sidney's leaving in 1580 was his family's dependence upon him. Languet's letter to Sidney of 28 October 1580 has a sharp comment on this aspect of Sidney's decision:

Illustrissimo tuo parenti, et aliis tuis necessariis, icucundum est frui tui ingenii praestantia et suavitate quomodocunque id fiat, quibus licet plurimum debeas, et praesertim Illustrissimo tuo parenti, puto tamen te adhuc plus debere patriae, cui cum videantur imminere saevae tempestates, tuum est te praeparare ad eas avertendas, quantum in te erit. . . .

I finding the specious fires of youth to prove far more scorching, then glorious, called my second thoughts to counsell, and in that Map cleerly discerning Action, and Honor, to fly with more wings then one: and that it was sufficient for the plant to grow where his Soveraignes hand had planted it; I found reason to contract my thoughts from those larger, but wandring Horizons, of the world abroad, and bound my prospect within the safe limits of duty, in such home services, as were acceptable to my Soveraigne.

In which retired view, Sir Philip Sidney, that exact image of quiet, and action: happily united in him, and seldome well divided in any; being ever in mine eyes, made me thinke it no small degree of honour to imitate, or tread in the steps of such a Leader. So that to saile by his Compasse, was shortly (as I said) one of the principall reasons I can alleage, which perswaded me to steale minutes of time from my daily services, and employ them in this kind of writing.

(Life of Sidney, pp. 171-2)

I should point out, however, that neither Greville nor Sidney left behind entirely his ideal of heroic action. Greville recounts several attempts over an extended period to go off to the wars. There is also evidence that Sidney, at the same time that he was writing the *Old Arcadia*, was hoping to be appointed to replace his father (who had been recalled by the Queen) as the military commander and governor of Ireland. Sidney lost the post to Lord Grey de Wilton, who was appointed Lord Deputy to succeed Sir Henry Sidney in July 1580.[1] Though the young men

---

[1] Sir Henry Sidney wrote to Lord Grey on 17 September 1580:

You shall have the beste Advice that I shalbe able to geve you; protestinge that if Philip Sidney were in your Place, who most ernestlie and often hath spoken and writen to doe this louinge Office, he I saie shold haue no more of me, then I moste willinglie will wright to you from Tyme to Tyme.   (Collins, p. 281)

Sidney seems to have known of his own ill-success in obtaining the office at the time he wrote to Edward Denny (22 May 1580). Denny, along with Spenser, was to accompany Lord Grey to Ireland. Sidney's tone in the letter indicates that some feeling of resentment had arisen among Sidney's friends over the preferment of Lord Grey, a resentment which Sidney tries to lay to rest:

And very willingly doe I beare the preferringe of the noble L. Gray; since so I preferre him to my selfe, as I will ever be most glad to doe him service with affectionate honor, which truly I am but to very fewe. And if you should doe otherwise, in steade of thankinge you, I should doute you might in like sorte dispence with your selfe to sett me behinde some other of lesse bothe acqueaintance & worthe. Honour him therfore still, and as you matche me with him, soe therein will I matche my selfe with you.

Lord Grey formed a model for Spenser's Artegall in Book Five of *The Faerie Queene*. After two years in Ireland, Lord Grey was recalled by the Queen because of his

failed, they did not stop trying for advancement. But basically they found themselves standing idly by—while the rest of Europe was in arms—serving, as Greville put it, 'a Soveraign, which rested with her sex at home' (*Life*, p. 110). Their task as courtiers, however, was to make the best of the given situation, not to rebel. Sidney understood that necessity, and was willing to adjust his views, even if it involved redefining somewhat the idea that heroism entailed heroic constancy to a single intention. This thinking is reflected in a letter of 1578 which Sidney wrote to his father about the latter's Irish reverses:

So strangely and dyversely goes the Course of the Worlde by the enter-changinge Humors of those that governe it, that thoughe it be most noble to have allweyes one Mynde and one Constancy, yet can it not be allwaies directed to one Pointe; but must needes sometymes alter his Cource, according to the Force of others Changes dryves it.

(Sidney to Sir Henry Sidney, 25 April 1578)[1]

In redefining his way of being useful to the state, Sidney had already before 1580 begun to gravitate towards performing services of a literary nature at court. As early as 1577 he gave a discourse before the Queen refuting charges made against his father's Irish policies. The Sidney family secretary greeted the undertaking with enthusiasm, for the young heir had returned from abroad, evidently possessed of the high polish which only a fine continental education could bestow at the time:

Before the arrival of Mr. Whitten, Mr. Philip had gatherid a Collection of all the Articlis, which have bene enviously objectid to your Govern-ment, wherunto he hath fraimid an Answer in Way of Discours, the most excellently (if I have eny Judgement) that ever I red in my Lief; the Substance wherof is now approvid in your Letters, and Notes, by Mr. Whitten. But let no Man compare with Mr. Philips Pen.

(Edward Waterhouse to Sir Henry Sidney, Last Sept. 1577)[2]

The fact that Sidney came to accept this designation as an eloquent and skilful advocate is suggested by the motto he chose for him-self. 'Vix Ea Nostra Voco' indicates generally, as I have remarked before, the desire of Sidney to excel as an individual, independ-

---

excessive cruelty (see Smith and De Selincourt edition of Spenser, p. xxiv), at which time Sir Henry Sidney attempted once again, and again failed, to obtain a post there for his son (see Collins, p. 295).

[1] Collins, p. 247.
[2] Collins, p. 228.

ent of his powerful family. But the well-known scene in Ovid's *Metamorphoses* from which he drew the motto gives a clue to the special way in which Sidney wished to excel, a way which would allow him to serve, but serve completely on his own merits, the interests of his family and their faction at court. For when, in contest with Ajax over the arms of Achilles, Ulysses discounts his noble ancestry in the words which Sidney took as his own, Ulysses does so in order that his *eloquence* in the debate may have full importance. That is the substance of the lines which precede 'vix ea nostra voco'. Here is Golding's translation:

> Ne let my wit (which ay hath done you good O Greekes)
>   hurt mee.
> But suffer this mine eloquence (such as it is) which now
> Dooth for his mayster speake, and oft ere this hath spoke
>   for yow,
> Bee undisdeynd. Let none refuse his owne good gifts he
>   brings.
> For as for stocke and auncetors, and other such like things
> Wherof ourselves no fownders are, I scarcely dare them
>   graunt
> Too bee our owne.
>
> (XIII. 169–75)

It is that power of eloquence which is vindicated when the judges rule in favour of Ulysses:

> The Lords were moved with his woordes, and then appeered
>   playne
> The force that is in eloquence. The lerned man did gayne
> The armour of the valeant.
>
> (XIII. 463–5)

The Ovidian Ulysses, it should be understood, was considered by the Elizabethans to be as important a model of heroism as his Homeric counterpart.[1] In the debate with and verbal victory over Ajax, Ulysses gave a significant lesson to Sidney and his contemporaries by affirming the heroism of wit and wisdom over

---

[1] I am indebted for this information, and for the interpretation of the debate as opposing the two kinds of heroism, to Reuben Brower, *Hero and Saint*, pp. 121, 123–4.

mere martial deeds. Sidney was also schooled by Languet against the Ajax-like heroism of brute force:

Most men of high birth are possessed with this madness, that they long after a reputation founded on bloodshed, and believe that there is no glory for them except that which is connected with the destruction of mankind. Ought not you, adorned as you are by Providence with all those splendid gifts of the mind, to feel otherwise than men feel, who are buried in the most profound shades of ignorance, and think that all human excellence consists in physical strength? And yet, let them be never so strong, in this respect they are inferior to many of the brutes. Make use then of that particle of the Divine Mind (as you beautifully express it) which you possess, for the preservation and not the destruction of men.

(Languet to Sidney, 2 May 1578, Pears, p. 147)

While Languet provided supportive arguments, the debate of Ulysses seems to have provided symbolic reassurance for Sidney that indeed service and an acceptable kind of heroism could lie in cultivating the role of the eloquent spokesman at court.

The *Letter to Queen Elizabeth*, which precipitated Sidney's personal crisis of 1580, should be recognized as an extension of the role that he followed in imitation of Ulysses.[1] By comparing the substance of the *Letter* with the *Old Arcadia*, we can at last begin to perceive Sidney's decision to withdraw to Wilton and write as more than a negative reaction against exile. It is also more than the abdication which Languet feared when he begged Sidney to come out of hiding:

[1] There is evidence that on one, possibly two other occasions Sidney offered to play Ulysses' part and to serve his family, friends, and country with the best of 'his owne good gifts'. In 1583, as reported by Nichols (II. 400), Burghley had decided to resign from the Privy Council under the pressure of some hostile rumour. Nichols gives a letter of encouragement written to him by the Queen in May 1583: 'Let never care appear in you for such a rumour: but let them well know, that you rather desire the righting of such wrong, by making known their error . . .' (p. 400). At around the same time, Sidney wrote to Burghley suggesting, 'Neither will I use more plenty of wordes, till God make me hable to print them in som serviceable effect towardes yowr Lordeshippe' (Sidney to Burghley, 20 July 1583, Letter No. LVIII in Feuillerat). Certainly in 1585 Sidney tried to serve his uncle when the libellous *Leicester's Commonwealth* was circulated. His *Defence of the Earl of Leicester* was the result. Probably because official word went out from the Privy Council itself on 26 June 1585 to put Londoners on notice that supporting the libel against Leicester would be considered an act of treason directly against the Queen, Sidney's defence was overshadowed and was not published as he had at first intended. There is no evidence that a defence of Burghley was ever written.

Consider well, I entreat you, how far it is honourable to you to lurk where you are, whilst your country is imploring the aid and support of her sons. If the advice which you offered, believing it to be good for England, was not received as it deserved, you must not therefore be angry with your country. . . . When Themistocles was proposing measures that were salutary to his country, Eurybiades threatened to strike him if he did not hold his peace; to which he replied, 'Strike, but hear.' Imitate Themistocles, and undeceive your countrymen. . . .

(Languet to Sidney, 24 Sept. 1580, Pears, p. 185)

From various passages of the two works, we can see that the eloquent spokesman in the public realm had a close relationship to the poet in his privacy. In the *Old Arcadia*, Sidney did not abandon the attempt to imitate Ulysses or, as Languet put it, to 'imitate Themistocles'. Indeed, the same general advice which, Languet remarks, 'was not received as it deserved' by the Queen, is boldly repeated in Philanax' speech to Basilius at the beginning of the *Old Arcadia*.[1] In the *Letter* Sidney's opening point to the Queen about her proposed marriage to Anjou is this:

. . . a man might well ask: 'What makes you in such a calm to change course? To so healthful a body, to apply such a weary medicine? What hope can recompense so hazardous an adventure?' Hazardous indeed, were it for nothing but the altering of a well maintained and well approved trade.[2]

The theme of the folly of changing the *status quo* is restated as Philanax' main argument to Basilius.

Why should you now seek new courses, since your own example comforts you to continue on, and that it is most certain no destiny nor influence whatsoever can bring man's wit to a higher point than wisdom and goodness? Why should you deprive yourself of governing your dukedom for fear of losing your dukedom, like one that should kill himself for fear of death?

(*Old Arcadia*, Bk. I, p. 7)

Philanax begins by trying to calm Basilius's fears of the oracle, which are driving him to seek solitude. Thus Sidney departs from the order of argument of the *Letter to Queen Elizabeth*, but the ideas and even the language he uses in each work about such

[1] This point has been made briefly by Marcus Goldman in *Sir Philip Sidney and the Arcadia* (Urbana, Ill., 1934) and by Richard Lanham in ' The Old Arcadia,' from *Sidney's Arcadia*.

[2] *Sidney's Miscellaneous Prose*, p. 47. Other page references in the text to the *Letter to Queen Elizabeth* will be to this edition.

fears are almost the same. Here is Sidney's statement about the
fears that have impelled the Queen to seek to change her state
through marriage: '. . . the causes that should drive you to this
are either fears of that which cannot happen, or by this means
cannot be prevented . . .' (*Letter*, p. 56). Philanax says something
very similar.

These kinds of soothsaying sorceries (since the heavens have left us in
ourselves sufficient guides) [are] nothing but fancies wherein there
must either be vanity or infallibleness, and so either not to be respected
or not to be prevented.

(Old Arcadia, Bk. I, p. 7)

Finally we should notice the exhortation to Basilius's better nature
which Philanax repeats at the opening of his digression about the
princesses and at the close of the discourse:

Let your subjects have you in their eyes, let them see the benefits of
your justice daily more and more; and so must they needs rather like
of present sureties than uncertain changes. . . . stand wholly upon
your own virtue as the surest way to maintain you in that you are,
and to avoid any evil which may be imagined.

(Old Arcadia, Bk. I, pp. 7–8)

This appeal is directly parallel in meaning and phraseology to the
last paragraph of the *Letter to Queen Elizabeth*:

Against contempt at home, if there be any, which I will never believe,
let your excellent virtues of piety, justice and liberality daily, if it be
possible, more and more shine. Let some such particular actions be
found out (which is easy, as I think, to be done) by which you may
gratify all the hearts of your people. Let those in whom you find trust,
and to whom you have committed trust in your weighty affairs, be
held up in the eyes of your subjects. Lastly, doing as you do, you shall
be as you be: the example of princes, the ornament of this age, the
comfort of the afflicted, the delight of your people, the most excellent
fruit of all your progenitors, and the perfect mirror to your posterity.

(Letter, pp. 56–7)

The imitation of the *Letter to Queen Elizabeth* in the opening of
the *Old Arcadia* functions on one level as Sidney's defence of himself and an assertion of his undiminished good will to serve his
sovereign. In this connection the portrait of Philanax as the honest
courtier and one true friend to the duke almost certainly carries a

hint of the way Sidney regarded the part he had played in trying to advise the Queen:

> ... Philanax, whom he [the duke] had ever found a friend not only in affection but judgement, and no less of the duke than dukedom—a rare temper, whilst most men either servilely yield to all appetites, or with an obstinate austerity, looking to that they fancy good, wholly neglect the prince's person. But such was this man; and in such a man had Basilius been happy if his mind, corrupted with a prince's fortune, had not resolved to use a friend's secrecy rather for confirmation of fancies than correcting of errors. . . .
>
> (*Old Arcadia*, Bk. I, pp. 5–6)[1]

'A friend's secrecy' has some relationship, I believe, to the opening of the *Letter to Queen Elizabeth*, where Sidney begs leave to give his reasons freely, 'as hoping they shall only come to your merciful eyes' (*Letter*, p. 46). Whether or not that was a true hope on Sidney's part, or only a rhetorical flourish, seems to have become a question which reflected badly on Sidney's honour when the letter was circulated widely at court. Principally, in fact, it was the circulation of the letter, not the writing of it, which seems to have aroused the anger of the Queen and the Duke of Anjou and brought Sidney to the point of choosing between exile or rustication.[2] Thus the claim of secrecy which Sidney makes for Philanax above has an important bearing on the case he is making by analogy for himself.[3]

---

[1] Greville, in the *Life of Sidney*, uses similar language to contrast the honesty of Sidney toward the Queen about the French marriage with the self-interest of 'the great, and wise men of the time' who were 'every one fishinge to catch the Queens humor in it . . .' (pp. 53–4).

[2] Languet's letter to Sidney of 22 October 1580 implies that the publication, more than the actual writing of the *Letter to Queen Elizabeth*, was the discreditable act:

I am glad you have told me how your letter about the Duke of Anjou has come to the knowledge of so many persons; for it was supposed before, that you had made it known to show that you despised him, and cared nothing for his dislike; which appeared to me by no means a safe proceeding, and inconsistent besides with your natural modesty. And therefore I suspected that you had been urged to write by persons who either did not know into what peril they were thrusting you, or did not care for your danger, provided they effected their own object.   (Pears, p. 187)

It is important to note, in this context, that the *Letter* was not an example of Sidney's personal policy or bravery. Indeed, Languet goes on to say (as Sidney had evidently told him) that Sidney was 'ordered to write as you did by those whom you were bound to obey', probably by Leicester.

[3] Languet's letter to Sidney of 22 October 1580 continues, in an untranslated

Another part of the scene which, I feel, has that same undertone of a personal explanation is Philanax' reaction when Basilius orders him 'especially to keep narrow watch of the frontiers'. The courtier,

acknowledging himself much honoured by so great trust, went with as much care to perform his commandment as before he had with faith yielded his counsel, which in the latter short disputations he had rather proportioned to Basilius's words than to any towardness ['overwillingness'—O.E.D.] of argument.

(*Old Arcadia*, Bk. I, p. 9)

The first lines about Philanax clearly match Sidney's own desire to serve in a similar capacity on the Queen's frontiers in Ireland. The final apology also seems related to a feeling of regret by Sidney about the nature of his advice to the Queen, most likely about the portrayal of Anjou in the *Letter*. Languet, in writing to Sidney, reflects his friend's basic worry about the *Letter*. Languet notes that the overstatements do require some explanation, but that once that explanation has been forthcoming from Sidney, 'no fair-judging man can blame you ... even for exaggerating some circumstances in order to convince them of what you judged expedient' (Languet to Sidney, 22 Oct. 1580, Pears, p. 187). One of the poems from the *Old Arcadia* may also reflect Sidney's feelings about the *Letter to Queen Elizabeth*, for it tells the fable of the swan who 'woulde sing' at court, 'but others were defaste' (*Old Arcadia*, No. 10, l. 76). The other birds, who have been slandered, call a parliament which deprives the swan of his dignity and sends him away from court in silence and disgrace. Of course, Sidney has followed conventional literary models here—Ovid's tale of the raven in the *Metamorphoses* (II. 667–795), Chaucer's *Manciple's Tale* and *Parlement of Foules*. But the fable is told with an unconventional, and possibly personal, mixture of feelings: bitterness and anger against the accusers at court combined with regret at the swan's descent from neutral advocacy into invective:

portion, to give proof that Sidney had intended the *Letter to Queen Elizabeth* to be a private communication, 'inter amicos':

Nam eiusmodi scripta sunt instar privatorum colloquiorum inter amicos, in quibus liberius proferre solemus quid de quolibet sentiamus, interdum enim virtutes laudamus, aut vitia detestamur, prout aliquos in odium adducere, aut eis benevolentiam conciliare volumus: quod si nobis coram pluribus de iis ferendum esset iudicium, non eodem modo sermonem nostrum institueremus.

I warne thee therefore (since thou maist have choice)
Let not thy tonge become a firy matche,
No sword soe bytes as that evill toole annoyes.
(*Old Arcadia*, No. 10. ll. 88–90)[1]

In a more general way, Philanax' speech also introduces the political analogy which runs throughout the *Old Arcadia*. This last provides a different measure of Sidney's continuing desire to serve his country by using the eloquence of advice and admonition, but now in fictional form. I have used the term analogy on purpose, rather than allegory, because I would resist any implication that a one-to-one correspondence exists between Basilius and Queen Elizabeth, for instance, or between Arcadia and England, or between the events in Arcadia and contemporary history. The seminal work on this subject, E. A. Greenlaw's article, 'Sidney's *Arcadia* as an Example of Elizabethan Allegory', assumes that such detailed correspondences can indeed be substantiated. But that assumption leads to a conclusion which comes close to a criticism, not just of Basilius, but of Arcadia in general and also of the young princes, who by some later commentators have been portrayed as entering Arcadia in order to indulge 'criminal' pursuits of 'amorous toying' similar to those which Greenlaw sees at the root of Basilius's political blundering:

At the very time when he was working on his book, Sidney was in disgrace because he had addressed a letter to the Queen protesting against the proposed French marriage. It is this sloth, this foolish fear of fate, this wasting of time in amorous toying while factions were multiplying and plots against the throne grew ripe, that the Basilius story shows forth. Sidney does not hold up the pastoral life of Basilius as a model; he does not find in it an admirable withdrawal from the cares of life; it is no idyllic existence in the forest of Arden, but a criminal evading of responsibility that will bring ruin to any state.[2]

---

[1] A trace of Sidney's anger about his treatment at court over the *Letter to Queen Elizabeth* is reflected, I think, in a short letter to his uncle, the Earl of Leicester, written in the summer of 1580. At that time Sidney was evidently being called back from retirement to court. I sense a double meaning, or perhaps a triple meaning (in that the role of spokesman was the *only* role he had been allowed) in Sidney's statement that he will not yet return to court because he is 'so full of the colde as one can not heere me speake: whiche is the cawse keepes me yet frome the cowrte since my only service is speeche and that is stopped' (Sidney to Leicester, 2 Aug. 1580, Feuillerat, No. XLI).

[2] *Kittredge Anniversary Papers* (Boston, 1913), p. 337.

Any reflection in the *Old Arcadia* of Sidney's opinions about the French marriage is bound to have some relationship to his contemporary *Letter to Queen Elizabeth*. But the appraisal in that work of the potential dangers of the match with Anjou makes no mention of the danger of wasting time in 'amorous toying.' Sidney concentrates instead on the possibility that Anjou might upset the carefully maintained balance between English factions. The secret of Sidney's persuasive force in the following passage from the *Letter* lies not only in the clarity of his analysis of the factions, but also in the imaginative empathy with which he manages to present various points of view. He brings before us vividly the attitudes of not only the 'very common people' in the Protestant camp, but also the highly educated, wealthy, and frighteningly sincere Catholics:

Your inward force ... consisteth in your subjects: your subjects generally unexpert in warlike defence, and, as they are, divided into two mighty factions, and factions bound upon the never ending knot of religion.

The one is of them to whom your happy government hath granted the free exercise of the eternal truth. ... These, how their hearts will be galled, if not aliened, when they shall see you take to husband a Frenchman, and a Papist, in whom, howsoever fine wits may find further dangers or painted excuses, the very common people well know this: that he is the son of the Jezebel of our age; that his brother made oblation of his own sister's marriage, the easier to make massacres of all sexes; that he himself, contrary to his promise, ... did sack La Charité and utterly spoil Issoire with fire and sword. ...

The other faction ... is of the Papists: men whose spirits are full of anguish; some being forced to oaths they account damnable; some having their ambition stopped ...; some in prison and disgrace; some whose best friends are banished practisers; many thinking you an usurper; many thinking the right you had, disannulled by the Pope's excommunication; all burdened with the weight of their consciences; men of great number, of great riches (because the affairs of the state have not lain on them); of united minds, as all men that deem themselves oppressed naturally are. With these, I would willingly join all discontented persons, such as want and disgrace keeps lower than they have set their hearts ... they want nothing so much as a head ....

(*Letter*, pp. 47, 48, 49)

The general political lesson of the *Old Arcadia* seems to me related to the argument of the *Letter to Queen Elizabeth*. That lesson, as I see it, concerns the danger to the state, in an unstable political situation, arising from powerful factions on one side and on the other, from the usually loyal 'very common people'. The dangers of confusion in the last group are exemplified by the Phagonian rebellion at the end of Book Two of the *Old Arcadia*.[1] About the first group, Sidney emphasizes in the *Old Arcadia* not religious divisions, but more generally the destructive influence of quarrelsomeness and ambition. The parliament which comes together after Basilius's supposed death in Book Four exemplifies the chaos which divided opinions and personal jealousies can produce among the powerful in the absence of a clear successor to the government.[2] The analogy with contemporary English politics and the warning which Sidney directs at his countrymen centre on these possible consequences of changing the *status quo*, not on the particular cause—retirement to the pastoral lodges—which precipitates the change in Arcadian politics. Basilius is a fool, but I do not think that Sidney meant to imply a similar idea about Queen Elizabeth. Nor did he wish us to draw a critical conclusion about Arcadia as a place. 'Long peace and fruits of peace' may necessitate greater vigilance against potential dangers, as Sidney points out in his discourse to the Queen (*Letter*, p. 50), but the country where such peace can be maintained has a value above other nations.

It is not only by developing the political theme of the *Old Arcadia* (a minor part of the book, after all) that Sidney can be regarded as fulfilling a positive ideal of service to other men.

---

[1] The Phagonian villagers are stirred to rebellion by the idea of a foreigner's taking control of the state: 'Certain of them of wretched estates . . . began to say a strange woman had now possessed their prince and government . . .' (*Old Arcadia*, Bk. II, p. 127). In the *Letter to Queen Elizabeth*, similarly, Sidney makes a point that the English common people had been discontented under Queen Mary because 'she had made an odious marriage with a stranger, which is now in question whether your Majesty should do or no' (*Letter*, p. 55). Interestingly enough, Sidney changed the rebellion in the *New Arcadia* to give it more topical flavour for the 1584, rather than the 1580 period. Whereas in the original version the villagers go rushing off with the cry, 'Let us deliver our prince from foreign hands . . .' (p. 127), in the *New Arcadia* their reason is changed to, 'Let us deliver our Prince from daunger of practises . . .' (*New Arcadia*, Bk. II, p. 323). By 1584, the prospect of the French marriage had failed, and a greater threat seemed to be from plots, like that of Throckmorton, against the throne (see Howell's account, pp. 78–9).

[2] About the problem of succession, Sidney has this to say in the *Letter*: 'Who would leave the beams of so fair a sun for the dreadful expectation of a divided company of stars?' (p. 54). It is that 'dreadful' eventuality which he imagines in the scene of the parliament in the *Old Arcadia*.

Sidney's main love theme also provides what Greville has described aptly as moral 'threads' (though not such direct threads, I think, as Greville assumes), '. . to guide every man through the confused Labyrinth of his own desires, and life' (*Life of Sidney*, p. 245). If we take as an example the advice of Languet, who as much as anyone schooled Sidney in his ideals, we will realize that a broad view of moral action was held up to Sidney's eyes. Increasingly as Languet came to understand the actual fringe position, instead of the expected central role, which his protégé held at the English court, the correspondence records a broadening of advice on the kinds of good works which Sidney might still perform. Languet was not, as we have seen earlier, afraid to contemplate the prospect of Sidney's leaving England altogether; indeed, sometimes he seems to have looked upon exile as a necessity to improve the young man's lot: 'You want another stage for your character, and I wish you had chosen it in this part of the world' (Languet to Sidney, 14 Oct. 1579, Pears, p. 165). Yet we have also seen that Languet did not believe in the heroism of warfare and brute physical strength. Many of these broader ideas come together in Languet's letter to Sidney of 2 May 1578, the letter which answers Sidney's mock defence of his 'indolent ease' at court (Sidney to Languet, 1 Mar. 1578, Pears, p. 143). Languet's reply is keyed to the undertone of frustration which is strong in Sidney's joking. With sympathy, and with humour that in the end matches Sidney's own, Languet proposes a course of home service which, though it takes no account of Sidney's writing, yet resembles the 'exact image of quiet and action' that Greville saw and emulated in Sidney's work as a poet:

If you marry a wife, and if you beget children like yourself, you will be doing better service to your country than if you could cut the throats of a thousand Spaniards or Frenchmen.

When the question was raised in Cambyses's presence at a banquet, whether he or his father Cyrus was the better prince, all the company, in fear of the tyrant's cruelty, pronounced him far superior to his father. But when it came to Croesus's turn to speak, he said, 'Sir, I consider that your father must be held to be your better, because he was the father of an admirable prince, whereas you have as yet no son like yourself.' You see I am not endeavouring, as you say, to cover faults with a splendid and specious colouring, nor am I recommending to you ease and idleness, at least if you believe the poet who advises any man that wishes plenty of trouble to get him a wife.

(Languet to Sidney, 2 May 1578, Pears, p. 148)

Sidney did not choose to follow Languet's advice immediately by starting a family. But in 1580 at Wilton, during the same period when his sister Mary was carrying her first child (a son was born on 8 April 1580), Sidney produced what he himself calls—perhaps with a humorous glance at his sister's condition and at his own ideas of poetry – 'this child which I am loath to father' (*Old Arcadia*, Prefatory Letter to Mary, the Countess of Pembroke). Even in Languet's terms, the *Old Arcadia* can be regarded as a 'child' of which Sidney could be proud. It has a lesson for England, and a greater lesson for human kind about the way love works in the fallen world.

Arcadia seems to have become the favourite of Sidney. It is the only one of his works which he chose to revise. At least four times he returned to the manuscript to make minor corrections to the text, before finally recasting the story completely.[1] As his art matured, so did his 'child'. It is that further process of growth which I shall now attempt to trace.

---

[1] The evidence for four distinct revisions (and the beginning of a fifth) of the *Old Arcadia*—before the writing of the *New Arcadia* was begun—is recorded by Ringler in his Commentary on the poems from the *Old Arcadia*, pp. 364–81, and by Robertson in her Textual Introduction to the *Old Arcadia*, especially pp. lii–lxiv. As for Sidney's other works, Ringler and the editors of *Sidney's Miscellaneous Prose* agree that no evidence survives of any revision.

CHAPTER V

Arcadia *Re-made*

IN THE previous chapter I attempted to show how the forces of circumstance and Sidney's personal inclinations interacted to produce his first important piece of poetry, the *Old Arcadia*. Circumstance intervened again at Sidney's death, leaving the incomplete *New Arcadia* as his last piece of original work. As he revised his story, Sidney remained true to the broad ideal of moral service through poetry which we have followed in its initial development. But while this aspect of the poetry stays the same, the revision also reveals the changes in Sidney's thought and art which took place during his brief career as a poet. It is that second aspect of Sidney's creative development which will be the focus of this chapter. The fact that Sidney remained content with a single basic story is an indication in itself that the changes with which we will be dealing here are subtle ones. Indeed, we will find that nothing substantial in the plot or theme has been lost from the *Old Arcadia* to the new version, but the whole has been enriched and expanded.

The literary sources which Sidney mined for his additions to the *New Arcadia* have received thorough study. Montemayor's *Diana* and Heliodorus's *An Aethiopian History* have been identified as major influences on the revision, with lesser contributions from Malory's Arthurian tales and Xenophon's *Cyropaedia*.[1] It

---

[1] Sidney's debt to Montemayor's *Diana* has been examined in detail by T. P. Harrison in 'A Source of Sidney's "Arcadia"', *University of Texas Studies in English*, VI (Dec. 1926), 53–71, also by H. Genouy in *L' 'Arcadia' de Sidney dans ses rapports avec l' 'Arcadia' de Sannazaro et la 'Diana' de Montemayor* (Montpellier, 1928), p. 112–22, and by Judith M. Kennedy in her edition of Bartholomew Yong's translation of Montemayor's *Diana* and Gil Polo's *Enamoured Diana* (Oxford, 1968), pp. xxxiii–xxxix. The importance of Heliodorus has been shown by S. L. Wolff in *The Greek Romances in Elizabethan Prose Fiction* (New York, 1912), pp. 307–66. The use of Malory in the *New Arcadia* has been documented by Marcus S. Goldman in *Sir Philip Sidney and the Arcadia*, and the influence of Xenophon's *Cyropaedia* has been noted by E. A. Greenlaw in 'Sidney's *Arcadia* as an Example of Elizabethan Allegory'. Evidence that Sidney had read these works years before the *New Arcadia* is supplied by references in *A Defence of Poetry* to Xenophon's Cyrus (p. 79), to 'honest

can be shown that Sidney had read all these by the time he had
written the *Old Arcadia*, *A Defence of Poetry*, and *Certain Sonnets*.
Yet from 1580 to late 1581 Sidney made only minor changes in
the text of the *Old Arcadia*. He did not begin remoulding the
story into the *New Arcadia* until several years later.[1] The question
why remains to be answered. Since we already have evidence that
Sidney created the *Old Arcadia* to be both useful and moral, it is
unlikely that he felt the story needed reformation in those general
areas. And since none of the outside sources Sidney used were
new to him, with the possible exception of Bartholomew Yong's
English translation of the *Diana* (completed May 1583), then the
new inspiration to change must have come from still another
quarter.[2] Most of the major developments represented by the *New*

King Arthur' (p. 105), and to Heliodorus's 'sugared invention of that picture of love'
(p. 81), and by the inclusion of translations of songs from Montemayor in *Certain
Sonnets* (Nos. 28, 29).

[1] The date 1584 is written on the first page of Cm, the unique surviving manuscript
of the *New Arcadia*. Robertson believes that this 'is too late a date for the beginning
of the revision' (p. lvii n.). Ringler, on the other hand, accepts the 1584 dating of the
New Arcadia, and gives solid evidence that Sidney must have begun the revision
at least after the year 1582 (pp. 365–6). During this later period of his poetic
career, Sidney continued as before to try to establish another career for himself at
court. Attempts in 1582 to follow his father in entering the Irish and Welsh ad-
ministrations failed. Throughout 1583 Sidney pursued the possibility of joining his
uncle, the Earl of Warwick, as Master of the Ordnance. After delays, Sidney did
obtain a subordinate position; and later, in the summer of 1585, he was made joint
Master of the Ordnance with his uncle. Contemporary records also show Sidney's
growing interest in the New World, where (to use Greville's metaphor, *Life*, p. 105)
the golden fleece that remained to be fetched away seemed increasingly attractive to
English Jasons as a source of personal riches as well as a way to strike at their enemy,
Spain. This interest on Sidney's part culminated in his attempt to sail secretly with Sir
Francis Drake in the autumn of 1585. With Drake's complicity, Sidney was prevented
from going, but he was offered instead the governorship of Flushing as part of an
English armed force being provided for the Netherlands. In that honourable capacity
he departed from England in November 1585, not to return again. Although Sidney
died almost a year later in the Low Countries, it can be assumed that he broke off
writing the *New Arcadia* and delivered the unfinished fair copy (of which Cm is a
rather poor transcript) to Greville before leaving England. Greville, who did not
accompany Sidney to the Netherlands, first reported the existence of the *New Arcadia*
a month after his friend's death: 'a correction of that old one don 4 or 5 years since
which he left in trust with me. . . .' (Greville to Sir Francis Walsingham, Nov.
1586, Ringler, p. 530).

[2] Sidney's early access to the Yong translation, which was not published until
1598, is made probable by the relationship he had established with Edward Bannister,
who was directly responsible for persuading Yong to begin the work. Thus Bannister
certainly would have had a copy of the completed translation (see Yong's Preface,
Kennedy edition, p. 5). I have cited before the copy of Sidney's *Certain Sonnets*, No.
30 which exists in a manuscript collection made by Bannister, with an attached note

Arcadia, however, can be related to Sidney's original ideas on love and poetry. Thus it seems to me the safest assumption that he undertook the revision not because he had discovered a new author, style, or genre, certainly not because he disapproved of his former work (the manuscript evidence for the *Old Arcadia* shows that Sidney made no attempt to recall copies which his friends had obtained), but because he had more to say on his original themes.[1]

The opening of the *New Arcadia* is an acknowledged instance of Sidney's borrowing, in this case from the opening of Montemayor's *Diana*. But having recognized that, we still need to seek out Sidney's reasons for borrowing. If we approach the scene with an eye towards identifying Sidney's imaginative growth, however, particularly with an eye for subtle changes in his attitudes to love and poetry, we will better be able to discover those reasons.

The shepherds Strephon and Klaius, whom Sidney singles out in the first scene to sound the keynote of the *New Arcadia*, appear only tangentially in the older version. They are introduced with a passing reference during the Third Eclogues, where they are associated with Philisides (*Old Arcadia*, Third Eclogues, p. 245). In the Fourth Eclogues they are allowed two fine songs, but only a short paragraph is devoted to their story. They are, in the *Old Arcadia*, not shepherds but gentlemen—strangers to Arcadia— who have entered the country and taken up the trade of shepherds out of love for an Arcadian maiden Urania, 'thought a shepherd's daughter, but indeed of far greater birth'. Each friend knows of the other's love, yet the strength of their mutual friendship is so remarkable 'that they never so much as brake company one from

signifying that Sidney personally gave the poem to the collector, 'Att pvttenye In svrrye Decembris x° Ann° 1584' (Ringler, p. 555).

[1] Several critics, notably R. W. Zandvoort in *Sidney's Arcadia: A Comparison between the Two Versions* (Amsterdam, 1929) and E. M. W. Tillyard in *The English Epic and Its Background* (London, 1954), have surmised generally about motives for the revision that 'Sidney found that he had more to say' (Tillyard, p. 296). But what precisely Sidney had to say in terms of his old topics of interest seems to me an important question which has so far remained obscured in comparative studies of the two *Arcadias* by the critical preoccupation with genre and sources and by the critical impulse to form a preference between the two versions where Sidney's intricate method of revision often makes it impossible to separate them. Kenneth Muir's pamphlet, *Sir Philip Sidney*, has an example of the last impulse. On p. 16, Muir argues for the superior style of the *New Arcadia*, citing phrases which came to the revision untouched from the *Old Arcadia*.

the other, but continued their pursuit, like two true runners both employing their best speed, but one not hindering the other'. Urania has now abandoned them in Arcadia, leaving a commandment that they wait there for her return. Thus the two friends remain, 'rather meaning to break their hearts than break her commandment, they bare it out as well as such evil might be . . .' (*Old Arcadia*, Fourth Eclogues, p. 328).

The love-relationship between Strephon and Klaius and Urania seems to have interested Sidney more than his cursory treatment of them in the *Old Arcadia* would suggest. For he returned to their story as his main subject in a lengthy unfinished poem (*Other Poems*, No. 4) written, according to Ringler, close to the time of *Astrophil and Stella*, sometime between 1581 and 1583, and most probably left in its present state before the *New Arcadia* was under way.[1] In the 544 extant lines of the poem (it is actually the longest piece of verse which Sidney produced), Sidney gives much fuller portraits than before of his three characters. Urania, in particular, is transformed into a charming and sympathetic figure. But the major change from the *Old Arcadia* is the emphatic lowliness of everyone's birth. Sidney seems to have conceived of his poem as something like an epic of love. He chose to write in the heroic metre, *ottava rima*; and by invoking not the conventional Muses but a well-born and happy audience, Sidney both differentiates his aims from the epic and aspires to its broad appeal:

> A SHEPHEARD'S tale no height of stile desires
> To raise in words what in effect is lowe:
> A plaining songe plaine-singing voice requires,
> For warbling notes from inward chearing flow.
> I then, whose burd'ned brest but thus aspires
> Of shepheards two the seely case to show,
> 　　Nede not the stately Muses' helpe invoke
> 　　For creeping rimes, which often sighings choke.
> But you, ô you, that thinke not teares too deare
> To spend for harms, although they touch you not:
> And deigne to deeme your neighbors' mischefe neare,
> Although they be of meaner parents gott:
> You I invite with easie eares to heare
> The poore-clad truth of love's wrong-ordred lot.　　(ll. 1–14)

---

[1] Ringler gives detailed evidence for this dating, p. 494.

Strephon and Klaius have become, for Sidney, representative of
a pervasive human truth. The gentlemen of the *Old Arcadia* are
transformed into authentic shepherds:

> Train'd in the life which on short-bitten grasse
> In shine or storme must sett the clowted shoe . . . . (ll. 19-20)

The woman they love is also no longer the lost child of a pastoral
romance, 'of far greater birth' than her situation would indicate.
Urania is simply a country girl, 'by fortune meane, in Nature
borne a Queene' (l. 91). From their minor role in the *Old Arcadia*,
Strephon and Klaius—in their new personification as low-born
shepherds in love with a low-born shepherdess—have developed
into Sidney's paradigm of all unhappy human affection.

    These clearly-realized symbols of 'love's wrong-ordred lot',
rather than the shadowy Strephon and Klaius of the *Old Arcadia*,
dominate the opening of the *New Arcadia*.[1] Like the doleful

---

[1] There is a measurable increase in Sidney's sympathy towards those 'of meaner
parents gott' from the *Old Arcadia* (where Sidney is rather supercilious toward the
shepherds) to *Other Poems*, No. 4 and the *New Arcadia*, where we have Strephon and
Klaius, as well as the kinder view of poverty expressed through Sidney's portraits of
Urania and Lalus in the tournament of Artesia (Bk. I, pp. 104, 106–7). Piers Ingersoll
Lewis, in *Literary and Political Attitudes in Sidney's Arcadia* (Harvard Doctoral Dissertation, 1964), has criticized Sidney on just this point, focusing his attack on the
'five memorable strokes' which are struck by the princes against the rebelling
commoners in Book Two of the *New Arcadia* (pp. 312–13). Lewis argues, 'Sidney
would not be able to turn slaughter into comedy if he did not feel that butchers,
bakers, tailors, farmers, etc., were too low and contemptible to become the objects
of pity or remorse' (p. 126). I think that the scene emanates less from Sidney's
aristocratic scorn of the mob than from an artistic need to represent civil dis-
order in a graphic yet also symbolic way. To do this, Sidney has chosen to follow
Ovid's method in the *Metamorphoses* (XII. 236–592), where the chaotic battle of the
Centaurs and the Lapiths at the wedding of Pirithous and Hippodame comes to
stand for all war, and for the Trojan War in particular. Sidney points to his source
when he describes the 'poore painter' who 'was to counterfette the skirmishing
betwene the *Centaures* and *Lapithes,* and had bene very desirous to see some notable
wounds, to be able the more lively to expresse them' (*New Arcadia*, Bk. II, p. 313).
A last blow by Musidorus cuts off both the painter's hands, so he ends the day, 'well
skilled in wounds, but with never a hand to performe his skill' (p. 313). The intense
yet half-comic cruelty of the blows matches closely the Ovidian portrayal of slaughter.
Sidney uses the same manner later in the *New Arcadia* to describe the disorderly
frays between the noble followers of Amphialus and Basilius in Book Three.
Policrates, for example, is an aristocrat but also a coward: '*Amphialus* with a memorable blowe strake of his head, where, with the convulsions of death setting his
spurres to his horse, he gave so brave a charge upon the enemie, as it grewe a
proverbe, that *Policrates* was onely valiant, after his head was off' (p. 389). My point
is that Sidney was following a literary, not a political convention in each instance.
Spenser makes use of the same convention when he contrasts the disordered image
of the Centaurs and Lapiths at the bridal feast with the essential order of the stars, and
by analogy of the Graces dancing on Mount Acidale:

Syrenus and Sylvanus in Montemayor's *Diana*, Sidney's shepherds announce, through their commiserations, the principal
themes of the book. Sidney departs slightly but significantly,
however, from what he found in Montemayor. He brings his two
shepherds on stage together at the outset, rather than have first
one, then the other appear; and he keeps the greater emphasis
throughout the scene on their continuing friendship and double
sorrow, rather than, as in the *Diana*, on their separate grief and
their rivalry in love. From the opening soliloquy by Syrenus in
the *Diana*, Sidney derived the address to 'remembrance' ('Memorie'
in Yong's translation of Montemayor) in his opening scene.[1] But
Sidney takes the theme beyond its use in the *Diana*. By repeating
the word 'remembrance' in the speeches of not just one, but both
shepherds, Sidney links the irredeemably sad memory of Urania's
departure, conjured up by Strephon, with Klaius's more com-
forting thoughts of Urania's beauty and of the improving effects
which love for her has had upon her lovers. This last speech
probably took its origin from Sylvanus's recitation in the *Diana* of
the contentment he has found in love despite his grief.[2] But in
Montemayor, after further songs and exchanges, the scene rises to
a crescendo of sorrow in the final duet sung by the shepherds.[3]

> Looke how the Crowne, which *Ariadne* wore
>   Vpon her yuory forehead that same day,
> That *Theseus* her vnto his bridale bore,
>   When the bold *Centaures* made that bloudy fray,
>   With the fierce *Lapithes*, which did them dismay;
> Being now placed in the firmament,
>   Through the bright heauen doth her beams display,
>   And is vnto the starres an ornament,
> Which round about her moue in order excellent.
>   (*The Faerie Queene*, VI.x.13)

[1] Kennedy edition, p. 12: 'Ah memorie (cruell enemie to my quiet rest) were not
thou better occupied to make me forget present corsies, then to put before mine
eies passed contents? What saiest thou memorie?'

[2] Kennedy edition, pp. 17–18. Sylvanus speaks:

Canst thou then thinke (*Syrenus*) that I would wish thee ill, bicause *Diana* loved thee?
. . . What man, my faith was never so basely poysed, but that it was ever so serviceable to my Mistresse humour, not onely in loving thee, but in loving and honouring
all that ever she loved. . . . I can say as much by my selfe, and thinke moreover that
there was never any, that casting his eies on *Dianas* peerelesse beautie, durst desire
any other thing, then to see her, and to converse with her.

[3] Kennedy edition, p. 27. Sylvanus sings:

> *Syrenus*, that most cruell love, engendring me
>   Such greefe, stints not, nor hindreth the perswading me
> Of so much ill: I die therein remembring me.
>   (ll. 34–6)

Sidney's scene ends on the more positive note supplied by Klaius, that even the sources of love's torment are arguments in favour of loving:

hath not shee throwne reason upon our desires, and, as it were given eyes unto *Cupid*? hath in any, but in her, love-fellowship maintained friendship betweene rivals, and beautie taught the beholders chastitie?
(*New Arcadia*, Bk. I, p. 8)

Sidney has thus remoulded (and considerably shortened) Monte-mayor's scene to create a sharper dramatic climax. Sidney's scene moves directly from the shepherds' grief to having them 'thinke with consideration, and consider with acknowledging, and acknowledge with admiration, and admire with love, and love with joy in the midst of all woes' (*New Arcadia*, Bk. I, p. 7).

It is this pattern of response to love—certainly not a response of rising hope among such hopeless lovers, but at least a rising understanding and acceptance of love's fruits, emerging from love's sorrow—which Sidney places as a prologue to his retelling of the original story of the *Arcadia*. Thus the opening scene announces, as I see it, a love-theme for the *New Arcadia* which complements and extends the original theme of the *Old Arcadia* without radically departing from it. The new dimensions of love which are revealed by Strephon and Klaius are endless pain and the endurance of pain, but those revelations only make more triumphant the continuance and renewal of love which the original story confirms.

Despite Neo-Platonic resonances in Urania's name (the same as Plato's Venus Urania, or Heavenly Beauty), the love which Strephon and Klaius hold for her seems to be no different in kind from the love of other men and women in Sidney's earlier poetry. Certainly this is true in the long unfinished poem where Sidney treats the unfortunate trio in detail. Strephon and Klaius are not Platonic lovers. Instead, like Astrophil, they are the victims of desire.[1] For example, Sidney offers this account of the growth of Strephon's love:

---

[1] An interesting coordinate to Sidney's preoccupation with desire in *Astrophil and Stella* is the tourney-play *The Four Foster Children of Desire*. There is some evidence that Sidney wrote it (Ringler, pp. 518–19) for a performance in which he participated on 15 May 1581. This work, conceived at the same time as the sonnet sequence, has the theme (which looks forward to the *New Arcadia* too) that 'the wing of memorie, alas, the sworne enimie unto the wofull man's quietnesse, being

. . . into none doubt of his love did sinke,
For not himselfe to be in love did thinke.
But glad Desire, his late embosom'd guest,
Yet but a babe, with milke of Sight he nurst:
Desire the more he suckt, more sought the brest,
Like dropsy folke still drinke to be a thyrst.
            (*Other Poems*, No. 4, ll. 199–204)[1]

Klaius's reactions to love are less naïve and less openly sensual than Strephon's, for Klaius is the older and more earnest of the two friends. But he too is described by Sidney in phrases that strongly echo Astrophil:

For then wise *Klaius* found no absence can
Help him, who can no more hir sight foregoe.
He found man's vertue is but part of man,
And part must folowe where whole man doth goe.
    He found that Reason's self now reasons found
    To fasten knotts, which fancy first had bound.
So doth he yeeld, so takes he on his yoke,
Not knowing who did draw with him therin. . . .
                    (ll. 419–26)[2]

As the lovers of Urania resemble Astrophil in their feelings, so Urania herself resembles Stella. Both women have heavenly names, but both arouse an earthly passion. The fact that Sidney conceived of them in similar terms is suggested by a number of

constantlie held by the hand of perfection' blows the coal of desire, 'this flame un-quenchable by anie means: till by death the whole fewell be consumed' (Nichols, II. 327). The pageant also presents another important idea, which has a relation to Astrophil's and to Strephon's and Klaius's feelings. It is that desire, by its very definition, can never be fulfilled. Thus someone who suffers from desire cannot be cured:

Of all affections that are, Desire is the most worthie to woo, but less deserves to win Beautie: for in winning his saint, he loseth himselfe: no sooner hath Desire what he desireth, but that he dieth presentlie: so that when Beautie yeeldeth once to Desire, then can she never want to be desired againe. Wherefore of force this principle must stand, it is convenient for Desire ever to wish, and necessarie that he alwaies want.
                                (Nichols, II. 325)

[1] See in relation to this passage *Certain Sonnets*, No. 6 ('Sleepe Babie mine, Desire, nurse Beautie singeth') and also *Astrophil and Stella*, No. 71 (' "But ah", Desire still cries, "give me some food." ') and No. 72 ('But thou Desire, because thou wouldst have all,/Now banisht art, but yet alas how shall?').
[2] There is an echo (l. 423) of *Astrophil and Stella*, No. 10:

For soone as they strake thee with *Stella's* rayes,
Reason thou kneel'dst, and offeredst straight to prove
By reason good, good reason her to love.

instances in the poetry where imagery and actions are repeated with reference to Stella and also to her country cousin.[1] For example, Urania is introduced in a charming scene with her pet sparrow. The same situation in the sonnet sequence (No. 83) stresses Astrophil's jealousy over the physical liberties which the sparrow is allowed to take with Stella. The sonnet is clearly indebted to Skelton's delightfully wanton poem *Philip Sparrow* (and ultimately to Catullus). With Stella and Skelton's Mistress Jane as immediate relations, Urania is an unlikely representative of Heavenly Love. And indeed Sidney uses the sparrow scene above all to give the shepherds a glimpse of Urania's ravishing breasts. In the lines that follow, her earthliness is never for a moment left behind:

> The happy wretch she putt into hir breast,
> Which to their eies the bowles of *Venus* brought,
> For they seem'd made even of skie-mettall best,
> And that the bias of hir bloud was wrought.
> Betwixt them two the peeper tooke his nest,
> 　　Where snugging well he well appear'd content
> So to have done amisse, so to be shent.
>
> 　　　　　　　　　　　　　(ll. 98–104)

In a later passage from the poem (ll. 145–60), Urania's irresistible physical beauty—dressed out with metaphors also used for Stella in *Astrophil and Stella*, No. 13—conquers the shepherds' hearts by 'cutting Reason's raines' (l. 158). Thus it cannot be said to be disembodied 'reasonable' love, in conventional Neo-Platonic terms, which Urania inspires.

Where Urania becomes symbolic of love generally, as I think she does in the opening of the *New Arcadia*, she does not stand in contrast to the earthly loves of the princes and princesses. I do not agree that, as some critics say, by beginning with Urania's departure from Arcadia, Sidney therefore implies that the rest of the love story will take place under the pall of an 'iron age' of sensuality.[2] His purpose, instead, seems to be to begin with love in

---

[1] Ringler details the repetitions, p. 494.

[2] K. Duncan-Jones, in 'Sidney's Urania', *Review of English Studies*, New Series XVII (1966), 123–132, states that, 'As far as the *Arcadia* is concerned, the point about Urania, above all, is that she has gone away. . . . this is rather a bitter complaint for a departed Muse than a hopeful address to a present one' (pp. 129–130). Urania was sometimes associated with Astrea, the virgin of classical mythology whose departure from earth signalled the end of the Golden Age. Duncan-Jones argues that

its essential sorrow, to begin with absence, with unattainable and unrequited affection. By attaching to his original love story these more tragic elements Sidney conveys, as far as the unfinished *New Arcadia* will allow, a more inclusive, but not a different theme from the *Old Arcadia* about the power and pervasiveness of love in the world.

This idea about Sidney's handling of the love-theme can further illuminate some changes he made in the *New Arcadia* in the characters of Pyrocles and Musidorus. For Sidney has added to their experiences and feelings in love precisely those elements which serve to bring them closer to Strephon and Klaius, as well as to Astrophil. One instance of a change is the tragedy which Pyrocles has lived through because of Zelmane's love and death for him. This takes place before he enters Arcadia and falls in love himself with Philoclea.[1] It is noteworthy that Sidney calls attention to the Zelmane incident in the first book of the *New Arcadia*, before we know the actual sequence of events, which is finally recounted in Book Two. To the uninitiated reader, then, the references in Book One seem more confused than purposeful. But Sidney's intention seems to be to indicate at the outset mysterious reserves of experience and wisdom in Pyrocles' character. That enables Sidney specifically to strengthen Pyrocles' position in the early debate with Musidorus on love. In the passage below from the debate as it stands in the *New Arcadia*, Pyrocles' lines from the original version, which signal less wisdom than the play of a ready wit, have been augmented by an emotional appeal addressed directly to his opponent (in italics, below). This addition implies strongly that some deeper reason centred in life, not just in the play of rhetoric, is compelling Pyrocles' actions and feelings.

Eagles we see fly alone; and they are but sheepe, which alwaies heard together; cōdemne not therefore my minde somtime to enjoy it selfe; nor blame not the taking of such times as serve most fitte for it. *And alas, deere Musidorus, if I be sadde, who knowes better then you the just causes*

there is a contrast 'between the effects of love described by Strephon and those which are seen in the main plot of the *Arcadia*. . . . It is clear, in the main plot, that we have to do with a different kind of love altogether', one of 'sensual enjoyment' (pp. 128–9). But the proofs for this interpretation are, by the critic's own admission, contradictory (p. 132).

[1] Montemayor's *Diana* includes the story of Felismena, who serves her lover, disguised as his page (Bk. II). This was clearly a model for the actions of Zelmane in giving proof of her love for Pyrocles (*New Arcadia*, Bk. II, pp. 290–9).

I have of sadnes? And here Pyrocles sodainly stopped, like a man un-satisfied in himselfe, though his witte might well have served to have satisfied another.

(*New Arcadia*, Bk. I, p. 56, emphasis mine)[1]

Another addition to Pyrocles' character is the initial opposition he gives to love. In the *Old Arcadia* he is an easy victim to the passion, as a result of youthful ignorance and a noble capacity for pity:

As the most noble heart is most subject unto it, from questions grew to pity; and when with pity once his heart was made tender, according to the aptness of the humour, it received straight a cruel impression of that wonderful passion which to be defined is impossible, by reason no words reach near to the strange nature of it. They only know it which inwardly feel it. It is called love. Yet did not the poor youth at first know his disease, thinking it only such a kind of desire as he was wont to have to see unwonted sights, and his pity to be no other but the fruits of his gentle nature.

(*Old Arcadia*, Bk. I, pp. 11–12)

But in the *New Arcadia* (although the passage above does remain in the revision) a further struggle takes place in Pyrocles' mind after he realizes that he is in love. The description which Sidney supplies is strongly reminiscent of Astrophil's internal struggles (in Sonnets Nos. 18 and 19, for example, among several sonnets on the subject early in the sequence). It is also close to the des-cription of Klaius's feelings in *Other Poems*, No. 4, whereas Strephon, in the same passage, seems like the more naïve Pyrocles of the older characterization:

---

[1] Another change which strengthens Pyrocles' position in the debate is the division of the scene into two parts in the *New Arcadia*. One part, up to the revelation that Pyrocles is a lover, takes place before Pyrocles has disguised himself (*New Arcadia*, Bk. I, pp. 54–9). But the actual discussion of love, under the force of Musidorus's disapproval, takes place after Pyrocles' transformation into an Amazon is an accom-plished fact which cannot be altered by argument (Bk. I, pp. 77–84). In lines which Sidney added at this point to Pyrocles' account of the birth and growth of his love, Zelmane again plays a part, as does Musidorus himself, in making the passion for Philoclea seem inevitable:

Cousin (saide hee) then began the fatall overthrowe of all my libertie, when walking among the pictures in *Kalanders* house, you your selfe delivered unto mee what you had understood of *Philoclea*, who muche resembling (though I must say much sur-passing) the Ladie *Zelmane*, whom too well I loved: there were mine eyes infected, & at your mouth did I drinke my poison.

(*New Arcadia* only, Bk. I, pp. 84–5)

Klaius streight felt, and groned at the blowe,
And cal'd, now wounded, purpose to his aide:
Strephon, fond boy, delighted did not knowe,
That it was Love that shin'de in shining maid . . .
(ll. 161–4)

*   *   *

Klaius in deede would faine have puld a way
This mote from out his eye, this inward burre,
And now, proud Rebell gan for to gainsay
The lesson which but late he learn'd too furre:
   Meaning with absence to refresh the thought
   To which hir presence such a feaver brought.
(ll. 171–6)

The result of the struggle of Astrophil, Klaius, and finally of Pyrocles, is only a more emphatic triumph for love, wherein the lover's reason itself conspires to effect his overthrow (see in this connection *Astrophil and Stella*, No. 10 and *Other Poems*, No. 4, ll. 423–4). That is the point of the passage which Sidney has added in the *New Arcadia* to the account of Pyrocles' response to love:

Yet I take to witnesse the eternall spring of vertue, that I had never read, heard, nor seene any thing; I had never any tast of Philosophy, nor inward feeling in my selfe, which for a while I did not call for my succour. But (alas) what resistance was there, when ere long my very reason was (you will say corrupted) I must needs confesse, conquered; and that me thought even reason did assure me, that all eies did degenerate from their creation, which did not honour such beautie?
(*New Arcadia* only, Bk. I, p. 85)

To Musidorus, who was recalcitrant towards love in the *Old Arcadia*, Sidney gives a pair of new speeches in Book One of the revision about the necessity of yielding to love. The first echoes the end of Pyrocles' speech above:

I now (woe is me) do try what love can doo. O *Zelmane*, who will resist it, must either have no witte, or put out his eyes? can any man resist his creation? certainly by love we are made, and to love we are made. Beasts onely cannot discerne beauty, and let them be in the role of Beasts that doo not honor it.
(*New Arcadia*, Bk. I, p. 113)[1]

---

[1] There is also an echo of *A Defence of Poetry* (p. 104), where Sidney, in defending love poetry, also defends love: 'But grant love of beauty to be a beastly fault (although it be very hard, since only man, and no beast, hath that gift to discern beauty). . . .'

The second speech by Musidorus echoes the Eleventh Song of
Astrophil and Stella, particularly in the central image of a person
shaking a stake and only succeeding in driving it further into the
ground.

> But alas, well have I found, that Love to a yeelding hart is a king; but
> to a resisting, is a tyrant. The more with arguments I shaked the stake,
> which he had planted in the grounde of my harte, the deeper still it
> sanke into it. But what meane I to speake of the causes of my love,
> which is as impossible to describe, as to measure the backside of
> heaven? Let this word suffice, I love.
>
> > *(New Arcadia*, Bk. I, p. 115)[1]

The sorrows and struggles which, in the first book of the *New
Arcadia*, Sidney added to Pyrocles' feelings and re-emphasized in
Musidorus, fit into the same pattern which we found in the
opening scene with Strephon and Klaius. It is a pattern which
rises from the painful experience of love to the magnifying of
love's power. Sidney reinforces that idea in the comment made
by the princes at the end of Book One. At the same point in the
Old Arcadia, the princes are simply apprehensive about the
future:

> Alas! What further evil hath fortune reserved for us, or what shall be
> the end of this our tragical pilgrimage? Shipwrecks, daily dangers,
> absence from our country, have at length brought forth this captiving
> of us within ourselves which hath transformed the one in sex, and the
> other in state, as much as the uttermost work of changeable fortune
> can be extended unto.
>
> > *(Old Arcadia*, Bk. I, p. 43)

In the comparable passage from the *New Arcadia*, the impulse to
lament remains—interestingly enough, without the stress on
fortune.[2] But it is accompanied by a more assured belief that the
ends of love are good.

---

[1] The parallel image in *Astrophil and Stella*, Eleventh Song, is this:

> 'But the wrongs love beares, will make
> Love at length leave undertaking'.
> No, the more fooles it do shake,
> In a ground of so firme making,
> Deeper still they drive the stake.　(ll. 31–5)

[2] This difference from Sidney's original version and from the romance tradition
has been noted by Richard A. Greer in *Adaptations of the Greek Romances in the
English Renaissance as Reflections of the Debate between Fortune and Virtue* (Harvard

O heaven and earth (said *Musidorus*) to what a passe are our mindes
brought, that from the right line of vertue, are wryed to these crooked
shifts? But ô Love, it is thou that doost it: thou changest name upō
name; thou disguisest our bodies, and disfigurest our mindes. But in
deed thou hast reason, for though the wayes be foule, the journeys end
is most faire and honourable.

(*New Arcadia* only, Bk. I, p. 117)

My larger argument about love in the *New Arcadia* is not that
these positive feelings are new, but that the positive aspect re-
ceives new emphasis because it is now achieved in the process of
enduring much greater difficulties. The nature of those difficulties
is important to notice. For the added troubles of Pyrocles and
Musidorus in the *New Arcadia* are clearly related to the troubles of
Astrophil and of Strephon and Klaius which Sidney explored in
poetry of the period intervening between the *Old Arcadia* and the
revision. Thus the love-theme developed in the *New Arcadia* represents an accommodation between the older theme of love's
folly and delight and the more recent and less joyful preoccupa-
tions of Sidney's poetry. In the following passage from the *New
Arcadia*, for example, the pangs of Astrophil and his sad encounter
with Stella's 'Tyran honour' (Eighth Song, l. 95) can be seen to
have a definite influence on the reflections uttered by Musidorus.
Sidney has carefully joined the sadder thoughts of the lover to his
original hopeful resolves, as taken from the *Old Arcadia* (added
material indicated by italics):

*Many times, when my masters cattle came hether to chewe their cudde, in this
fresh place, I might see the young Bull testifie his love. But how? with proud
lookes, and joyfulnes. O wretched mankind (said I then to my selfe) in whom
witte (which should be the governer of his welfare) becomes the traitor to his
blessednes. These beasts, like children to nature, inherite her blessings quietly; we,
like bastards, are layd abroad, even as foundlinges to be trayned up by griefe and
sorrow. Their mindes grudge not their bodies comfort, nor their sences are letted
from enjoying their objects:* we have the impediments of honor, and the torments
of conscience. Truely in such cogitatiōs have I . . . long stood. . . . But Love,
(which one time layeth burthens, another time giveth wings) when I was at the
lowest of my downward thoughts, pulled up my harte to remēber, that nothing

Doctoral Dissertation, 1972), p. 82. Greer sees love in Sidney's *Arcadia* as having
many affinities to fortune and as being only imperfectly reconciled by Sidney to the
opposite of fortune, virtue. Duncan-Jones takes the exclamation by Musidorus as
an ironic commentary on the blindness of the princes to the sensuality of their
passion ('Sidney's Urania', p. 129).

is atchieved before it be throughlie attempted; and that lying still doth never goe forward. . . .

(*New Arcadia*, Bk. II, p. 154, emphasis mine)[1]

Through Sidney's additions here, the pattern of movement from sorrow towards comfort, which was introduced by Strephon and Klaius in the first scene of the *New Arcadia*, is repeated once again.

The opening scene of the *New Arcadia* not only reveals a development in Sidney's attitude to love, but also announces a shift of emphasis in his approach to poetry in the revision. 'Remembrance', which figures so often in the speeches of Strephon and Klaius, serves both to unify the shepherds' presentation of love and to introduce what proves to be an important poetic principle in the rest of the work. In terms of the general effect of the *New Arcadia* on readers, the 'call to memorie' (p. 7) in the opening scene establishes the dominance of the fictional mode—which appeals specifically to the memory. In the *Old Arcadia*, on the other hand, we feel a strong accompanying effect of music, 'the most divine striker of the senses' (*Defence*, p. 100); for Sidney

[1] In discussing the development of the love-theme in the *New Arcadia*, I have concentrated on Sidney's slightly different, but still comparable handling of the characters of the princes. There is a much greater difference between the *Old* and the *New Arcadia* in Sidney's characterizations of the princesses. In fact, the detailed and sympathetic portraits in the *New Arcadia* are hardly comparable at all to the original Pamela and Philoclea. But that difference in the treatment of the women in the revision is also related to Sidney's expansion of the original love-theme to bring it into line with poetry of the intervening period. There Stella's honour looms large as an aspect of the female psyche with which her lover must learn to reckon. In the *Old Arcadia* there is an inconsistency in Sidney's snickering at Andromana ('she should have done well to have been sure of the church before he had been sure of the bed', *Old Arcadia*, Second Eclogues, p. 154), then placing his heroine Philoclea in the same situation. But in his revision the 'impediments of honour', on the women's part, are carefully assimilated into the plot. Some critics persist in calling the revised *Arcadia* the Countess of Pembroke's book (see for example C. S. Lewis, *English Literature in the Sixteenth Century Excluding Drama* [Oxford, 1954], p. 333); furthermore, it is widely presumed that her prudish objections influenced Sidney (if she did not make the changes herself) to omit the explicit sexual activities by which the princesses are compromised in the *Old Arcadia* (the consummation by Pyrocles and Philoclea of their love, and the near-rape of Pamela by Musidorus). She seems to have known nothing about the revision, however, until Greville revealed its existence and edited the 1590 *Arcadia*, which the Countess was content simply to reprint in her own 1593 *Arcadia*. Since the 1593 changes in later books of the *Arcadia*, among which the sexual omissions are conspicuous, can be proved to be authorial (see Ringler, pp. 377–8 and Robertson, pp. lx–lxii), they deserve to be admitted as genuine developments in Sidney's attitude towards women. Penelope Rich and, later, Frances Walsingham could have had as much influence on that change of attitude as the Countess of Pembroke herself.

brings together in the first version more than seventy songs and eclogues.

The manuscript evidence for the *New Arcadia* bears out this impression of a changed approach to the poetry. The original transcript prepared or authorized directly by Sidney (Cm is a witness to its state) left out the Eclogues, though there are two distinct pauses in the story where 'pastorals' seem to be called for and where the editors of 1590 did insert Eclogues (*New Arcadia*, pp. 125 and 338). The narrative itself has room for twenty-two of the *Old Arcadia* poems; some of them, especially in the later parts of the story, have been taken from the Eclogues, thus destroying the original symmetry of Sidney's groups of verses and raising questions about his intentions for using these groupings. Sidney's lack of interest in the poems is remarked by Ringler, whose textual evidence strongly suggests that Sidney did not stop to copy the verses into his narrative. He simply instructed the scribe who was preparing the fair copy to write down the texts from Sidney's personal manuscript of the *Old Arcadia*, with its several revisions in the margins.[1] When Sidney needed an extra poem for his new Book Three, he chose not to write another one, but went back to his earlier collection *Certain Sonnets* to find Amphialus's love song.[2]

Other than a one-line motto for Dametas, six lines of an eclogue associated with the appearance of Philisides, and possibly the simple epitaph for Argalus and Parthenia (included in the 1593 edition only), Sidney wrote no new verses for the *New Arcadia*. Instead, he concentrated on adding action and exemplary stories. Especially in the first two books of the revision, Sidney gives an extraordinary development to the theme of 'remembrance' by interweaving his original Arcadian material and his additions, largely in a series of remembered tales.[3]

The existence of a special tie between fiction and memory was a conventional idea in literary criticism before Sidney, but he declares an especially strong allegiance to the idea in *A Defence of*

---

[1] Ringler, pp. 371–2.

[2] *Certain Sonnets*, No. 3 appears in the *New Arcadia*, Bk. III, p. 442.

[3] The examples of both Heliodorus and Montemayor probably influenced Sidney's decision to suppress the original narrator of the *Old Arcadia* in favour of an indirect narrative structure where the characters tell the story in their own voices. For a further statement of this idea, see the Kennedy edition of Yong's *Diana*, pp. xxxvi–xxxvii.

Poetry. There Sidney argues that the essential virtue of 'the speaking picture of poesy' is that it inspires, rather than simply burdens the memory with wisdom (*Defence*, p. 86).[1] Thus poetry makes its feigned images more readily useful to the judgement than the real images of history or the abstract precepts of philosophy. A sign that Sidney's basic opinions on the subject had not changed from the *Defence* to the *New Arcadia* is conveyed by a passage Sidney added in the revision. There Musidorus explains, in terms that recall the *Defence*, the importance of fictional examples and tales in the education of the princes. An echo of more than one theme of the earlier essay can be heard here:

> ... images of battailes, & fortificatiōs being then delivered to their memory, which after, their stronger judgemēts might dispens, the delight of tales being cōverted to the knowledge of al the stories of worthy Princes, both to move them to do nobly, & teach them how to do nobly; the beautie of vertue still being set before their eyes, & that taught them with far more diligent care, then Grāmatical rules. . . .
> (*New Arcadia* only, Bk. II, pp. 189–90)

Granted that Sidney's inward sense of the purpose and the effects of fiction had not changed; nevertheless his handling of the same story in two versions of *Arcadia* does show a marked outward difference. Put as simply as possible, there seems to be *more* of everything in the *New Arcadia*—more of everything except verse. There are more heroic adventures, more tales of love, and for the original lovers, as I have noted before, more 'impediments of honor, and . . . torments of conscience' (*New Arcadia*, Bk. II, p. 154). There is also a greater number of small realistic details in the *New Arcadia* than in the original version. These last changes have led at least one important commentator to see the *New*

---

[1] The Commentary on the *Defence* in *Sidney's Miscellaneous Prose*, p. 192, gives the background to Sidney's use of memory in the ancient *ars memoriae* practised by rhetoricians. Another Renaissance version of the art of memory which has a similarity to Sidney's use of it in poetry is Giulio Camillo's symbolic Theatre of the World, described by Richard Bernheimer in 'Theatrum Mundi', *The Art Bulletin*, XXXVIII. iv (Dec. 1956), especially pp. 228–31. Camillo's idea was to create a visible image of everything in the universe by placing each thing in its 'natural seat' in an amphitheatre. Thus the whole as well as the relationship between parts could easily be perceived. Whereas Camillo uses an architectural emblem, Sidney uses a dramatic one, the speaking picture; but the connection between making things visible and making them memorable remains the same. A more recent work on this subject is F. A. Yates, *The Art of Memory* (Chicago, 1966).

Arcadia as approaching the fullness, the approximation to real life, which is a defining quality of the novel. The *Old Arcadia*, however, should not be dismissed by comparison, as the same critic has done, as a 'primitive' narrative which lacks verisimilitude.[1] There is evidence, in fact, that Sidney was striving for verisimilitude in both *Arcadias*, but in slightly different ways. The evidence I will use here concerns only one minor area of change in Sidney's handling of the fiction, his use of geography in each work. Through that small but clear-cut example, however, we can see a basic shift in Sidney's concept of verisimilitude, a shift which, in my opinion, also helped to dictate larger changes in the revision.

In the *Old Arcadia* there are the names of twenty-three countries, seven cities, two rivers, and one valley; whereas in the *New Arcadia* the action is localized even more by Sidney's adding to the original group at least thirty other place-names.[2] But plausibility, rather than historical accuracy in the geographical references, seems to have been Sidney's aim in the *New Arcadia*. In contrast, when Sidney wrote the *Old Arcadia*, verisimilitude seems to have meant to him a careful reproduction of actual Ptolemaic geographical names (no longer in use by the Renaissance) and an exact physical location of each country mentioned in his story. In setting about this, Sidney used real maps of the Ptolemaic geography which had only recently appeared in Europe. I should emphasize again that the underlying purpose in using geographical details is no different in either version of the *Arcadia*. Sidney wished to appeal to the memory and touch the judgement of his reader. The following statement from Sidney's letter to Edward Denny, which is contemporary with the *Old Arcadia*, suggests what Sidney may have thought he was accomplishing by his careful use of maps in his book. Clearly, in terms of general purpose, there is a correspondence between the ideas here and those of the *Defence*, as well as the ideas stated about tales by Musidorus in the *New Arcadia*. Sidney wrote to Denny: '. . . provide your selfe of an Ortelius, ᵗᵧ when you reed of any place, you

---

[1] Zandvoort, p. 102.

[2] Ringler, p. 376. Ringler is moved, by his count of the frequency of geographical details in the *New Arcadia*, to assume that 'Sidney must have made a special study of the geography of Greece and Asia Minor in order to give his action a local habitation as well as a name' (p. 376). He does not recognize the fact that the details of geography in the *Old Arcadia*, while they are fewer, are more accurate.

may finde it out, & have it, as it were before your eyes; For it doth exceedingly confirme, both the iudgement, & memory' (22 May 1580).

Abraham Ortelius's popular atlas *Theatrum Orbis Terrarum* (first published in 1570) had included in the 1579 edition three new maps using the ancient place-names, along with a listing of Ptolemaic nomenclature.[1] If we approach the *Old Arcadia*, heeding Sidney's advice to 'take . . . your Ortelius, to knowe the places you reed of' (Sidney to Denny, 22 May 1580), we shall find that we have the locales of the main action brought sharply before our eyes. At the opening of Book One, for example, Sidney states that Euarchus's kingdom of Macedonia was invaded 'three sundry ways . . . at one time' (*Old Arcadia*, Bk. I, p. 10) by the armies of Pannonia, Thrace, and Epirus. On Ortelius's Map No. 92 of the Roman Empire (see Map 1), Pannonia appears to the north-west above Macedonia, while on Map No. 93 of Ancient Greece (see Map 2), Thrace is easily seen in the north-east of Macedonia, and Epirus in the south-west. Thus only the south-east corner of Macedonia, where the land-locked province of Thessalia lies, would have been safe from the invaders. There Euarchus sent his son Pyrocles to escape danger. Incidentally, the description of Pyrocles in the *Old Arcadia* as 'younger, but chiefer' than Musidorus (Bk. I, p. 9) is correct according to the maps and Ortelius's accompanying commentary. For Pyrocles was heir to an entire kingdom in Macedonia, whereas Musidorus's Thessalia was only a province, and thus only a ducal inheritance like Arcadia itself. In

---

[1] Both Ringler (p. 376) and Robertson (p. x) indicate that in 1578 Mercator brought out several maps using the Ptolemaic place-names. These were issued separately at Cologne. Several bits of evidence, however, point to Ortelius as being more likely to have been Sidney's source. The first is the letter of Sidney to Denny, where 'an Ortelius' is synonymous with an all-purpose series of maps. Second, a letter exists from Sidney to the publisher and bookseller Christopher Plantin of Antwerp requesting 'Les mappes de lortelius en la plus nouvelle édition'. Although the letter is undated, Feuillerat places it in his edition as No. XLIII, among the letters of 1580. According to the rather complete catalogue of 'Orteliuses' in the British Library, Plantin was not the source of the book until the 1579 edition appeared, with its special 'Parergon Theatri' (added ornament to the Theatre) of (Map No. 91) The Travels of Saint Paul, (Map No. 92) The Roman Empire, and (Map No. 93) Ancient Greece. The only other edition of Ortelius that appeared afterwards during Sidney's lifetime (also from Plantin) was the edition of 1584, which merely repeated the Ptolemaic features which had been new in the 1579 edition. Another link between Sidney and Ortelius is the fact that a commendatory poem by Sidney's friend Daniel Rogers appears at the opening of the *Theatrum*.

the *New Arcadia* Sidney did not make such distinctions, but took the liberty of making all these locations kingdoms and their rulers kings. In the *Old Arcadia* Sidney was also careful to chart his princes' travels as they skirted the Aegean and the Mediterranean seas. From their initiation into the events of romance—their shipwreck 'upon the coast of Lydia' (*Old Arcadia*, Bk. I, p. 11, Sidney's one slip, for Lydia is landlocked, with Aeolis being on the sea) —they venture up to Paphlagonia to slay a dragon and a giant (*Old Arcadia*, Second Eclogues, p. 153), then down to Syria, then on to Palestina, across the Arabian desert and into Egypt, whence they set sail for Greece, 'so taking Arcadia [in the centre of the Peloponnesus] in their way, for the fame of the country' (*Old Arcadia*, Bk. I, p. 11).[1]

In the *New Arcadia* the address to the memory and judgement of the reader takes another form. The number of geographical names and details is greatly increased, thus confirming the aura of real life about the fiction. But Sidney departs freely from Ortelius's maps, preferring to locate two notable scenes in settings borrowed strictly from classical literature. It was Ovid, in the *Fasti* and the *Metamorphoses*, who provided the imaginary Arcadian locale where Musidorus first discovers the disguised Pyrocles, 'under the side of the pleasaunt mountaine *Maenalus*' (*New Arcadia*, Bk. I, p. 75), and also the pretty river Ladon where the princesses bathe under the gaze of Pyrocles and Amphialus in Book Two. These place-names were not on the maps of Arcadia which were available to Sidney.[2]

If we turn back to a letter which Sidney wrote at the time of the

[1] Only one name in the *Old Arcadia* seems to be a pure coinage of Sidney's brain. Phagona, from the Greek word for glutton, is the town from which the drunken mob issues in Book Two to rebel against the duke Basilius. In the *New Arcadia* the name is changed to Enispus, from the Greek word for strength or opposition. Samothea is the homeland of Philisides in the *Old Arcadia* and is the only other spot named in the book which cannot be located on Ortelius's maps. Katherine Duncan-Jones, in 'Sidney in Samothea: A Forgotten National Myth', *Review of English Studies*, New Series XXV (1974), 174–7, shows that this was a name for ancient Britain—'a place where learning and justice flourished, and which declined under the conqueror Albion' (p. 175). The name Samothea was used by Holinshed, Languet, and other historians whose works were available to Sidney.

[2] These locations are not on the map of Arcadia as pictured either by Ortelius or by Mercator. The geographical liberties taken in the *New Arcadia* are numerous, but only a few examples need be mentioned here. We have the princes setting sail from the shore of land-locked Thessalia (*New Arcadia*, Bk. II, p. 191); we have Lycia (on the southern coast of Asia Minor near the Mediterranean), Iberia (near the Caspian

Old Arcadia, however, we can see that even at that period he was conscious of the value of the poetical or fictional appearance of truth, as distinct from the truth itself. The context of the letter is actually a discussion of writing history; but Sidney lists, besides the bare recording of dates, several devices of fiction which the historian may use to help his work take a firmer hold in the memory. In one sense, Sidney states, the historian may even make himself

a poet, in painting forth the effects, the motions, the whisperings of the people, which though in disputation one might say were true, yet who will mark them well, shall find them taste of a poetical vein, and in that kind are gallantly to be marked: for though perchance they were not so, yet it is enough they might be so.

(Sidney to Robert Sidney, 18 Oct. 1580)[1]

I think it is significant that Sidney returned to emphasize the value of plausibility again in 1584, at the same time as he was writing the *New Arcadia*. For when Sidney defends his uncle against the libellous fiction *Leicester's Commonwealth*, one of the first objections he makes to the work is a purely literary one—that the story is patently improbable. Reading a passage like the one below from the *Defence of Leicester*, we should remember that simultaneously with his critique of the unknown libeller, Sidney was revising his own *Arcadia*, as we have seen, with a view towards greater plausibility of detail. And he was also working out the brilliant characterizations of the revision, like those of Amphialus, Cecropia, and Clinias. In them Sidney studiously avoids the crudities which he notes here with contempt:

Perchance he had read the rule of that sycophant, 'that one should backbite boldly, for though the bite were healed, yet the scar would remain'. But sure that schoolmaster of his would more cunningly have carried it, leaving some shadows of good, or at least leaving out some evil, that his treatise might have carried some probable show of it. . . . For through the whole book, what is it else but such a bundle of railings as if it came from the mouth of some half drunk scold in a tavern, not regarding, while evil were spoken, what was fit for the

Sea), and Bythinia (northern Asia Minor, near the Hellespont) all bordering on each other (in the heroic stories of Bk. II); and we have the King of Iberia going hawking in Asia Minor (Bk. II, p. 277).

[1] Pears, p. 200.

person of whom the railing was, so the words were fit for the person of an outrageous railer.[1]

The stress on memory, the striving for greater plausibility, those are specific aspects of Sidney's conception of poetry in the *New Arcadia* which need serious attention in detail. But far more endearing in the *New Arcadia* is Sidney's display of a more pronounced general attitude of acceptance toward his 'unelected vocation' as a poet. The mouthpiece for these mellower feelings is the aged Arcadian gentleman Kalander. In one passage particularly, a passage from the first book of the revision, Kalander excuses himself to Musidorus for his garrulousness in telling long tales about Arcadia. The 30-year-old Sidney must have enjoyed playing the old man's part here, for he expatiates with engaging humour on several reasons for the talkative nature of old age. But the climactic and final reason is the one which follows. It can be taken, without doing violence to the actual context, as indicating Sidney's own feelings toward those poetical 'children' which formerly (half in jest, half in truth) he had been 'loath to father' (*Old Arcadia*, Prefatory Letter). The mood is less reluctant now in Kalander's remark

. . . that mankinde by all meanes seeking to eternize himselfe so much the more, as he is neere his end, dooth it not only by the children that come of him, but by speeches and writings recommended to the memorie of hearers and readers.

(New Arcadia only, Bk. I, p. 27)[2]

Shortly afterwards Sidney again makes Kalander his spokesman about poetry, this time transferring to the mouth of the old gentleman the introduction to the First Eclogues of the *Old Arcadia*. Sidney prefaces this with an added passage wherein Kalander refers specifically to the elevated wit of Strephon and Klaius, those symbols in the *New Arcadia* of the pains and the inspiration— now including poetic inspiration—of love. Kalander notes that 'it is a sporte to heare howe they impute to love, whiche hath indewed their thoughts (saie they) with suche a strength'

---

[1] The *Defence of Leicester*, in *Sidney's Miscellaneous Prose*, pp. 130–1.
[2] Sidney's conception of poetry in the *New Arcadia* had not changed so much, however, that he could not still satirize the poetical pretension to a divine fury. When Pyrocles-Zelmane sees the naked body of Philoclea as she is bathing, Sidney notes that the lover's 'wit began to be with a divine furie inspired' (Bk. II, p. 218) to sing a blazon of his earthly muse.

(*New Arcadia*, Bk. I, p. 27). The passage goes on to describe the 'sportes of the witte' characteristic of all the Arcadian shepherds, love once more playing an equal role with 'ease' in nourishing poetry:

> But certainely, all the people of this countrie from high to lowe, is given to those sportes of the witte, so as you would wonder to heare how soone even children will beginne to versifie. Once, ordinary it is among the meanest sorte, to make Songes and Dialogues in meeter, either love whetting their braine, or long peace having begun it, example and emulation amending it. Not so much, but the clowne *Dametas* will stumble sometimes upon some Songs that might become a better brayne: but no sorte of people so excellent in that kinde as the pastors; for their living standing but upon the looking to their beastes, they have ease, the Nurse of Poetrie.
>
> (*New Arcadia* only, Bk. I, pp. 27–28)

Sidney also appends another new sentence to the original words from the *Old Arcadia*, a sentence which is definitely intended to steer the reader towards a more positive view of the Arcadian poets: 'There is no cause to blame the Prince for somtimes hearing them; the blame-worthinesse is, that to heare them, he rather goes to solitarinesse, then makes them come to companie' (*New Arcadia*, Bk. I, p. 28).

Sidney clearly makes an effort through Kalander at this point to impute a greater role to love in inspiring poetry. And we can also see elsewhere in the *New Arcadia* Sidney's effort to bring together the follies of love, which he exposes and celebrates in the *Old Arcadia*, with the follies of poetry, which he exposes and affirms in the *Defence*. Several passages occur only in the revision where the passion of the lovers is given a semi-humorous treatment. In those passages, it is the verbal and poetical fireworks, in particular, on which Sidney trains his subtle wit. On two occasions an opening for humour is provided by the structural change in the *New Arcadia* from having an outside narrator to having the participants themselves tell their own stories. For example, in the *Old Arcadia* the narrator describes the first appearance of Philoclea, whereas in the *New Arcadia*, it is Pyrocles, the lover of Philoclea, who takes over that pleasant task. Sidney embellishes his original description with festoons of superlatives, in keeping with Pyrocles' extreme enthusiasm. Thus the passage generates a delicate irony about the lover's eloquence. But self-directed irony by Sidney is also present. For many of the added images have been lifted directly from his own love-sonnets in *Astrophil and Stella*.

But when the ornament of the Earth, *the modell of heaven, the Triumphe of Nature, the light of beauty, Queene of Love*, yoūg *Philoclea* appeared in her Nimphe-like apparell, so neare nakednes, as one might well discerne part of her perfections; & yet so apparelled, as did shew she kept best store of her beuty to her self: her haire (*alas too poore a word, why should I not rather call thē her beames*) drawē up into a net, *able to take Jupiter when he was in the forme of an Eagle*; her body (*O sweet body*) covered with a light taffeta garment, so cut, as the wrought smocke came through it in many places, inough to have made your restraind imaginatiō have thought what was under it: with the cast of her blacke eyes; blacke indeed, *whether nature so made them, that we might be the more able to behold & bear their wōderfull shining, or that she, (goddesse like) would work this miracle in her selfe, in giving blacknes the price above all beauty*. Then (I say) indeede me thought *the Lillies grew pale for envie, the roses me thought blushed to see sweeter roses in her cheekes, & the apples me thought, fell downe frō the trees, to do homage to the apples of her breast*; Then the cloudes gave place, that the heavēs might more freshly smile upō her. . . .

(*New Arcadia*, Bk. I, p. 90, added material in italics)[1]

In another passage Musidorus recounts his effort to win Pamela by pretending to woo Mopsa. The *Old Arcadia* has the narrator report simply that Dorus made 'store of love songs unto her' (*Old Arcadia*, Bk. II, p. 99). But in the *New Arcadia*, Dorus himself recites examples of his poetical flights. The fact that his praises, though aimed at Pamela, are actually received by the clownish Mopsa implies a gentle irony on Sidney's part in adding the passage, a commentary on the exaggerations possible to skilful and love-blinded admirers of women. As in the first example above, however, Sidney does not exclude himself from the irony, for once again the additions resemble strongly his own love poetry:

I cryed out of nothing but *Mopsa*: to *Mopsa* my attendance was directed: to *Mopsa* the best fruites I coulde gather were brought: to *Mopsa* it seemed still that mine eye conveyed my tongue. So that *Mopsa* was my saying; *Mopsa* was my singing; *Mopsa*, (that is onely suteable in laying a foule complexion upon a filthy favour, setting foorth both in sluttishnesse) she was the load-starre of my life, she the blessing of

[1] There are echoes here of *Astrophil and Stella*, No. 7 (on black eyes), No. 12 (on the lady's hair as a shining trap), and No. 68 ('STELLA, the onely Planet of my light,/ Light of my life, and life of my desire').

mine eyes, she the overthrowe of my desires, and yet the recompence of my overthrowe; she the sweetnesse of my harte, even sweetning the death, which her sweetnesse drew upon me. In summe, what soever I thought of *Pamela*, that I saide of *Mopsa*. . . .

> (*New Arcadia* only, Bk. II, pp. 154–5)[1]

A third instance in the *New Arcadia* where Sidney treats love and poetry as related forms of folly is the description, in Book Three, of Musidorus's attempt to apologize in verse to Pamela. Dorus is at this point both desperate and ashamed, for he has tried to kiss Pamela and has been rebuffed by her. Sidney's tone towards him in the passage below is a charming mixture of sympathy and humour, as the grief-stricken lover summons up the powers of poetry on his own behalf:

At last he yelded, since he was banished her presēce, to seeke some meanes by writing to shew his sorrow, & testifie his repentance. Therfore getting him the necessarie instruments of writing, he thought best . . . to put it in vers, hoping, that would draw her on to read the more, chusing the *Elegiac* as fittest for mourning. But pen did never more quakingly performe his office; never was paper more double moistned with inke & teares; never words more slowly maried together, & never the *Muses* more tired, then now with changes & rechanges of his devises: fearing howe to ende, before he had resolved how to begin, mistrusting ech word, condemning eche sentence.

> (*New Arcadia* only, Bk. III, p. 356)[2]

Besides considering the development and indeed the points of convergence in Sidney's attitudes to love and poetry, we must glance briefly at an important aspect of the *New Arcadia* which is closely related to these attitudes. That is Sidney's general moral viewpoint in the work. I believe that it too matches the pattern of change which we have seen before, where earlier ideas, represented in the *Old Arcadia*, are carried forward into a more complex and more inclusive, yet always benevolent vision. We have already discussed why Sidney adapted the opening of Montemayor's *Diana* for his first scene in the revision. But we should further recognize that the second scene of the book was also plucked by Sidney from an outside source. The bloody shipwreck, through

---

[1] There are parallels in this passage to *Astrophil and Stella*, No. 68, No. 79 (sweetness), and Eighth Song (ll. 29–34).

[2] J. G. Nichols cites the same passage in illustration of his thesis that 'we should take Sidney seriously as a poet, but should always beware of taking him solemnly' (p. 50).

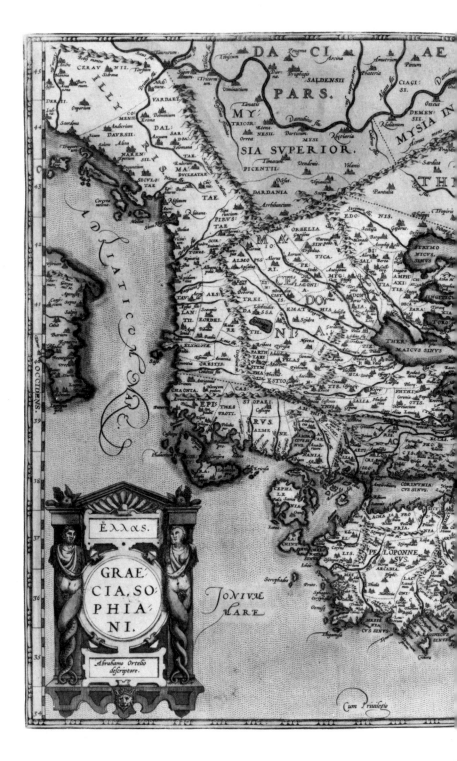

which Musidorus and Pyrocles are introduced, is modelled upon the beginning of Heliodorus's *An Aethiopian History*. The question arises, naturally, why Sidney chose two opening scenes from separate romances and attached them both to his own romance. The answer seems to me to lie in the growth of Sidney's imagination towards greater inclusiveness. I have argued before that the original love story of the *Old Arcadia* is carried forward in the *New Arcadia* in a different emotional atmosphere, one where not just the painful prelude to love's success (as in the *Old Arcadia*), but the really tragic possibilities of passion are allowed to enter. The opening on that emotional world is provided by Strephon and Klaius in the first scene. Next to it the shipwreck stands, I think, as a second opening on the different physical and moral world of the *New Arcadia* in which the original story will also be working itself out. This is a world where violence is more frequent and more menacing than it is in the *Old Arcadia*. And like 'a shipwrack without storme or ill footing: and a wast of fire in the midst of water', that violence seems more horribly inexplicable because it is not caused by nature, but is 'growen of humane inhumanitie' (*New Arcadia*, Bk. I, p. 10).[1] The *Old Arcadia* is not devoid of violence, but the line of moral responsibility runs straight and clear between Basilius's foolishness in retiring to the unguarded lodges, and the exposure which his family suffers as a result. The rebellion of the villagers in Book Two of the *Old Arcadia*, for example, can be understood as a perfectly logical consequence of the first action of the story. But the unreasoned hatred of Cecropia is a new and unsettling force in the revision. The fact that she is given a part in fomenting the uprising

---

[1] Heliodorus, at least in the translation of Underdowne, puts more emphasis on the incongruities of the shipwreck scene than on the moral turpitude which it represents:

To be briefe, God shewed a wonderfull sight in so shorte time, bruing bloude with wine, joyning battaile with banketting, mingling indifferently slaughters with drinkings, and killing with quaffinges, providing such a sight for the theeves of Egypt to gaze at. (p. 8)

Sidney had already used this idea of simple incongruity in the *Old Arcadia*, without the moral outrage which animates his presentation in the *New Arcadia*. When the Phagonians rebel in the *Old Arcadia*, Book Two (p. 128), the narrator remarks, 'Thus was their banquet turned to a battle, their winy mirths to bloody rages, and the happy prayers for the duke to monstrous threatening his estate; the solemnizing his birthday tended to the cause of his funerals'. S. L. Wolff (p. 360) notes that the close verbal parallels here indicate that Sidney did in fact know the translation of Underdowne.

of the Arcadians complicates the moral statement originally implied in the event, for now the monster of human evil is set
against the mere thoughtlessness of a foolish king. In addition,
moral cause and effect in the *New Arcadia* are turned completely
awry by the wrong-headed passion of Basilius and Amphialus,
and by the fortune of war. The result is the killing of the innocent
and happy lovers Argalus and Parthenia. Epitaphs and tombs enriched with marble images may do honour to their death (*New
Arcadia*, Bk. III, p. 449), but nothing can compensate for the
senselessness of it. Unlike the *Old Arcadia*, then, the *New Arcadia*
opens a darker perspective on human experience. In connection
with that view of life, Sidney's words in a late letter are striking:
'. . . be not troubled with my trouble for I have seen the worst in
my judgment before hand, and wors then that can not bee'
(Sidney to Sir Francis Walsingham, 24 Mar. 1586).[1]

Against the darker background of the *New Arcadia*, however,
human love, foolish and fragile though it is, shines more brightly.
Indeed, there are signs that, even after the massive dislocation of
action away from the original story which takes place in the third
book of the revision, Sidney intended to return to the original
finale of Love tried, condemned, pardoned, and blessed. A key
indication of this intention is the additional oracle which Sidney
placed near to the point where the revision breaks off, at a point,
nevertheless, where one feels sure the third book is actually
drawing to a close. In a distinct change from the sceptical attitude
towards oracles in the *Old Arcadia*, Sidney here sends Philanax, an
open disbeliever, to learn at Delphos, 'that reason cannot shewe
it self more reasonable, then to leave reasoning in things above
reason' (*New Arcadia*, Bk. III, p. 510). More important for our
present considerations, however, is the celestial commandment
which Philanax brings back, that Basilius 'should keepe on his
solitary course, till bothe *Philanax* and *Basilius* fully agreed in the
understanding of the former prophecie' (*New Arcadia*, Bk. III,
p. 510). Thus, in effect, Sidney has committed himself to the task
of forcing the action back into its old path. It should also be noted
that the 'former prophecie', the oracle which frightened Basilius
into retirement in the first place, has been changed significantly in
the *New Arcadia*, changed, as I see it, especially to emphasize the
final events of the original version and their happy outcome.

[1] Feuillerat, No. LXXXIX.

In the *Old Arcadia*, the oracle stands at the opening of the book. The positioning and the stark syntax of the poem are appropriate to its purpose and contents, a series of potential hammer-blows by fate which will drive Basilius immediately to seek for cover:

> Thy elder care shall from thy careful face
> By princely mean be stolen and yet not lost;
> Thy younger shall with nature's bliss embrace
> An uncouth love, which nature hateth most.
> Thou with thy wife adult'ry shalt commit,
> And in thy throne a foreign state shall sit.
> All this on thee this fatal year shall hit.

In the *New Arcadia*, on the other hand, the oracle is not revealed until the end of the second book.

> Thy elder care shall from thy careful face
> By princely meane be stolne, and yet not lost.
> Thy yonger shall with Natures blisse embrace
> An uncouth love, which Nature hateth most.
> Both they themselves unto such two shall wed,
> Who at thy beer, as at a barre, shall plead;
> Why thee (a living man) they had made dead.
> In thy owne seate a forraine state shall sit.
> And ere that all these blowes thy head doo hit,
> Thou, with thy wife, adultry shall commit.

The additions here, lines 5–7, explicitly predict the trial and also point to its happy ending. We can now safely anticipate Basilius's awakening—'Why thee (a living man) they had made dead'— and the marriages of the princes and princesses—'Both they themselves unto such two shall wed.' Moreover, the order of the original series has been reversed so that the love theme—'Thou, with thy wife, adultry shall commit'—takes precedence of last place over the political blow which was formerly the crowning one—'In thy owne seate a forraine state shall sit.' Generally, we can say that the change of position and the additions to the oracle in the *New Arcadia* make it less menacing. Rather than setting in motion the beginning of an action, it now looks toward the end, and a joyful end at that.[1]

---

[1] I have been influenced in my discussion of the oracles in the *Arcadia* by Mary Lascelles, 'Shakespeare's Pastoral Comedy', in *More Talking of Shakespeare*, edited by John Garrett (London, 1959), pp. 70–86. Both Ringler (p. 379) and Robertson (p. lxii) take the oracle of the *New Arcadia*, with its added lines about the trial, as

In sum, the line of Sidney's growth, as it can be perceived in differences between the two *Arcadias*, tends towards more in-clusiveness, particularly of the crueller truths about humanity and human passion. But the essential positiveness of Sidney's vision, born out of tolerance and assured faith, remains constant in the *New Arcadia*, as in the original story.

proof that Sidney intended to 'remedy a serious flaw in the ending of the *Old Arcadia*' (Robertson, p. lxii). That is, they believe that Sidney meant to try the princes only for murdering Basilius, not for their love of the princesses. Thus when Basilius awakened, there would be no need to set aside the just judgement of Euarchus. This interpretation seems to me based on a fundamental misunderstanding of the close relationship between the trial and Sidney's theme about love in the *Arcadia*, as well as a misunderstanding of the final necessity that, in order to fulfil the love-theme, the fool must be seen to set right the very same situation which the wise man cannot.

Honouring the Heavenly Maker

IN THE poetry as in Sidney's life, to which the poetry continually refers us, we can see a unified spirit at work. Sidney's habit of mind is to join contradictory tendencies of thought and feeling, always keeping hold on the facts of earthly experience. Thus we find in Sidney the consciousness of human folly coexisting with the belief in the wisdom of that folly, the serious love of truth coexisting with the sophistication of courtly and humanistic games, the appreciation of peace coexisting with the anticipation of war, and finally, the certitude of tragedy and evil in the world coexisting with a triumphant comic and heroic affirmation. The presupposition that such contradictions are somehow reconcilable within a benevolent scheme underlay much Renaissance thought. For Sidney, in particular, it seems to have been not only a reflex of his reason but a conscious article of his faith. This last is made explicit in the argument against atheism in the *New Arcadia*. One of the religious principles which Sidney articulates there is that, precisely because things in nature are contradictory, the fact that all these contraries are contained within 'this fayre estate' proves that 'a right heavenly Nature' must exist to bridle them into the unity, harmony, and beauty perceivable on earth (*New Arcadia*, Bk. III, pp. 408-9).

In the revision of the *Arcadia*, there are signs that Sidney had come to depend more heavily than before on heaven's power to resolve the complexities and contradictions of the world. I have already noted the new attitude of belief which is directed, in Book Three, towards the oracle that Philanax brings back from Delphos. In addition, I would point to Sidney's revision of the opening of Book Four, a change which only appears in the 1593 edition of the *Arcadia*.[1] The original fourth book begins thus:

[1] It bears repeating that the most recent and thorough research on the revisions in Books III–V of the *Old Arcadia* (revisions which first appeared in the 1593 edition) holds that they are indeed authorial and that they were made by Sidney in connection with his first two books of the *New Arcadia*. Ringler notes (pp. 377-8) that two passages appearing only in the 1593 edition—the account of the intended journey

The everlasting justice (using ourselves to be the punishers of our faults, and making our own actions the beginning of our chastisement, that our shame may be the more manifest, and our repentance follow the sooner) took Dametas at this present (by whose folly the others' wisdom might receive the greater overthrow) to be the instrument of revealing the secretest cunning. . . .

(*Old Arcadia*, Bk. IV, p. 265)

of Pyrocles after he has eloped with Philoclea, and the actual journey of Euarchus to Arcadia—are related to each other by references in each to a second uprising of the Helots. These references tie the passages directly to the *New Arcadia*, where the first uprising of the Helots takes place in Book One. Ringler concludes, as does Robertson, who follows the same argument (pp. lx–lxi), that only Sidney himself, not an editor, would have written these extra passages of completely gratuitous narrative and descriptive material. Thus if Sidney changed the purpose of Pyrocles toward Philoclea (to elope with her, rather than simply to lie with her), he probably also at least authorized the omission of Musidorus's corresponding attempt (in the *Old Arcadia*, Bk. III) on Pamela, as well as a host of small revisions in the trial scene which are related to these larger omissions.

Ringler and Robertson have a further argument to prove that the revisions are Sidney's, an argument which seems to me to be weak. It is that these revisions could only have been made by someone who had studied Mercator's Ptolemaic maps, which they contend Sidney did for the *New Arcadia*, but not for the *Old*. I have already shown, however, that Sidney used the Ptolemaic place-names in both *Arcadias*; in fact he used them far more accurately in the *Old Arcadia* than in the revision. But there is an additional argument to be made—I think, a stronger one—for Sidney's authorship of the revisions.

In Book Two of the *New Arcadia* Sidney creates a scene where the two princes, walking under some palm trees symbolic of their friendship, discuss the progress of their loves (pp. 152–4). This short scene of companionship is not modelled after anything in the original Book Two of the *Old Arcadia*, but after the original opening of Book Three (*Old Arcadia*, pp. 168–72).

In the 1593 edition the bulk of the opening scene of Book Three between Pyrocles and Musidorus has been deleted (see Robertson, pp. 168 and 172, notes on variant readings). This tends to substantiate the idea that Sidney himself made the 1593 revisions (comprising *Old Arcadia*, Books Three onwards), and that he made them in conjunction with revising Books One and Two. A further proof is the fact that a small phrase from the deleted material—'the heart stuffed up with woefulness is glad greedily to suck the thinnest air of comfort' (*Old Arcadia*, Bk. III, p. 172)—reappears in one of the two added passages of the 1593 edition (Bk. III) which Ringler and Robertson noted as significant. In this Pyrocles, having tried and failed to rouse the sickly Philoclea to elope with him, watches her sleeping and ponders his rashness in coming to her chamber. He considers the chances that he may not have compromised her, if only Gynecia and Basilius do not betray him. Having gained some comfort from this last thought—'as naturally the heart stuffed up with woefulness is glad greedily to suck the thinnest air of comfort'—Pyrocles falls asleep beside the still-virginal Philoclea (see Robertson, p. 237, notes on variant readings).

It does not seem to me likely or even possible that the intricate method of intertwining old and new phrases, which Sidney practises consistently in the first two books of the *New Arcadia*, and of which this passage provides an example in the revisions of Books Three to Five (1593), could have been imitated by an editor without some explicit directions left by the author himself.

In the 1593 *Arcadia*, however, the wording and the spirit of this passage have undergone a modification, one which shifts the seat of punishment and amendment away from our own human level toward the supernal one.

The almighty wisdom evermore delighting to show the world that by unlikeliest means greatest matters may come to conclusion; *that human reason may be the more humbled, and more willingly give place to divine providence*; as at the first it brought in Dametas to play a part in this royal pageant, so having continued him still an actor, now that all things were grown ripe for an end, made his folly the instrument of revealing that which far greater cunning had sought to conceal. . . .

(*Arcadia*, 1593 edition, emphasis mine)[1]

Actually this change has little effect on the way the reader comes to regard the final sequence of events in the *Arcadia*. Human reason is not more humbled in the 1593 version, but retains its original function in the trial scene, pointing out the spots of earthly love. Moreover, Basilius, after his awakening, acknowledges both human and divine influences in reaching his final edict of mercy: 'considering all had fallen out by the highest providence, and withal weighing in all these matters his own fault had been the greatest . . .' (1593 edition, wording unchanged from *Old Arcadia*, Bk. V, p. 416). But the desire which Sidney shows in his late revisions, to give place 'more willingly . . . to divine providence', does draw us beyond the *Arcadia* itself, to look at Sidney's last poetic labour—his versification of the *Psalms of David*. Even here, however, the conflict-ridden human element is not completely obliterated. Rather it is subsumed in a traditional form of religious poetry.

The forty-three poems of the *Psalms* which Sidney completed cannot be considered original. For Sidney did not attempt a new English version, only a careful reproduction, in a variety of metres suitable for singing, of translations which already existed.[2]

---

[1] I have quoted the 1593 revisions of *Arcadia* from the source where their differences from the *Old Arcadia* are most easily visible, that is, from the textual apparatus of Robertson's edition of the *Old Arcadia*, here from the notes on variant readings, p. 265.

[2] Ringler (pp. 505–6) lists the four texts which Sidney can be said with certainty to have used. 'He probably had the English prose Psalter [1539], the Geneva version [1560], the Marot-Beza French metrical Psalter [1562], and Beza's *Paraphrasis* [1580] open before him, and read each Psalm through carefully in all four texts before making his own metaphrase' (p. 506).

But in the rare instances where Sidney did heighten the imagery
beyond what he found in his sources, his personal mood seems to
have been congenial to the darker, questioning tone of the Psalms
with which he was dealing. In them, by and large, the poet
struggles to believe in God against a growing sense of the menace
of the world. One example where Sidney elaborated on his sources
is this:

> Link not me in self same chain
>   With the wicked working folk
>   Who, their spotted thoughts to cloak,
>   Neighbors friendly entertain
>   When in hearts they malice meane.
>   (Psalm XXVIII, 11–15)[1]

The mood here is not that joy of the Psalmist which had attracted
Sidney's notice earlier, in *A Defence of Poetry*:

He maketh you, as it were, see God coming in His majesty, his telling
of the beasts' joyfulness and hills leaping, . . . a heavenly poesy, wherein
almost he showeth himself a passionate lover of that unspeakable and
everlasting beauty to be seen by the eyes of the mind, only cleared by
faith.

(Defence, p. 77)

Instead, a stanza like the one above matches the troubled feelings
expressed in Sidney's last letters, written from his embattled post
of command in the Low Countries: 'I understand I am called very
ambitious and prowd at home, but certainly if thei knew my ha[rt]
thei woold not altogether so judg me' (Sidney to Sir Francis
Walsingham, 24 Mar. 1586).[2]

In the ancient complaint of the Psalmist, Sidney found an
acceptable expression in poetry of both questioning and assured
belief. The lines from Psalm XXXVII below, for example, provide a formula of religious fortitude which is calming and austerely
beautiful:

> Frett not Thy self, if thou do see
>   That wicked men do seeme to flourish,
>   Nor envy in thy bosome nourish
>   Though ill deeds well succeeding be.

---

[1] Ringler, in his commentary on this poem (also No. 28 of Sidney's series),
notes that Sidney invented the images of the chain and 'spotted thoughts' (p. 514).
[2] Feuillerat, No. LXXXIX.

> They soone shall be cutt down like grasse
> And wither like green herb or flower;
> Do well and trust on heavnly power,
> Thou shalt have both good food and place.

(ll. 1–8)

Sidney matches that tone in his explanation to Walsingham of his personal desire to persevere against all odds:

For me thinkes I see the great work indeed in hand, against the abusers of the world, wherein it is no greater fault to have confidence in mans power, then it is to hastily to despair of Gods work. I think a wyse and constant man ought never to greev whyle he doth plai as a man mai sai his own part truly though others be out but if him self leav his hold becaws other marrin[ers] will be ydle he will hardli forg[ive] him self his own fault. For me I can not promis of my own cource no nor of the my[   ] becaws I know there is a hyer power that must uphold me or els I shall fall, but certainly I trust, I shall not by other mens wantes be drawn from my self.

(Sidney to Sir Francis Walsingham, 24 Mar. 1586)

The character of Sidney's imaginative vision never let him lose sight of the fact that men are no more (as he put it in the *New Arcadia*) than 'the children of the Earth' (Bk. II, p. 192). But he also believed, with that acceptance of paradoxes which was characteristic of his age, that in weakness and dependence on God lay the greatest strength, that in the foolishness of love lay the best human wisdom, and that in making poetry a man might both woo beauty and father it.

Bibliography

PRIMARY SOURCES

Works by Sidney and Contemporary Records Bearing Directly on his Life

BRADLEY, WILLIAM ASPENWALL, ed. *The Correspondence of Sir Philip Sidney and Hubert Languet*. Vol. V in The Humanist's Library. Boston, 1912.

BUXTON, JOHN. 'An Elizabethan Reading-List: An Unpublished Letter from Sir Philip Sidney', *Times Literary Supplement*. 24 Mar. 1972, 343–4.

Calendar of Letters and State Papers Relating to English Affairs, Preserved Principally in the Archives of Simancas. Edited by Martin A. S. Hume. Vols. II, III, IV, 1568–1603. London, 1894.

Calendar of State Papers, Colonial Series, America and West Indies, Addenda 1574–1674, Preserved in the Public Record Office. Edited by W. Noel Sainsbury. London, 1893.

Calendar of State Papers, Domestic Series. Edited by Robert Lemon. Vol. 1581–90. London, 1865.

Calendar of State Papers, Foreign Series. Vols. 1578–9 and 1584–5. Edited by A. J. Butler. London, 1903.

Calendar of the State Papers Relating to Scotland and Mary, Queen of Scots. Vols. VII, VIII, IX, 1584–8. Edited by William K. Boyd. Edinburgh, 1913–15.

CAMDEN, WILLIAM. *Remains Concerning Britain*. London, 1870.

CAMERARIUS, P. *The Living Librarie, or Meditations and Observations Historical, Natural, Moral, Political and Poetical*. Translated from Latin by John Molle. London, 1621.

A Collection of State Papers Relating to Affairs in the Reign of Queen Elizabeth, from the year 1571–1596 . . . Left by William Cecill Lord Burghley, and Reposited in the Library at Hatfield House. Edited by William Murdin. Vols. I and II. London, 1759.

COLLINS, ARTHUR. *Letters and Memorials of State*. London, 1746.

GIFFORD, GEORGE. *The Manner of Sir Philip Sidneyes Death*. Private Printing of the Juel-Jensen Manuscript. Oxford, 1959.

GREVILLE, FULKE, BARON BROOKE. *The Life of the Renowned Sir Philip Sidney*. London, 1652.

HILLIARD, NICHOLAS. 'Treatise concerning "The Arte of Limning", with Introduction and Notes by Philip Norman', *The Walpole Society*, I (1911–12), 27–32.

Huberti Langueti, Viri Clarissimi, Epistolae Politicae et Historicae Scriptae Quondam ad Illustrem et Generosum Dominum Philippum Sydnaeum, Equitem Anglum. Frankfort, 1633.

Huberti Langueti, Epistolae Secretae ad Principem suum Augustum Sax. Ducem. Halae Hermunduror[um], 1699.

LANT, THOMAS. *The Funeral of Sir Philip Sidney.* London, 1587.

LEVY, CHARLES S. 'The Sidney-Hanau Correspondence', *English Literary Renaissance*, II.i (Winter 1972), 19–28.

MOFFET, THOMAS. *Nobilis or A View of the Life and Death of a Sidney* and *Lessus Lugubris.* Translated with introduction and notes by Virgil B. Heltzel and Hoyt H. Hudson. San Marino, Calif., 1940.

NICHOLS, JOHN. *The Progresses and Public Processions of Queen Elizabeth.* 1823 edition. 3 vols. New York, 1966.

OSBORN, JAMES M. 'New Light on Sir Philip Sidney', *Times Literary Supplement*, 30 Apr. 1970, 487–8.

OSBORN, JAMES M. *Young Philip Sidney, 1572–1577.* New Haven, Conn., 1972.

Pears, Steuart A., trans. and ed. *The Correspondence of Sir Philip Sidney and Hubert Languet.* London, 1845.

RATHMELL, J. C. A. *The Psalms of Sir Philip Sidney and the Countess of Pembroke.* The Stuart Editions. New York, 1963.

Sidneiana. Edited by Revd. Samuel Butler. London, 1837.

Sidney Family Correspondence, 1558–1709. British Library Additional MS. No. 15. 914.

Sidney Papers. British Library Additional MS. No. 17520.

Sidney Papers. British Library Additional MS. No. 18675/665 c.i.

SIDNEY, PHILIP; Robert, Late Earl of Essex; and Secretary Davison. *Profitable Instructions; Describing what speciall Observations are to be taken by Travellers in all Nations, States, and Countries, Pleasant and Profitable.* London, 1633.

SIDNEY, Sir PHILIP. *An Apology for Poetry.* Edited by Geoffrey Shepherd. London, 1965.

SIDNEY, Sir PHILIP. *The Apology for Poetry.* The Norwich Sidney manuscript, edited by Mary R. Mahl. Northridge, Calif., 1969.

SIDNEY, Sir PHILIP. *Astrophil and Stella.* Edited by Max Putzel. New York, 1967.

SIDNEY, Sir PHILIP. *The Defence of Poesie, Political Discourses, Correspondence, Translation.* Edited by Albert Feuillerat. Vol. III of *The Prose Works of Sir Philip Sidney.* (4 vols.) Cambridge, 1923.

SIDNEY, Sir PHILIP. *The Countess of Pembroke's Arcadia (The Old Arcadia).* Edited with Introduction and Commentary by Jean Robertson. Oxford, 1973.

SIDNEY, Sir PHILIP. *The Countesse of Pembrokes Arcadia* [*The New Arcadia*]. Edited by Albert Feuillerat. Vol. I of *The Prose Works of Sir Philip Sidney* (4 vols.). Cambridge, 1965.

SIDNEY, Sir PHILIP. *Miscellaneous Prose of Sir Philip Sidney.* Edited by Katherine Duncan-Jones and Jan van Dorsten. Oxford, 1973.

SIDNEY, Sir PHILIP. *The Poems of Sir Philip Sidney.* A critical edition by William A. Ringler. Oxford, 1962.

SIDNEY, Sir PHILIP. *Selected Poetry and Prose.* Edited by David Kalstone. A Signet Modern Classic. New York, 1970.

SIDNEY, Sir PHILIP. *Selected Prose and Poetry.* Edited by Robert Kimbrough. New York, 1969.

SIDNEY, Sir PHILIP. *Selections from Sidney's Arcadia.* Edited by Rosemary Syfret. London, 1966.

SIDNEY, Sir PHILIP. *Selected Poetry and Prose.* Edited by T. W. Craik. London, 1965.

OTHER PRIMARY SOURCES

APULEIUS, LUCIUS. *The Golden Ass.* Translated by William Adlington. (1566). Edited with an introduction by Harry C. Schnur. New York, 1962.

BULLETT, GERALD, ed. *Silver Poets of the Sixteenth Century.* Everyman's Library. New York, 1947.

BUXTON, JOHN, ed. *A Draught of Sir Philip Sidney's Arcadia* (1644). Oxford, 1961.

CALDWELL, MARK LEONARD, ed. *The Prose of Fulke Greville.* Unpublished Doctoral Dissertation, Harvard Univ., 1973.

CASSIRER, ERNST; KRISTELLER, PAUL OSKAR; and RANDALL, JOHN HERMAN, Jr., eds. *The Renaissance Philosophy of Man.* Chicago, 1948.

CASTIGLIONE, BALDESSAR. *The Book of the Courtier.* Translated by Sir Thomas Hoby (1561). In *Three Renaissance Classics,* edited by Burton A. Milligan. New York, 1953.

CASTIGLIONE, CONTE BALDESSAR. *Il Libro del Cortegiano.* Padua, 1766.

CHAUCER, GEOFFREY. *The Works of Geoffrey Chaucer.* Edited by F. N. Robinson. 2nd edn. Boston, Mass., 1957.

DONNE, JOHN. *The Elegies* and *The Songs and Sonnets.* Edited by Helen Gardner. Oxford, 1965.

ELYOT, Sir THOMAS. *The Book Named the Governor.* Edited with an introduction by S. E. Lehmberg. Everyman's Library. New York, 1962.

ERASMUS, DESIDERIUS of Rotterdam. *The Praise of Folie.* Translated by Sir Thomas Chaloner (1549). Edited by Clarence H. Miller. The Early English Text Society, No. CCLVII. London, 1965.

FICINO, MARSILIO. '*Commentary on Plato's Symposium*, the Text and a Translation, with an Introduction by Sears Reynolds Jayne', *The University of Missouri Studies*, XIX. i. Columbia, Mo., 1944.

GILBERT, ALLAN H. *Literary Criticism: Plato to Dryden*. New York, 1940.

GREVILLE, FULKE, First Lord BROOKE. *Caelica*. British Library Additional MS. No. 54570, Vol. V 'E'. The Warwick Castle Manuscript.

GREVILLE, FULKE, First Lord BROOKE. *Poems and Dramas of Fulke Greville, First Lord Brooke*. Edited by Geoffrey Bullough. 2 vols. New York, 1945.

GREVILLE, FULKE, First Lord BROOKE. *Selected Poems*. Edited with an Introduction by Thom Gunn. London, 1968.

HELIODORUS. *An Aethiopian History*. Translated by Thomas Underdowne (before 1587). The Abbey Classics, No. XXIII. London, 1925.

LAMB, CHARLES. *Works*. Edited by Thomas Hutchinson. Oxford, 1924.

MERCATOREM, GERARDUS. *Tabulae Geographicae C. Ptolemei ad mentem auctoris restitutae & emendate*. Cologne, 1578.

MERCATOREM, GERARDUS. *C. Ptolemei . . . geographiae libri octo. . . .* Cologne, 1584.

MONTEMAYOR, GEORGE of, and POLO, GIL. *Diana* and *Enamoured Diana*. A critical edition of Bartholomew Yong's translation, edited by Judith M. Kennedy. Oxford, 1968.

ORTELIUS, ABRAHAM. *Theatrum Orbis Terrarum*. 90 maps with a Parergon of 3 Maps, Portrait of Ortelius, and List of Ptolemaic Nomenclature. Antwerp, 1579.

PETRARCH, FRANCIS. *Selected Sonnets, Odes and Letters*. In translation. Edited by Thomas G. Bergin. A Crofts Classic. New York, 1966.

PLATO. *The Dialogues of Plato*. Translated by Benjamin Jowett. *Great Books of the Western World*, Vol. VII. Chicago, 1952.

PLUTARCH. *Essays and Miscellanies*. First Volume (in 5 vols.) Edited by A. H. Clough and Prof. William W. Goodwin, with introduction by Ralph Waldo Emerson. New York, 1905.

PUTTENHAM, GEORGE. *The Arte of English Poesie* (1589). English Linguistics Series, 1500–1800, No. CX. Menston, England, 1968.

ROBBINS, ROSSELL HOPE, ed. *Secular Lyrics of the XIVth and XVth Centuries*. 2nd edn. Oxford, 1955.

ROUSE, W. H. D., ed. *Shakespeare's Ovid: Arthur Golding's Translation of the Metamorphoses*. The Norton Library. New York, 1966.

SANNAZARO, JACOPO. *Arcadia and Piscatorial Eclogues*. Translated by Ralph Nash. Detroit, 1966.

SHAKESPEARE, WILLIAM. *Complete Works*. Edited by Alfred Harbage. Baltimore, 1969.

SHAKESPEARE, WILLIAM. *The Tempest*. Edited by Frank Kermode. The Arden Edition of the Works of William Shakespeare. London, 1966.

SPENSER, EDMUND. *Poetical Works*. Edited by J. C. Smith and E. De Selincourt. London, 1924.

WYATT, Sir THOMAS. *Collected Poems of Sir Thomas Wyatt*. Edited by Kenneth Muir and Patricia Thomson. Liverpool, 1969.

SECONDARY SOURCES

ABETTI, GIORGIO. *The History of Astronomy*. Translated by Betty Burr Abetti. New York, 1952.

ALPERS, PAUL J. 'Narrative and Rhetoric in *The Faerie Queene*', *Studies in English Literature*, II. i (1962), 27–46.

Anonymous Review, 'Energia and Inertia of *Sidney's Poetic Development*', *Times Literary Supplement*, 14 Dec. 1967, 1206.

Anonymous Review, 'Istevan Gal: "Sir Philip Sidney's Guide to Hungary"', *Times Literary Supplement*, 29 Jan. 1970, 116.

BANKS, THEODORE HOWARD. '"Astrophil and Stella" Reconsidered', *PMLA*, L (1935), 403–12.

BERGER, HARRY, Jr. 'The Renaissance Imagination: Second World and Green World', *The Centennial Review*, IX. i (Winter 1965), 36–78.

BERGERON, DAVID M. *English Civic Pageantry, 1558–1642*. London, 1971.

BERNHEIMER, RICHARD. 'Theatrum Mundi', *The Art Bulletin*, XXXVIII. iv (Dec. 1956), 225–48.

BOAS, FREDERICK S. *Sir Philip Sidney: Representative Elizabethan*. London, 1955.

BOND, WILLIAM H. *The Reputation and Influence of Sir Philip Sidney*. 2 vols. Unpublished Doctoral Dissertation, Harvard Univ., 1941.

BRADBROOK, M. C. *Shakespeare and Elizabethan Poetry*. London, 1951.

BRIE, FRIEDRICH. *Sidneys Arcadia: Eine Studie zur Englischen Renaissance*. Quellen und Forschungen zur Sprach—und Culturgeschichte der Germanischen Völker. Strassburg, 1918.

BRONSON, BERTRAND H. *In Search of Chaucer*. Toronto, 1960.

BROWER, REUBEN A. *Hero and Saint: Shakespeare and the Graeco-Roman Heroic Tradition*. New York, 1971.

BROWN, RUSSELL M. 'Astrophil and Stella, I', *The Explicator*, XXXII. iii (Nov. 1973), Article 21.

BURCKHARDT, JACOB. *The Civilization of the Renaissance in Italy*. Translated by S. G. C. Middlemore. New York, 1935.

BUSH, DOUGLAS. *Mythology and the Renaissance Tradition in English Poetry*, Revised edition. New York, 1963.

BUXTON, JOHN. *Sir Philip Sidney and the English Renaissance*. London, 1965.

CASSIRER, ERNST. 'Giovanni Pico della Mirandola', *Renaissance Essays from the Journal of the History of Ideas*. Edited by Paul O. Kristeller and Philip P. Wiener. New York, 1968.

CHEVREUL, HENRI. *Hubert Languet: Étude sur le XVIᵉ Siècle*. Paris, 1852.

COLIE, ROSALIE L. *Paradoxia Epidemica: The Renaissance Tradition of Paradox*. Princeton, N.J., 1966.

COOPER, SHEROD M., Jr. *The Sonnets of Astrophil and Stella: A Stylistic Study*. The Hague, 1968.

COULMAN, D. 'Spotted to Be Known', *Journal of the Warburg and Courtauld Institutes*, XX (1957), 179–80.

DANBY, JOHN F. *Elizabethan and Jacobean Poets* (formerly entitled *Poets on Fortune's Hill*): *Studies in Sidney, Shakespeare, Beaumont and Fletcher*. London, 1965.

DAVIS, WALTER R. 'Actaeon in Arcadia', *Studies in English Literature*, II (1962), 95–110.

DAVIS, WALTER R. 'A Map of Arcadia: Sidney's Romance in its Tradition', in *Sidney's Arcadia*. New Haven, Conn., 1965.

DAVIS, WALTER R. *Idea and Act in Elizabethan Fiction*. Princeton, N.J., 1969.

DENKINGER, EMMA MARSHALL. *Immortal Sidney*. New York, 1931.

DOBELL, BERTRAM. 'New Light upon Sir Philip Sidney's "Arcadia"', *The Quarterly Review*, No. 420 (July 1909), 74–100.

DONOW, HERBERT S. *A Concordance to the Sonnet Sequences of Daniel, Drayton, Shakespeare, Sidney, and Spenser*. Carbondale and Edwardsville, Ill., 1969.

DORAN, MADELEINE. *Endeavors of Art: A Study of Form in Elizabethan Drama*. Madison, Wis., 1964.

DUNCAN-JONES, K. 'Sidney in Samothea: A Forgotten National Myth', *Review of English Studies*, N.S. XXV (1974), 174–7.

DUNCAN-JONES, K. 'Sidney's Urania', *Review of English Studies*, N.S. XVII (1966), 123–32.

ESLER, ANTHONY. *The Aspiring Mind of the Elizabethan Younger Generation*. Duke Historical Publications. Durham, N.C., 1966.

FABRY, FRANK J. 'Sidney's Poetry and Italian Song-Form', *English Literary Renaissance*, III. ii (Spring 1973), 232–48.

FRYE, NORTHROP. *Anatomy of Criticism: Four Essays*. Princeton, N.J., 1957.

FRYE, NORTHROP. 'The Argument of Comedy'. In *Shakespeare: Modern Essays in Criticism*. Edited by Leonard F. Dean. New York, 1961.

GENOUY, H. *L"Arcadia' de Sidney dans ses rapports avec l"Arcadia' de Sannazaro et la 'Diana' de Montemayor*. Montpellier, 1928.

GODSHALK, WILLIAM L. *Sidney and Shakespeare: Some Central Concepts*. Unpublished Doctoral Dissertation, Harvard Univ., 1964.

GOLDMAN, MARCUS S. *Sir Philip Sidney and The Arcadia*. Urbana, Ill., 1934.

GOMBRICH, E. H. *Art and Illusion*. New York, 1960.

GOMBRICH, E. H. 'Botticelli's Mythologies; A Study in the Neoplatonic Symbolism of His Circle', *Journal of the Warburg and Courtauld Institutes*, VII (1945), 7–60.

GREEN, PAUL DAVID. *'Long Lent Loathed Light': A Study of Suicide in Three English Nondramatic Writers of the Sixteenth Century*. Unpublished Doctoral Dissertation, Harvard Univ., 1971.

GREENLAW, E. A. 'Sidney's *Arcadia* as an Example of Elizabethan Allegory', in *Kittredge Anniversary Papers*. Boston, 1913.

GREER, RICHARD ALLEN. *Adaptations of the Greek Romances in the English Renaissance as Reflections of the Debate Between Fortune and Virtue*. Unpublished Doctoral Dissertation, Harvard Univ. 1972.

GREG, WALTER W. *Pastoral Poetry and Pastoral Drama: A Literary Inquiry, with Special Reference to the Pre-Restoration Stage in England* (1905). New York, 1959.

HAMILTON, A. C. 'Sidney's *Arcadia* as Prose Fiction: Its Relation to Its Sources', *English Literary Renaissance*, II. i (Winter 1972), 29–60.

HARDISON, O. B. Jr. 'The Two Voices of Sidney's *Apology for Poetry*', *English Literary Renaissance*, II. iii (Autumn 1972), 83–99.

HARRISON, T. P., 'A Source of Sidney's "Arcadia"', *University of Texas Studies in English*, VI (Dec. 1926), 53–71.

HAUSER, ARNOLD. *The Social History of Art*. Translated by the author in collaboration with Stanley Godman. 2 vols. London, 1951.

HOWELL, ROGER. *Sir Philip Sidney: The Shepherd Knight*. London, 1968.

HUIZINGA, JOHAN. *Address delivered on the Occasion of Uncovering a Memorial to Sir Philip Sidney at Zutphen*. 2 July 1913. Translation from the Dutch.

HUIZINGA, JOHAN. *Homo Ludens: A Study of the Play Element in Culture*. Boston, 1960.

JUDSON, ALEXANDER C. *Sidney's Appearance: A Study in Elizabethan Portraiture*. Indiana University Publications Humanities Series No. XLI. Bloomington, Ind., 1958.

KAISER, WALTER. *Praisers of Folly: Erasmus, Rabelais, Shakespeare*. Cambridge, Mass., 1963.

KALSTONE, DAVID. *Sidney's Poetry: Contexts and Interpretations*. Cambridge, Mass., 1965.

KIMBROUGH, ROBERT. *Sir Philip Sidney*. Twayne's English Authors Series, No. CXIV. New York, 1971.

KOLVE, V. A. *The Play Called Corpus Christi*. Stanford, Calif., 1966.

LANHAM, RICHARD. '*Astrophil and Stella:* Pure and Impure Persuasion', *English Literary Renaissance*, II. i (Winter 1972), 100–15.

LANHAM, RICHARD. 'The *Old Arcadia*', in *Sidney's Arcadia*. New Haven, Conn., 1965.

LASCELLES, MARY. 'Shakespeare's Pastoral Comedy', in *More Talking of Shakespeare*, edited by John Garrett. London, 1959.

LAWRY, JON S. *Sidney's Two Arcadias: Pattern and Proceeding*. Ithaca, N.Y., 1972.

LEVI, F. J. 'Sir Philip Sidney Reconsidered', *English Literary Renaissance*, II. i (Winter 1972), 5–18.

LEVINE, ROBERT E. 'A Comparison of Sidney's *Old* and *New Arcadia*', *Salzburg Studies in English Literature*, No. XIII. Salzburg, 1974.

LEWIS, C. S. *The Allegory of Love*. London, 1936.

LEWIS, C. S. *English Literature in the Sixteenth Century Excluding Drama*. Oxford, 1954.

LEWIS, PIERS INGERSOLL. *Literary and Political Attitudes in Sidney's Arcadia*. Unpublished Doctoral Dissertation, Harvard Univ., 1964.

LINCOLN, ELEANOR TERRY, ed. *Pastoral and Romance: Modern Essays in Criticism*. Englewood Cliffs, N.J., 1969.

LINDHEIM, NANCY R. 'Vision, Revision, and the 1593 Text of the *Arcadia*', *English Literary Renaissance*, II. i (Winter 1972), 136–47.

MAHL, MARY R. 'A Treatise of Horsman Shipp', *Times Literary Supplement*, 21 Dec. 1967, 1245.

MALLOCH, A. E. 'John Donne and the Casuits', *Studies in English Literature*, II. i (1962) 57–76.

MARENCO, FRANCO. *Arcadia Puritana: L'uso della tradizione nella prima Arcadia di Sir Philip Sidney*. Bari, 1968.

McCLUNG, WILLIAM A. *The English Country House in Literature of the Renaissance*. Unpublished Doctoral Dissertation, Harvard Univ., 1972.

MILLER, PERRY. *The New England Mind: The Seventeenth Century*. New York, 1939.

MONTGOMERY, ROBERT L., Jr. *Symmetry and Sense: The Poetry of Sir Philip Sidney*. Austin, Tex., 1961.

MUIR, KENNETH. *Sir Philip Sidney*. Writers and Their Work Series, No. CXX. London, 1960.

MUIR, KENNETH, and DANBY, JOHN F. '"Arcadia" and "King Lear"', *Notes and Queries*, CXCV (1950), 49–51.

MUSCATINE, CHARLES. *Chaucer and the French Tradition, a Study in Style and Meaning*. Berkeley, Calif., 1957.

MYRICK, KENNETH. *Sir Philip Sidney as a Literary Craftsman*. 2nd edn. Lincoln, Neb., 1965.

NICHOLS, J. G. *The Poetry of Sir Philip Sidney: An Interpretation in the Context of his Life and Times*. Liverpool, 1974.

ORGEL, STEPHEN. 'Sidney's Experiment in Pastoral: *The Lady of May*', *Journal of the Warburg and Courtauld Institutes*, XXVI (1963), 198–203.

ORGEL, STEPHEN. *The Jonsonian Masque*. Cambridge, Mass., 1965.

OSBORN, ALBERT W. *Sir Philip Sidney en France*. Paris, 1932.

OTIS, BROOKS. *Ovid as an Epic Poet*. Cambridge, 1966.

PANNEKOEK, A. *A History of Astronomy*. New York, 1961.

PANOFSKY, ERWIN. *Meaning in the Visual Arts*. A Peregrine Book. Harmondsworth, Middlesex, England, 1970.

PANOFSKY, ERWIN. 'Renaissance and Renascences', *Kenyon Review*, VI (Spring 1944), 201–36.

PANOFSKY, ERWIN. *Renaissance and Renascences in Western Art*. Harper Torchbooks. New York, 1960.

PANOFSKY, ERWIN. *Studies in Iconology: Humanistic Themes in the Art of the Renaissance*. Harper Torchbooks, The Academic Library. New York, 1962.

POIRIER, MICHEL. *Sir Philip Sidney: Le Chevalier Poète Élisabéthain*. Travaux et Mémoires de l'Université de Lille Nouvelle Série—Droit et Lettres No. XXVI. Lyons, 1948.

PRICE, H. T. 'Like Himself', *Review of English Studies*, XVI (1940), 178–81.

PURCELL, JAMES MARK. 'Sidney's *Astrophil and Stella* and Greville's *Caelica*', *PMLA*, L (1935), 413–22.

QUINONES, RICARDO J. *The Renaissance Discovery of Time*. Cambridge, Mass., 1972.

REBHOLZ, RONALD A. *The Life of Fulke Greville, First Lord Brooke*. Oxford, 1971.

REES, JOAN. *Fulke Greville, Lord Brooke 1554–1628: A Critical Biography*. London, 1971.

REEVES, ROBERT NICHOLAS III. *The Ridiculous to the Delightful: Comic Characters in Sidney's New Arcadia*. The LeBaron Russell Briggs Honors Essay in English, 1973. Cambridge, Mass., 1974.

RICE, EUGENE F., JR. 'Erasmus and the Religious Tradition', *Renaissance Essays from the Journal of the History of Ideas*. Edited by Paul O. Kristeller and Philip P. Wiener. New York, 1968.

ROBERTS, MARK. 'The Pill and the Cherries: Sidney and the Neoclassical Tradition', *Essays in Criticism*, XVI. i (1966), 22–31.

ROBERTSON, JEAN. 'Macbeth on Sleep: "Sore Labour's Bath" and Sidney's "Astrophil and Stella" xxxix', *Notes and Queries*, XIV. i (1967), 39–41.

ROBERTSON, JEAN. 'Sidney and Bandello', *The Library*, XXI (1966), 326–8.

ROBERTSON, JEAN. 'Sir Philip Sidney and Lady Penelope Rich', *Review of English Studies*, N.S. XV (1964), 296–7.

ROBINSON, FORREST G. *The Shape of Things Known: Sidney's Apology in Its Philosophical Tradition.* Cambridge, Mass., 1972.

ROSE, MARK. *Heroic Love: Studies in Sidney and Spenser.* Cambridge, Mass., 1968.

ROSE, MARK. 'Sidney's Womanish Man', *Review of English Studies*, N.S. XV (1964), 353–63.

ROTA, FELICINA. *L'Arcadia di Sidney e il Theatro.* Con un testo inedito, 'Love's Changelings Change'. Biblioteca di studi inglesi No. VI. Bari, 1966.

RUDENSTINE, NEIL L. *Sidney's Poetic Development.* Cambridge, Mass., 1967.

SARGENT, RALPH M. *At The Court of Queen Elizabeth: The Life and Lyrics of Sir Edward Dyer.* London, 1935.

SELLS, A. LYTTON. *The Italian Influence in English Poetry: From Chaucer to Southwell.* Bloomington, Ind., 1955.

SEZNEC, JEAN. *The Survival of the Pagan Gods: The Mythological Tradition and Its Place in Renaissance Humanism and Art.* Harper Torchbooks, The Bollingen Library. New York, 1953.

SIEBECK, BERTA. *Das Bild Sir Philip Sidneys.* Schriften der Deutschen Shakespeare-Gesellschaft, Neue Folge, III. Weimar, 1939.

SMITH, HALLETT. *Elizabethan Poetry: A Study in Conventions, Meaning, and Expression.* Ann Arbor, Mich., 1952.

SOUTHALL, RAYMOND. *The Courtly Makers: An Essay on the Poetry of Wyatt and His Contemporaries.* Oxford, 1964.

STEVENS, JOHN. *Music and Poetry in the Early Tudor Court.* London, 1961.

STEVENSON, DAVID LLOYD. *The Love-Game Comedy.* Columbia Univ. Studies in English and Comparative Literature, No. CLXIV. Morningside Heights, New York, 1946.

SYMONDS, JOHN ADDINGTON. *Sir Philip Sidney.* Makers of Literature Series. New York, 1886.

THOMAS, DYLAN. 'Sir Philip Sidney', BBC Radio Broadcast of 1947, in *Quite Early One Morning.* New York, 1960.

TILLYARD, E. M. W. *The English Epic and Its Background.* London, 1954.

TRAFTON, DAIN A. 'Structure and Meaning in *The Courtier*', *English Literary Renaissance*, II. iii (Autumn 1972), 283–97.

TURNER, MYRON. 'The Disfigured Face of Nature: Image and Metaphor in the Revised *Arcadia*', *English Literary Renaissance*, II. i (Winter 1972), 116–35.

TUVE, ROSEMOND. *Elizabethan and Metaphysical Imagery.* Chicago, 1947.

TUVE, ROSEMOND. 'Imagery and Logic: Ramus and Metaphysical Poetics', *Renaissance Essays from the Journal of the History of Ideas.* Edited by Paul O. Kristeller and Philip P. Wiener. New York, 1968.

VAN DORSTEN, J. A. *Poets, Patrons and Professors: Sir Philip Sidney, Daniel Rogers and the Leiden Humanists*. Published for the Sir Thomas Browne Institute. London, 1962.

WAITH, EUGENE M. *The Herculean Hero in Marlowe, Chapman, Shakespeare, and Dryden*. New York, 1962.

WALLACE, MALCOLM. *Life of Sir Philip Sidney*. Cambridge, 1915.

WARREN, C. HENRY. *Sir Philip Sidney: A Study in Conflict*. New York, 1936.

WILEY, MARGARET. *The Subtle Knot*. Cambridge, Mass., 1952.

WILSON, MONA. *Sir Philip Sidney*. New York, 1932.

WIND, EDGAR. *Pagan Mysteries in the Renaissance*. New Haven, Conn., 1958.

WOLFF, SAMUEL LEE. *The Greek Romances in Elizabethan Prose Fiction*. New York, 1912.

YATES, FRANCES A. *The Art of Memory*. Chicago, 1966.

YATES, FRANCES A. 'Elizabethan Chivalry: The Romance of the Accession Day Tilts', *Journal of the Warburg and Courtauld Institutes*, XX (1957), 4–25.

YATES, FRANCES A. 'Queen Elizabeth as Astrea', *Journal of the Warburg and Courtauld Institutes*, X (1947), 27–82.

ZANDVOORT, R. W. *Sidney's Arcadia: A Comparison Between the Two Versions*. Amsterdam, 1929.

Index

(Main discussions are indicated in **bold** type.)